A Guide to Field
Experiences and Careers in

Sport and
Physical *Activity*

2nd Edition

Glenna G. Bower

UNIVERSITY OF SOUTHERN INDIANA

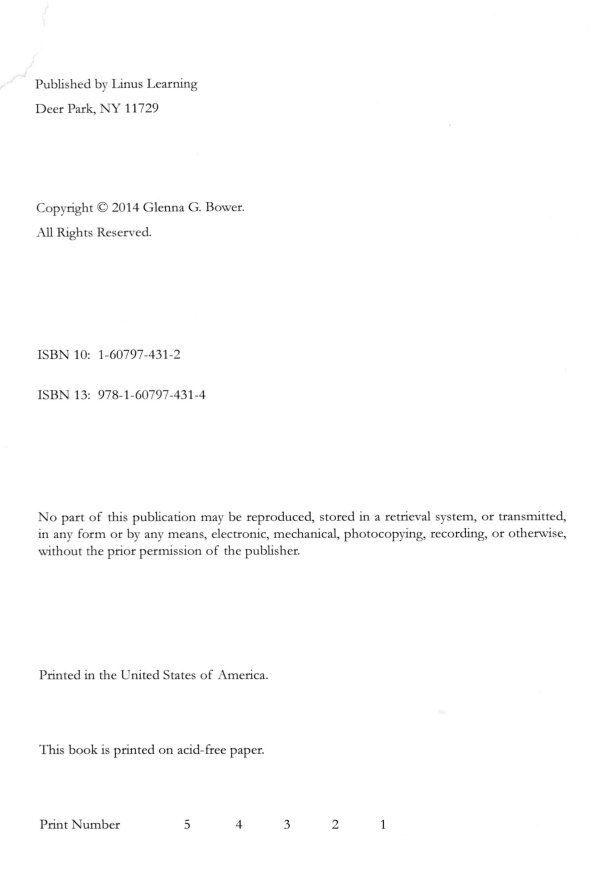

Published by Linus Learning

Deer Park, NY 11729

ISBN 10: 1-60797-431-2

ISBN 13: 978-1-60797-431-4

Printed in the United States of America.

This book is printed on acid-free paper.

Print Number   5   4   3   2   1

Table of Contents

SECTION One

Selecting a Career Path

SECTION Two

Professional Development Tools

SECTION Three

Making the Right Impression

SECTION Four

From College Graduate to Career

Appendices

Preface

A Guide to Field Experiences and Careers in Sport and Physical Activity *is a simple, hands-on guide for students pursuing a career in sport and physical activity. The book was written as a "how to" guide in making a successful move from college to the "real world." The book is like no other on the market because of the depth of information related specifically to the professional development of students in sport and physical activity. The book has many features including chapter scenarios, frequently asked questions, student learning activities, and career highlights. The chapter scenarios offer you a series of fictitious students who walk you through career exploration exercises while the frequently asked questions provides you with answers you may be seeking. The student learning activities provides hands-on assignments to reinforce each chapter while the career highlights introduce you to professionals working in sport and physical activity. Finally, the appendix and companion CD introduces 24 resume and cover letter templates and samples from all different sport and physical activity jobs.*

The book is divided into three major sections. Part I (Chapters 1-2) focuses on selecting a career path. Chapter 1 introduces you to the field experience, which is one of the most important educational experiences to help you get a job. Chapter 2 introduces you to potential career opportunities in sport and physical activity.

Part II (Chapters 3-5) focuses on professional development tools. Chapter 3 and 4 teach you how to write personalized, effective resumes, cover letters and other correspondence with easy to follow steps and guidance. Chapter 5 introduces you to the content of student portfolios which allows you to shine when walking into an interview.

Part III (Chapters 6-8) stresses the importance of "Making the Right Impression" explores networking and interviewing. Chapter 7 introduces you to social networking, a web-based tool to connect with the people for the purposes of reaching your career and business goals. Chapter 7 asks you to explore, build, and maintain networks while chapter 8 provides you with strategies to help you substantially improve your interview skills.

Part IV (Chapters 8-9) guides you along the path of successfully completing your field experience, graduating, and pursuing your career in sport and physical activity. Chapter 9, "Potential Field Experience Opportunities in Sport and Physical Activity," introduces you to the steps in securing a field experience. Chapter 10, "Finding and Accepting Employment in Sport and Physical Activity," encourage you to be pro-active in setting specific job objectives, effective methods for finding employment, tips on applying and being offered a position in sport management and exercise science.

This book is the early step in what could be a rewarding career for you in sport and physical activity. You need to devote time and energy to building a solid base of knowledge, skills, and hands-on experience. The knowledge, skills, and hands-on experience you develop can make it easier to obtain a job that is intellectually challenging while providing professional growth, personal satisfaction, and financial rewards.

Acknowledgements

I want to thank my mentors, Dr. Mary Hums, Professor, University of Louisville Sport Management program, who taught me how to be a writer and instilled confidence through all of my academic endeavors. I also want to thank Dr. Scott Gordon, Dean of the Pott College of Science, Engineering, and Education and Dr. Jane Davis-Brezette, former Chair of the Department of Kinesiology and Sport, for providing me opportunities and giving me the support I need to succeed within academia. All of these individuals have stood by my side throughout my academic career as mentors and colleagues. These individuals have truly impacted my life, and it is great to have the chance to work and learn from three of the best in the field.

A special thanks goes out to Lacey Houle who inspired and supported me during a time when there were many obstacles to overcome throughout the process of writing the book. You do not meet too many people like Lacey. She is one in a million, and I am fortunate to have her in my life!

In addition, this book would not have been possible without the encouragement of family, friends and colleagues who made a difference during my educational endeavors. To my parents, Gary and Debbie Bower, who have been genuine supporters throughout my whole life. I also want to thank Patty Marcum for supporting me throughout my career as the Chair of the Department of Kinesiology and Sport at the University of Southern Indiana. No matter what I could count on Patty to be a team player and provide the genuine support needed as an administrator. Finally, I want to thank Connie Houle for listening and encouraging me to be the best that I can be throughout my academic journey. I can always count on Connie to be there when I need her and that speaks volumes.

Finally, I want to thank all of those students who have inspired me through their hard work and dedication. I could not ask for better students than the ones at the University of Southern Indiana. These students have truly inspired me to be the scholar I am today. I especially want to thank Randy Butcher, a sport management student at the University of Southern Indiana, for his hard work in assisting me with the editorial updates for the 2nd edition of the book.

SECTION I

SELECTING
A
CAREER PATH

INTRODUCTION TO FIELD EXPERIENCES

SCENARIO #1 – FIELD EXPERIENCE/OBSERVATION - SOPHOMORE

Jacob

Jacob is a sophomore and currently enrolled in a sport and physical activity field experience course (20 hours- 1 credit hour). Jacob has enjoyed learning everything he can about personal training. He wants to obtain additional experience by completing a field experience at a local gym.

SCENARIO #2 – PRACTICUM - JUNIOR

Chris

Chris is a junior enrolled in a practicum course (150 hours – 3 credit hours). Chris is interested in working for a sports club. Chris has been an avid golfer and is a member University of South Carolina golf team. Chris wants to be a professional golf instructor for a vacation resort. Chris has the opportunity to complete his practicum at the Dayside Country Club.

SCENARIO #3 – INTERNSHIP - SENIOR

Heather

Heather is a senior enrolled in an internship course (450 hours – 9 credit hours). Heather is preparing to complete her internship with the Southern Illinois Athletic Department. Heather wanted to work alongside Brooke Morgan, the Life Skills Coordinator, within the Southern Illinois Athletic Department, after reading her career highlight (end of chapter). This internship experience reinforced the fact that Heather wants to pursue a similar career.

There are many ways to learn and some of the most important ones are often learned outside the classroom. Experiential learning allows you to learn by doing and is associated with being in touch or actively engaged (Bethell & Morgan, 2011). These experiential learning experiences may result in a change in your feelings, judgments, and/or skills (Foster & Dallas, 2010). You may learn from on-the-job training, participation in practical simulations or observations such as with role playing, volunteer work, and/or field experiences. Academic programs are utilizing experiential education in the form of field experiences, such as observations, practica, and internships as part of your professional or career preparation (Bethell & Morgan, 2011; Shoepfer & Dodds, 2010; Bower, 2013). The field experience is an experiential learning experience often referred to as experiential education. Experiential education is active participation in events or activities that allow students to acquire knowledge and skills for the real world (Bower, 2013). Hence, you have the opportunity to obtain hands-on experience in your potential career.

Field Experience/Observation

The field experience/observation may be the first course students take during their major. The field experience/observation course usually takes place during the first semester of your sophomore year. This field experience is an off campus activity that allows you to observe for a short period of time. You observe professionals in a career you are interested in pursuing. This field experience is completed early in the curriculum so you can make a decision if this is actually a career that you want to continue to pursue. For example, Jacob thinks he wants to pursue a career as a personal trainer. Jacob is not sure if he wants to train in a commercial, corporate, or independently owned facility and therefore decides to complete his field experience/observation at a commercial gym.

The Practicum

Some universities require several practica experiences before the field experience. A practicum usually occurs on a part-time basis, at different stages within the academic program, and focuses on the specific objectives (Foster & Dallas, 2010). You are usually allowed to take other coursework with the practicum, and therefore the sites are within a reasonable driving distance of the university you are completing the academic program. Although policies are different from each sport and physical activity program students are usually allowed to complete the practicum only after completing a certain amount of university core and/or major courses. The practicum usually constitutes at least three academic credit hours although this could be different depending on university requirements. For example, Chris is a junior and has to complete a practicum (150 hours – 3 credit hours) along with his coursework (9 credit hours). Chris takes advantage of a practicum opportunity offered to him at the Dayside Country Club.

The Internship

The internship is a field experience which typically takes place upon completion of all coursework and exposes you to a practical learning environment through which you apply classroom theory to reality (Foster & Dallas, 2010; Bower, 2013). In most cases the field experience is a full-time (40 hours/week) work experience for a minimum of 400 hours (American Society for Exercise Physiologist, 2006; NASPA/NASSM, 2000) although the CAAHEP for the American College of Sports Medicine (American College of Sports Medicine, 2013) standards and guidelines do not have a set amount of hours. You may participate in field experiences that fall into several categories including cooperative education, service learning, and academic service learning (Foster & Dallas, 2010). Cooperative education is also known as a paid internship, and falls into two categories: alternating and parallel (Foster & Dallas, 2010). Alternating cooperative education allows you to alternate between full-time paid work and full-time course work at your university. Parallel cooperative education allows you to attend classes while getting paid to work (Foster & Dallas, 2010). Heather is fortunate to have finished all of her coursework and is able to complete her internship within the Southern Illinois Athletic Department. Heather is able to devote all of her energy to the job without having additional stress if she had to complete coursework as well.

Exhibit 1.1 What Does the Field Experience do for You?

1. You can screen a career choice to determine if it meets job expectations

2. You can apply classroom experience to a "real world" situation

3. Allows you to make mistakes, critical decisions, and develop ideas and beliefs about a work settings in sport and physical activity.

4. If you obtain an "alternate" or "parallel" cooperative field experience then you receive course credit, gain practical experience, and get paid while working in a sport and physical activity setting.

5. You may develop a mentoring relationship or build networks with employers and supervisors that may lead to a potential career.

6. You may realize what it is to be professionally committed to something.

7. You may be assessed by a practitioner rather than a professor. This may provide additional insight on your strengths and weaknesses.

8. You may add this experience to your resume.

Benefits of the Field Experience

The field experience is valuable for you, the sponsoring agency, and the university in that each entity plays a part in helping you complete the responsibilities of the sport and physical activity position (Barclay, 2009). Therefore, a more in-depth look at the benefits to you, the sponsoring agency, and university are warranted. Exhibit 1.1 provides a list of how the completion of the field experience is crucial to your success in sport and physical activity.

There are several practical advantages provided to businesses and universities offering a field experience in sport and physical activity which are listed in Exhibit 1.2.

Exhibit 1.2 Practical Advantages of a Field Experience

1. You receive on-the-job training while the host site has the opportunity to evaluate potential employees.

2. You provide additional help to the business. As with academic service learning this additional help is without compensation.

3. You may provide creative ideas to programs and/or services offered for sport and physical activity sites.

4. The agency gains a presence on the university campus which may provide additional exposure.

5. The academic curriculum can stay current by keeping up with the latest trends in sport and physical activity. This connection with the "real world" helps the university department by exposing you to new and innovative equipment and up-to-date information that may improve classroom instruction.

6. The university develops a community network that helps you gain exposure resulting in future placement. Thus, these relationships could result in community research groups.

Summary

The field experience is an essential link between classroom knowledge and the "real world." There are many benefits of the field experience for you, the agencies, and the university.

A well-planned field experience search and selection process illustrates you are taking responsibility in defining direction for your future career. It is now up to you to take full advantage of what the field experience has to offer. The end result may be the job of your dreams!

Frequently Asked Questions

What is the difference between a practica and internships?

With the practicum you can take additional coursework and the number of hours is significantly lower than that of an internship. The practicum usually is 3-5 hours (150-250 hours) and the internship is usually 450 hours depending on the university.

When do most students complete their field experience?

It depends on the field experience. However, the field observation may be completed during the first semester of your sophomore year while the practicum is completed during your junior year and the internship during your senior year. There are some universities that only offer practica all throughout the major curriculum.

Can students complete more than one practicum or internship?

Students may complete multiple practica and/or internships throughout their academic career. The amount of practia or internships a student can take is dependent upon the major requirement.

Student Learning Activities

Talk to your advisor about what kind of field experiences is required. Ask the advisor what semester you will be completing each field experience.

➢ Field Experience Checklist
❑ Check with advisor on types of field experiences required
❑ Determine when you will be taking each field experience course

ASSOCIATE ATHELIC DIRECTOR

Christine Moeller

Assistant Director of Athletics/Student Services/SWA

Cleveland State University

Cleveland, Ohio

Education And Certifications

Master of Education, Sport Management

Bachelor of Arts, Communication

Years In Position

1 year

Previous Positions

Athletic Academic Advisor, Athletic Academic Coordinator, Compliance Coordinator

Current Job Responsibilities And Hours

I coordinate all auxiliary student services, overseeing the department's compliance program. I have supervisory oversight of volleyball, softball and men's and women's swimming. I have set on multiple Horizon League committees.

Greatest Challenges

Never know what you are going to get! Never have 2 days that are totally alike with the same duties. So many things come up in this field and most of the people that are in this field really just want to help support the student-athletes and staff in order to help them be as successful as possible, so the work could never end in order to do that. Always need to having the thinking cap on to be able to think outside the box and always be on toes. Never know which hat to wear and for how long. It is hard sometimes maintaining the importance of open and strong communication as that is the key to be able to work successfully with so many different people and their personalities/mindsets.

Career Advice

I always tell people that are looking to get into this field to NETWORK. Make sure you try to get a graduate assistantship, and/or do a practicum/internship in the different areas of collegiate athletics that you are interested in. I would suggest going to the different conferences that are offered, as well. I would advise someone entering the field to be open-minded and be able to roll with the punches. Stand strong, yet know that there will have to be flexibility. Lastly, to truly enjoy working with the student-athletes, coaches, and staff. It definitely is hard work, but I feel so fortunate to be working with the people I work with everyday and I think that is what makes all the difference – just enjoy!

CAREER HIGHLIGHT – COORDINATOR OF LIFE SKILLS

Brooke Morgan

Coordinator of Life Skills

Southern Illinois University

Carbondale, Illinois

Education And Certifications

Bachelor of Arts - Communication

Master of Science - Sport Administration

Years In Position

Starting my seventh year at Southern Illinois University.

Previous Positions

Previously held a Graduate Assistant/Assistant Academic Counselor at the University of Louisville for 2 years

Current Job Responsibilities And Hours

Coordinate community service, tutor coordinator, hire tutors, hire monitors for our academic center. Academically I work with volleyball, swimming and diving, softball, golf, tennis and assist with football teams. I have individual academic meetings with all freshman of these teams. I bring in national speakers to talk to our students about anything from leadership to alcoholism. I work with SIU's career services to make sure our student-athletes are attending job fairs and other activities they hold. I work on NCAA clearinghouse/admission status weekly reports, eligibility, APR, schedule classes. Basically you name it and I do it! Typically works 50 plus hours a week, depending on what part of the semester it is and what is going on.

Greatest Challenges

Students who are really smart and have the ability to do great in school but instead are lazy and do not give it their all. Time is also a challenge because I do so much but I refuse to work all the time. As much as I would like to bring work home I do not because I think work needs to be done at work and on the other hand have time to do important things with your family and friends at home.

Career Advice

Prepare to work a lot. This career path is not one for someone who wants to make a lot of money, but someone who really likes to help others succeed. This is sometimes a thankless job but deep down it is really great to have a kid succeed and that is the best part for me.

References

American College of Sports Medicine. (2013). *ACSM's guidelines for exercise testing and prescription, 9th edition.* Baltimore, Maryland: Lippincott Williams & Wilkens.

Barclay, B. (2009). Implementing experiential learning courses to teach students leadership principles *MAHPERD Journal, 6*(1), 3.

Barr, A. B., Walters, M.A., & Hagan, D. W. (2002). The value of experiential education dietetics. *Journal of the American Dietetic Association, 102*(10), 1458-1460.

Bethell, S. & Morgan, K. (2011). Problem-based and experiential learning: Engaging students in an undergraduate physical education Theory. *Journal of Hospitality, Leisure, Sport, & Tourism Education, 10*(1), 128-134.

Bower, G. G. (2013) Utilizing Kolb's Experiential Learning Theory to implement a golf scramble. *International Journal of Sport Management, Recreation, and Tourism,* 12, (1), 29-56.

Commission on Sport Management Accreditation. (2013). *COSMA accreditation principles and self-study preparation,* June 2010. Retrieved December 28, 2013, from http://www.cosmaweb.org/accredmanuals

Foster, S. B., & Dollar, J. E. (2010). *Experiential learning in sport management: Internships and beyond.* Morgantown: WV: Fitness Information Technology.

Schoepfer, K. L., & Dodds, M. (2010). Internships in sport management curriculum: Should legal implications of experiential learning result in the elimination of the sport management internship. *Marquette Sports Law Review, 21*(1), 182-201.

POTENTIAL CAREER OPPORTUNITIES IN SPORT AND PHYSICAL ACTIVITY

SCENARIO #1 – FIELD EXPERIENCE/OBSERVATION - SOPHOMORE

Pete

Pete is a sophomore and currently enrolled in a sport and physical activity field experience course (20 hours - 1 credit hour). Pete has been around sports all of his life. He is currently a student athlete on the University of Alabama men's tennis team. His father has been a high school athletic director for the past 10 years. Pete decides he wants to follow in the footsteps of his father in pursuing a career as an Athletic Director. He decides to observe members of the University of Alabama's Athletic Department to complete his 20 hour field experience.

SCENARIO #2 – PRACTICUM – JUNIOR

Samantha

Samantha is a junior enrolled in a practicum (150 hours – 3 credit hours). Samantha completed a field experience observing a recreational at UNC hospital. Samantha realized after completing her field experience that she wanted to assist with the individual development of people with physical limitations and therefore decided to resume her practicum at the UNC hospital.

SCENARIO #3 – INTERNSHIP – SENIOR

Joe

Joe is a senior enrolled in an internship (450 hours – 9 credit hours). Joe is interested in working within an intercollegiate athletic department. Joe would like to eventually become a Sports Information Director and is inspired after reading about Jenna Willhoit and Nells career highlights (end of chapter). Jenna is completing her assistant Sports Information Director internship at Xavier University. She has only 3 ½ months of experience but provides Joe with some insight on potential internships in the area of sports information director. Nells has been a sports information director at Bellarmine University for the past 3 years and provided additional insight about the career.

Participation in sport and physical activity at all levels continues to increase. With this increase in participation, career opportunities have never been greater. According to the U.S. Department of Labor (2013), career opportunities related to sport and physical activity are expected to increase faster than the average for all occupations through the year 2014. This rapid increase continues for many reasons including: (a) the growth of the general public participating in organized sport for entertainment, recreation, and physical conditioning, (b) the increased participation in organized sports for girls and women, (c) the increased number of baby boomers approaching retirement which may require additional instruction in leisure activities such as golf and tennis, and (d) the large number of children of baby boomers participating in high school and college athletics (Hatfield & Hatfield, 2005). The increase in career opportunities in sport and physical activity is an exciting development. However, selecting a career from the available options in sport and physical activity requires careful consideration of a number of factors which are explored in this chapter.

Careers in Sport and Physical Activity

Choosing a career in sport and physical activity is a decision-making process which entails gathering information in the areas of strengths, abilities, interests, educational experiences, and career expectations. You may begin to identify potential careers in sport and physical activity by having a realistic perspective in these areas. The process begins through an ongoing self-assessment process. Your self-assessment begins by completing the Career Exploration steps in Exhibit 2.1 to plan your career in sport and physical activity.

Exhibit 2.1 Career Exploration Steps
1. Identify career opportunities in sport and physical activity
2. Identify strengths, abilities, and interests
3. Identify educational experiences
4. Identify work experiences
5. Identify career expectations
6. Identify career goals
7. Develop a four-year career plan

Step 1 – Identify Career Opportunities in Sport and Physical Activity

With such a broad array of opportunities, the first step in your career exploration is to identify specific career opportunities in sport and physical activity (AKA, 2011; Wuest & Fisette , 2012; ACSM, 2013; Huntington College, 2013). Pete already has his sights set on a university athletic director position, but he realizes the importance of researching job responsibilities including the hours, qualifications, earnings, opportunities for advancement, and greatest challenges. Pete researched his potential job by obtaining information from multiple sources:

- Foundations of sport and physical activity course
- Occupational handbook
- A career counselor
- Talking with a professional already in the field (Pete's father and those within the University of Alabama's Athletic Department)

Pete completed his research and developed Exhibit 2.2 that provided him a detailed list of potential careers in sport and physical activity.

Step 2 – Identify Skills, Abilities, and Interests

One key factor in defining an ideal career is to identify your skills, abilities, and interests. Knowing what you are good at is half the battle in choosing a career. More than 90% of employers indicate potential job seekers do not know how to present their skills, abilities, or interests effectively (Farr, 2009). According to a study conducted by the U.S. Department of Labor and the American Association of Counseling and Development (Farr, 2009), employers have identified the top eight skills employers would like to see in a prospective employee:

- Learn to learn
- Basic academic skills (reading, writing)
- Good communication skills (listening and speaking)
- Creative thinking and problem solving

- Self-esteem, motivation, and goal setting
- Personal and career development skills
- Interpersonal skills and teamwork
- Organizational effectiveness and leadership

Exhibit 2.2 Sport and Fitness Center Careers

Academics
Sport Management Professor
Sport Management Researcher
Sport Department Administrator
Kinesiology Professor
Kinesiology Researcher
Kinesiology Department Administrator

Clinical
Clinical Exercise Physiologist
Certified Clinical Exercise Specialist
Medical and Osteopathic Physicians
Sport Medicine Clinical Director
Occupational Physiologist
Cardiopulmonary Rehabilitation Specialist
Medical Doctor
Physicians Assistant
Exercise Physiologist
Sport Psychologist

Corporate/Commercial/Campus Recreation Fitness
Group Exercise Instructor
Employee Fitness Director
Personal Trainer
Sport Dietitian/Sports Nutritionist
Health Promotion Specialist
Fitness Specialist
Fitness Leaders in Gerontology Settings
Sport Instructor

Facility Management
Facility Program Management
Facility Physical Management
Facility Emergency Management
Fitness Facility Management
Building/Vendor Services Manager
Ballpark/Field/Arena Management
Sports Convention Management
Data Network Surveillance

Sport Business
Entrepreneurial Opportunities
Youth Sports Entrepreneurship
Fitness Entrepreneurship
Sport/Recreation Equipment Small
    Business Entrepreneurship
Sports Equipment: Manager, Sales,
    Entrepreneurship
Sports Apparel Sales, Entrepreneurship
Merchandise Services

Sport Communication
Sports Information Director
Sport Media
Communications Manager
Public Relations
Sport Journalist

Sport Event Management
Event-City Liaison
Sport Hospitality Management
Sport Guest Management & Services
Olympic/Paralympic Management
    Program Operations
Special Olympics Programming &
    Operations
Youth Development Programming
Sports Trade Show Management
Sport Convention Planner
Safety Surveillance
Sport Conference Planner/Manager
Director of Operations
Sport Tourism
Event Tour Services

Sport And Fitness Administration
High School/College Athletic Director
Hall of Fame Administration
Amateur Sports Administration
Coach

cont'd

Exhibit 2.2 Sport and Fitness Center Careers

Recreation Management
Aquatic Director
Corporate Fitness Program Coordinator
Health Spa, Fitness Facility Director
Recreational Sports Management
Municipal, State, or National Program
    Manager
Aquatic and Waterfront Management
Specialized Sport Facility Management/
    Ownership
Retirement Community Recreation
    Administrator
Community Recreation Facility Management
Resort Management
Prison/Rehabilitation Recreation
    Administrator
Community Recreation Facility Programmer
Camp Director
Camp Management and Programmer
Special Needs Recreation Facilitator
Cruise Ship Recreation Management/
    Programmer
Amusement Park Management/Programmer
Youth Agency Management/Programmer
Extreme Sports Management Programmer
Health Spa, Fitness Programmer
Assisted Living Recreation/Activities
    Programmer
Paralympics Programming
Special Needs/Disabilities Programming
Recreational Festival Programming
Community Recreation Facility Programmer
Municipal, State, or National Park Director
Therapeutic Recreation
Armed Forces Recreation Administration/
    Programming
Travel and Tourism Programmer
Real Estate/Housing Recreation
    Programming
Corporate Recreation Administrator/
    Programmer
US Ranger
Outdoor Preservationist
Recreation Advocacy Specialist
Wilderness Programming/Specialist
Playground Equipment Development/
    Specialist
DNR Interpreter

Sport Official
Campus Recreation Director
Strength and Conditioning Coach
Fitness Center Owner of Manager
Corporate Fitness Program Coordinator

Sport Law
Sport Law Specialist

Sport Marketing
Marketing Manager
Sports Advertising
Web Developer
Client Services
Athletic, VIP Services
Membership Services

Sport Publicity And Promotions
Sports Promotion
Corporate Promotions
Promotion Material Editor
Sales Analyst
Ticket Sales
Sponsorship Sales
Sponsorship Services
Director of Annual Giving
Sports Fundraising
Alumni/Donor Relations

Therapy
Physical Therapist
Occupational Therapist
Chiropractor
Athletic Trainer (College/High School/
    Physical Extender, clinical)
Biomechanist

Complete Exercise 2.1 to help you identify a career.

Exercise 2.1 Identification of Career

1. What career would you like to research? _____
   _____

2. What are the job responsibilities of this career? _____
   _____

3. What are the approximate hours you will be working in this career?
   _____

4. What are the qualifications for this career? _____
   _____

5. What is the salary range for this career? _____
   _____

6. What are the opportunities for advancement within this career? _____
   _____

7. What are the greatest challenges within this career?_____
   _____

Joe identified his strengths and interests by reflecting on his experiences with professors, previous employers, peers, and parents. Joe asked himself the following questions:

- **What are your strengths (skills/abilities)?** Joe identified hardworking, reliable, punctual, and pay attention to detail.

- **What are your interest areas? What do you like to do?** Joe likes to attend all sporting events at his college, keep scoreboard for the men's basketball games, and enjoys his opportunity to promote intramural activities as a recreational sports marketing student worker.

- **What makes you a good worker?** Joe identified highly motivated team player and strong work ethic as his personal attributes

- **What personal abilities are reflected in your accomplishments?** Joe earned the volunteer award for his dedication to keeping scoreboard for the men's basketball team and the supervisor of the year for his dedication, punctuality, and customer service skills while serving the intramural department.

Complete Exercise 2.2 to identify your strength and interests.

Exercise 2.2 Strengths and Interest

1. What are your strengths (includes skills and abilities)? _____
   _____

2. What are your interest areas? What do you like to do?
   _____

3. What makes you a good worker? _____
   _____

4. What personal abilities are reflected in your accomplishments? _____
   _____

Step 3 – Identify Educational Experiences

Success throughout college can greatly facilitate the achievement of your career goals. Since you spent the majority of your life in school, identifying educational experiences may provide you with additional information on choosing a career. For example, Samantha is the president of the sport and physical activity club at her university. Samantha is also an active volunteer for all of the Sport and Human Performance Department activities such as the health fair, the after-school sports programs, the major's yearly fitness assessment, and family day.

There are also curriculums geared toward preparing for a career in sport and physical activity. These curriculums do vary from one university to the next but they all have some commonalities in terms of the core, major courses, minor courses, and field experiences. The core or liberal arts courses provide the base knowledge and usually consist of classes from the sciences, math, English, art, languages, and music. The major courses are specifically focused on sport and physical activity and provide you with knowledge relative to your discipline and prepare you for your chosen career. Electives are offered for several reasons, including enhanced marketability, prerequisites for graduate school, to fulfill the degree, and to strengthen your career preparation. You may also use electives to help fulfill a minor, concentration, or specialization. The minor, concentration, or specialization may broaden your career options while increasing your marketability. For example, Samantha pursues a degree as a recreational therapist and has the expectations to manage a facility in the future; therefore she opts to pursue a specialization in sport management. Complete Exercise 2.3 to identify educational experiences to help you choose a career in sport and physical activity.

Exercise 2.3 Educational Experiences

1. What are some of the extracurricular activities you are participating in during your educational experience?

   _____

2. What specific courses are related and provide relevant information for your potential career? What courses do you have interest in the most?

   _____

3. What are your academic strengths? What area of study do you enjoy most?

   _____ _____

   _____

Step 4 – Identify Work Experiences

Your work experience may provide you with some insight on special skills that may lead to a career. Work experience may include on-the-job training, volunteer work, and/or field experiences. You want to begin by listing each job and specific skills you learned from these experiences. Next, identify skills that directly relate to your job objective. For example, Joe realized his skills specific to a Sports Information Director included keeping stats for the Men's Basketball games and promotion intramural events. Complete Exercise 2.4 to identify work experiences from on-the-job training, volunteer work, and/or field experiences

Exercise 2.4 Work Experience

Experience 1

Name of organization_____

Job Title _____

_____

Employment Dates _____

_____

Identify skills specific to sport and physical activity _____ __

_____

Identify what you learned from this experience _____

_____

_____

How would you summarize your employer evaluation? _____

_____

Experience 2

Name of organization _____

_____

Job Title _____

_____

Employment Dates _____

_____

Identify skills specific to sport and physical activity _____

_____

Identify what you learned from this experience _____

_____

How would you summarize your employer evaluation? _____

_____

Step 5 – Identify Career Expectations

Your career expectations are important to identify your ideal job. The career expectations include the following variables:

- Preferred earnings
- Work hours
- Work environment
- Vacation accrual
- Level of responsibility
- Location

Pete reflected on his career expectations by asking himself the following questions:

- **What are your salary expectations?** Pete wanted to be associated with a successful athletic program and therefore salary was not a factor.

- **What is your hour expectations?** Pete identified with the long hours of an Athletic Director because an his experience as a student-athlete. Pete knew he would need to be working 60+ hours a week depending on the sport season.

- **How much vacation time would you prefer?** Pete liked the idea of having the opportunity to have three weeks of vacation during the summer months.

- **What kind of environment do you want to work in?** Pete learned to be a team player because of his experience as a student-athlete. Pete wanted the same team environment in the workplace.

- **Do you want to be in charge?** As the team captain, Pete enjoyed acting as a leader and wants to pursue a position as an Assistant Athletic Director.

- **Do you want to work in an urban, suburban, or rural area?** Pete does not have a preference on where he lives.

Complete Exercise 2.5 in deciding what is important to you when choosing a career.

Exercise 2.5 Career Expectations

1. What are your salary expectations? _____
   _____

2. What are your hour expectations? _____
   _____

3. How much vacation time would you like in a year?_____
   _____

4. What kind of environment do you want work in? Do you prefer to work with a team or an individual basis? What population do you prefer working with (youth, teens, young adults, middle age)?_____
   _____

5. Do you prefer to be in charge? Are you good at supervising others?
   _____

6. Do you want to work in an urban, suburban, or rural setting?
   _____
   _____

Step 6 — Identify Career Objective and Goals

After you identified career opportunities, strengths/abilities/interests, educational experiences, and expectations you need to develop career goals based upon your career objective. The career objective is specific and consists of particular outcomes. Joe used the guidelines in Chapter 3, Exercise 3.2 to develop his objective. For example, Joe states his career objective is "To obtain a Sports Information Director position where I can utilize my skills in writing, designing, keeping stats, and acting as a liason between coaches, student-athletes, and members of the media."

To complement the objective, specific goals provide you with a guide to accomplish the objective. Goal setting is instrumental in assessing your abilities and interests while establishing short and long-term expectations. Short-term goals are accomplishments occurring within a day, week, or month whereas long-term goals are often larger in scope thus taking longer to accomplish (Lumpkin, 2013). Short-term and long-term goals are essential to achieving a career. Joe had to ask himself what he needed to do in order to accomplish his objective. For example, Joe decided on the goals below to complement his objective:

1.   To complete an internship specific to career choice.

2.   To send resume and cover letter to specific schools offering a graduate assistantship.

3.   To post resume and cover letter on specific sports sites.

4.   To attend job fairs and submit resumes.

5.   To attend conferences, submit resumes, and interview for jobs.

Notice how Joe combined his objective and career goals together in Exhibit 2.3.

Exhibit 2.3 Career Goals Sample

Career Objective: To obtain a Sports Information Director position where I can utilize my skills in writing, designing, keeping stats, and acting as a liason between coaches, student-athletes, and members of the media.

Long-Term Goal: To become a Sports Information Director within a university setting.

Short-Term Goals:

1.   To complete an internship specific to his career choice.

2.   To send a resume and cover letter to specific schools offering a graduate assistantship.

3.   To post my resume and cover letter on specific sports sites – August 2014 until obtained.

4.   To attend conferences, submit resumes, and interview for jobs

---

Complete Exercise 2.6 to develop your career objective and goals. You need to refer to Chapter 3, Exercise 3.2, to determine your objective. Next, you need to follow Joe and determine how you can accomplish your objective through your long and short-term goals.

Exercise 2.6 Career Goals

Career Objective: _____

_____

Long-Term Goal: _____

_____

Short-Term Goals:

1._____

2._____

3._____

Step 7 — Develop the Four - Year Career Plan

You have completed STEPS 1-6 to determine what career you would like to pursue. Where do you go from here? Joe, Pete, and Samantha began the process by developing a four-year career plan when they were freshmen. A four-year plan provides you with a detailed example of how you can prepare for the career you want to obtain in sport and physical activity. Joe, Pete, and Samantha had to meet with professors, talk to professionals, conduct research, and take advantage of opportunities to learn more about becoming a professional in their prospective career. For example, Exhibit 2.4 provides a four-year career plan Joe used to develop his final objective and goals as mentioned previously in Exhibit 2.3.

Exhibit 2.4 Four - Year Career Plan

I. **Freshman Year**
    A. **Academics** – to develop an academic plan in sport management through the guidance of my advisor

    B. **Goals**
    Long-term – to obtain a 20 hour field experience/observation within a university athletic department
    Short-term –
        1. to interview an Athletic Director at a local university
        2. to ask about potential student-worker positions
        3. to network with as many administrators and coaches as possible in the athletic department by attending athletic events and/or functions.

    C. **Related Work Experience** – to volunteer to work summer sports camps and obtain a 20 hour field experience/observation working within the athletic department

D. **University/Professional Activities** – to join the sport management club

E. **Certifications/Memberships/Conferences** – to research College Sports Information Directors of America (CoSIDA) the North American Society for Sport Mangement (NASSM) organizations and to obtain a first aid/CPR/AED certification

F. **Career Strategies** – to visit the career services center on campus to find out about services offered and specific jobs in sport and physical activity; to begin a professional portfolio

II. **Sophomore Year**

A. **Academics** – to determine a minor or specialization (Communications) to complement my major (sport management)

B. **Goals**
Long-term - to obtain a practicum as a Sports Information Director intern at local university.The focus of this practicum is to compile statistics, personal information about players and teams, to provide postgame data, and to publicize upcoming events.
Short-term –
   1. to interview for the Sports Information Director Field Experience;
   2. to show my interest in working with the University of Alabama's Sports Information Director.

C. **Related Work Experience** – to obtain a practicum with the Sports Information Director

D. **University/Professional Activities** – to run for Treasure of the Sport Management Club

E. **Certifications/Memberships/Conferences** – to attend the NASSM conference and network with other students in the field of sport management. To renew CPR/First Aid/AED Certification.

F. **Career Strategies** – to complete a professional development course to prepare my resume and cover letter; to update professional portfolio

III. **Junior Year**

A. **Academics** –to begin to think about graduate school. To obtain informatioin about potential graduate assistantship opportunities and requirements.

B. **Goals**
Long-term - to obtain an additional practicum with a Sports Information Director. The focus of this practicum is press releases and team brochures
Short-term -
   1. to express an interest in helping with press release and team brochures.
   2. to remind the Sports Information Director of my minor in Communications

C. **Related Work Experience** – to complete a practicum with a Sports Information Director

D. **University/Professional Activities** – to run for Vice President of the Sport Management Club

E. **Certifications/Memberships/Conferences** - to join NASSM as a student member; submit a poster presentation conference to NASSM; renew first aid/CPR and AED certification

F. **Career Strategies** – to fine-tune interview skills (mock interviews); to update professional portfolio

IV. **Senior Year**

A. **Academics** – to apply for graduate assistantships.

B. **Goals**

Long-term - to obtain a Sports Information Director position where I can utilize my skills in writing, designing, keeping stats, and act as a liason between coaches, student-athletes, and members of the media.

Short-term –

1. to complete an internship specific to Sports Information Director

2. to send resume and cover letter to specific schools offering a graduate assistantship.

3. to post resume and cover letter on specific sport sites

4. to attend job fairs and submit resumes.

5. to attend conferences, submit resumes, and interview for jobs

C. **Related Work Experiences** – to complete an internship where I may strengthen my skills to obtain a graduate assistantship.

D. **University/Professional Activities** – to run for President of the Sport Management Club

E. **Certifications/Memberships/Conferences** – to renew at NASSM membership; to renew first aid/CPR/AED certification

G. **Career Strategies** – to update professional portfolio; to contact individuals in your network

Complete Exercise 2.7 to develop your four-year career plan. If you are not a freshman begin the plan with your academic year in school.

Exercise 2.7 Four-Year Career Plan

I. Freshman Year
   A. Academics

_____

   B. Goals
      Long-term

_____

Short-term

1. _____

2. _____

3. _____

C. Related Work Experience

_____

D. University/Professional Activities

_____

E. Certifications/Memberships/Conferences

_____

F. Career Strategies

_____

II. Sophomore Year

A. Academics

_____

B. Goals

Long-term

_____

Short-term

1._____

2._____

3._____

C. Related Work Experience

_____

D. University/Professional Activities

_____

E. Certifications/Memberships/Conferences

_____

F. Career Strategies

_____

III. Junior Year

A. Academics

_____

B. Goals

Long-term

_____

Short-term

1. _____

2. _____

3. _____

C. Related Work Experience

_____

D. University/Professional Activities

_____

E. Certifications/Memberships/Conferences

_____

F. Career Strategies

_____

IV. Senior Year

A. Academics

_____

B. Goals

Long-term

_____

Short-term

1. _____

2. _____

3. _____

C. Related Work Experience

_____

D. University/Professional Activities

_____

E. Certifications/Memberships/Conferences

_____

F. Career Strategies

_____

Where Do You Go From Here?

In this chapter, you identified a variety of information to help you define an ideal career in sport and physical activity. Joe, Pete, and Samantha wanted to connect their characteristics with their potential career choice. Joe, Pete, and Samantha used Figure 2.1 to complete this task. For example, Pete summarized the following information to make a clear connection between his characteristics and career:

■ Sport or Physical Activity Career – University Athletic Director

Connecting characteristics specific to this job that make Pete an ideal candidate for the position

■ Educational Experiences

• Major in Sport Management

• Member of men's tennis team

■ Work Experience

• School system summer position in the athletic department (works with father)

• University summer tennis camps

■ Career Expectations

• Salary not a factor

• 60+ hours a week during sport season

• 3-weeks summer vacation

■ Career Goals

• To complete an internship within a university athletic department

• To apply for a graduate assistantship by contacting schools and posting resumes on appropriate websites

■ Four-Year Plan

• Attach a copy of four-year plan to the career wheel (Figure 2.1).

Notice how Pete included a maximum of three responses for each characteristic located on the wheel. Use Figure 2.1 to completing Exercise 2.8 to make sure you have made a clear connection between your career characteristics and potential career.

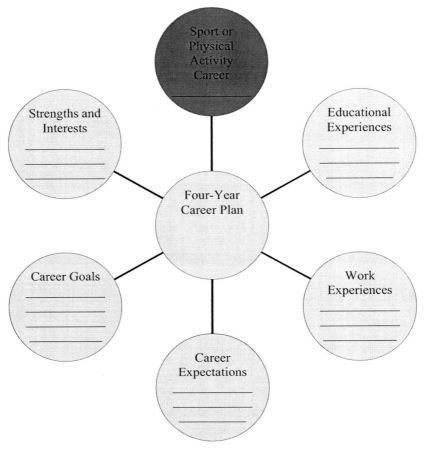

Figure 2.1 Career Wheel

1. Career Choice _____

_____

2. Educational Experiences _____

_____

3. Work Experience _____

_____

4. Career Expectations _____

_____

5. Career Goals/Objectives _____

_____

6. Strengths and Interests_____

Summary

Selecting a career path requires careful consideration of academic and experiential learning experiences. You were able to evaluate your career opportunities, strengths, abilities, interests, educational experiences, work experiences, and career expectations. Once the career wheel exercise was completed you need to ask yourself, "Am I headed in the right direction in pursuing this career?" Regardless if the answer to this question is "yes" or "no," you want to begin thinking about additional ways to prepare yourself for the career of your choice. The remainder of this book focuses on professional development tools (resume, cover letter, student portfolio, networking, interviewing) to help you obtain a field experience so you can land the job of your dreams!

Frequently Asked Questions

How do you choose a career?

You need to select a career as opposed to a position. The first step is finding out about you. Understanding your interests, abilities, values and personality is crucial to making good decisions.

What if I choose the wrong career?

That's a perfectly normal fear, but unfortunately you may never be 100% sure that you are doing the right thing. Making a good decision means that you have researched majors and occupations enough to feel that you are ready to take a reasonable risk and at least check it out. And remember, nothing is forever - you can always change your mind

What happens if I can't get into the major I really want? Is it the only door to that career?

Keep in mind that you may be able to reach your career goal from a variety of different majors. Doing some further exploration about the career of interest may provide you with alternative ways to achieve your goal.

Student Learning Activities

Complete the Career Exploration Exercises throughout this chapter.

Interview two people (one male and one female) of that potential career. Use questions from Exercise 2.1 to help identify a career and interview two people (one male and one female) within that area.

Get into small groups and solicit each other's input regarding a potential career choice.

Develop a four-year career plan.

> **Potential Career Opportunities Checklist**

❏ Identified career opportunities in sport and physical activity

❏ Identified strengths, abilities, and interests

❏ Identified educational experiences

❏ Identified work experiences

❏ Identified career expectations

❏ Identified career goals

❏ Developed a four-year career plan

CAREER HIGHLIGHT - ASSOCIATE SPORTS INFORMATION DIRECTOR

Jenna Willhoit

Sports Information Intern Assistant

Xavier University

Cincinnati, OH

Education And Certifications

BA in English from the University of Kentucky

MA in sport administration from the University of Louisville

Years In Position

2 years

Previous Positions

Previously held positions at Tennessee Tech and at the University of Louisville as a Sports Information Assistant (Intern)

Current Job Responsibilities And Hours

I am the primary sports information contact for women's basketball as well as the web site coordinator. I act as a liason between the coaches and student-athletes and members of the media. I design and write media guides, write game/match recaps for www.GOXAVIER.com, keep stats at home events using a statistical program called Statcrew, design and write match/game programs, design and write game/match notes and any other press releases. My average work week is 40-50+ hours per week (depends on what sports are in season).

Greatest Challenges

Time management!!!! Also, as a woman in a male dominated field, I sometimes have to work twice as hard to get the same recognition as a man.

Career Advice

I would advise that one start volunteering as soon as possible. I didn't know until I was 25 that I wanted to work in sports information and you have to have at least two years of experience to get a full-time, salaried position. The sooner you start working/volunteering in your desired field the better.

CAREER HIGHLIGHT – DIRECTOR OF ATHELTICS – INTERCOLLEGIATE ATHLETICS

Jon Mark Hall

Director of Athletics, University of Southern Indiana

Education and Certifications

Ohio State University

Masters of Art Sport Management

Murray State University

Bachelor of Art Business

Certification – Graduate of Sport Management Institute (SMI – University of Notre Dame and University of South Carolina)

Years in Position

Athletic Director for 12 years (January 2002) at the University of Southern Indiana

Previous Position:

Assistant Athletic Director at the University of Southern Indiana

Assistant Athletic Director at University of South Carolina-Spartanburg (now University of South Carolina-Upstate)

Current job responsibilities and hours:

Oversee all operations of athletic department. Head Coaches of all sports report to me as well as Associate AD, Training Staff, and other Administrative personnel. Normal work day is 8 – 4:30, but many weekend and evening hours are required.

Greatest Challenges

Greatest challenge is trying to accomplish what you want to accomplish with limited resources. You cannot make excuses and have to be creative in making things happen.

Career Advice

Hard work is necessary to be successful in whatever you may do. But most importantly, be passionate about what you do. If you aren't passionate about your profession, tough roads can lie ahead. Do want you want to do and don't let people tell you that it can't happen.

References

American College of Sports Medicine. (2013). *Careers in sports medicine and exercise science.* Retrieved December 28, 2013 from www.acsm.org.

American Kinesiology Association. (2011). *Careers in sport, fitness, and exercise.* Champaign, IL: Human Kinetics.

Farr, M. (2009). *The Very Quick Job Search.* Indianapolis, IN: JIST Publishing, Inc.

Halvorson, R. (2011). *Spring-clean your resume.* Retrieved December 28, 2013, from, http://www.ideafit.com/fitness-library/spring-clean-your-resumeacute

Huntington College. (2013). *Sport Management & Recreation Management Career Opportunities.* Retrieved December 28, 2013, from http://www.huntington.edu/uploadedFiles/Kinesiology_and_Recreation_Management/Programs2/Career%20Possibilities.pdf

Lumpkin, A. (2013). *Introduction to physical education, exercise science, and sport, 9th edition.* New York: NY: McGraw-Hill.

U.S. Department of Labor (2013). *2012-2013 Occupation outlook handbook.* Retrieved December 28, 2013, from www.bls.gov/es/ooh.

Wuest, D. A., & Fisette, J. L. (2012). *Foundations of physical education, exercise Science, and sport.* New York: NY: McGraw-Hill.

—

SECTION II

PROFESSIONAL DEVELOPMENT TOOLS

WRITING A RESUME

SCENARIO #1 – FIELD EXPERIENCE/OBSERVATION - SOPHOMORE

Andrea

*Andrea is a sophomore and currently enrolled in a sport and physical activity field experience course (20 hours-1 credit hour). Andrea has only worked odd jobs during the summer that are not related to sport and physical activity. Andrea wants to use this field experience to add valuable knowledge and skills to her resume while networking with professionals in recreational sports. Her professor introduces her to the **skills resume** since Andrea has limited experience. The skills resume will allow Andrea to present herself by highlighting what she has done under specific skills rather than under previous work experience.*

SCENARIO #2 – PRACTICUM - JUNIOR

Stephanie

*Stephanie is a junior enrolled in a practicum course (150 hours – 3 credit hours). Stephanie does have work experience related to the position she is applying for at a local health and fitness facility. Since Stephanie has some work related experience, extracurricular activities, professional memberships, and personal achievements she decides to develop a **combination resume**.*

SCENARIO #3 – INTERNSHIP - SENIOR

Mark

*Mark is a senior enrolled in an internship course (450 hours – 9 credit hours). Mark has accumulated three years of work-related experience by taking advantage of his part-time positions, his work-related volunteer and field experiences within sport and physical activity. Mark has a desire to work in Sport Marketing and is inspired by career highlights of Beth Johnson and James Breeding (end of the chapter). Beth is currently a Marketing Assistant Intern at Xavier University and James is the Director of Sales for the Louisville Riverbats. After careful consideration, Mark decides to pursue an internship as a Sport Advertising Associate for a minor league baseball team. Unlike Andrea, Mark has previous experience related to the internship and he decides to use a **reverse chronological resume** to show his experience in the field.*

Creating a resume is one of the most important tasks you will develop whether seeking a field experience or full-time job in sport and physical activity. A resume "is an accurate account of educational and professional qualifications, accomplishments, and experiences" (Pierce & Snyder, 2006, 19). The resume serves several purposes :

- Presents you to perspective employers

- Used as a screening tool

- Used as a promotion tool to help you achieve career goals

- Helps in organizing an effective job search

The purpose of this chapter is to help you identify the types of resumes and strategies for writing an effective resume. It also introduces resumes for sport and physical activity jobs to make the process of writing your resume easier and faster.

Types of Resumes

There are four basic types of resume formats including, skill (functional), combination, reverse-chronological, and Curriculum Vita (CV) (Salvador, 2006). In choosing the type of resume to prepare, you need to consider how well your skills and experiences match the job you are seeking. If you have little or no relevant work experience, a skills format is appropriate. If you have at least three relevant work experiences, a reverse-chronological format is preferable. Finally, if you have both work experience and skills then you may choose a combination resume. The standard length for the first three resume types is one page while the CV has no preferred length.

Skills or Functional Resume

As the name suggests, this type of resume focuses on the skills and strengths you may have related to the position for which you are applying. In this resume, the skills are clustered under major skill areas (Kursmark, 2011). For example, if leadership is a skill required for the job, you may list the skill and experiences that helped you develop it, such as being the leader of a sport and physical activity majors' club, for a specific group project, or at a summer sports camp. Ultimately, this resume allows you to emphasize the skills you may offer employers and de-emphasize limited work experience. The scenario of Andrea provides a good example of the limited experience she has in applying for a position with a University Recreational Sports Department. Andrea is encouraged to develop a skills resume. Andrea has several skills resume templates to choose from including the one in Exhibit 3.1 and

---

Exhibit 3.1 Skills or Functional Resume Template

NAME

| Phone | Address, City, State, Zip | Email Address |

OBJECTIVE

Skills and Career Achievements

Leadership	Paragraph describing skills and related experiences
Management	Paragraph describing skills and related experiences
Marketing	Paragraph describing skills and related experiences
Computer Applications	Paragraph describing skills and related experiences

EDUCATION

Degree, Name of School

    Anticipated graduation Date

    GPA or academic honors

Research project; Academic Honors

Professional Memberships

List organization

Extracurricular Activities

Name of activity, date

Name of activity, date

---

additional options in Appendix A. Andrea finally decides on one of the skills resume templates (Appendix A – Sample 1) and begin using the step-by-step procedures and guidelines in writing her resume (Appendix B – Sample 1). Notice how the her skills resume allowed Andrea to highlight her strengths in relation to skills without emphasizing limited work experience. Andrea mentions her exposure to a variety of short-term positions (Amigo Freshmen Orientation Counselor, Lifeguard, Summer Camp Counselor), but does not mention for how long.

Reverse - Chronological Resume

The reverse-chronological resume is the most traditional in organizing information by work experience. The objective of this type of resume is to list related work experiences and/or field experiences in reverse order from most recent to least recent (Halvorsa, 2011; Kursmark, 2011). The objective of the resume is for the employer to see a career progression, thus allowing for a quick screening to see if you meet the preferred profile. Although reverse-chronological is preferred most often by employers, this type of resume may not be appropriate if you are beginning your job search. The scenario of Mark provides a good example of a student with work-related experience specific in obtaining a sport marketing position with a minor league baseball team. Mark has several reverse-chronological resume templates to choose from including the one in Exhibit 3.2 and additional options in Appendix A. Mark finally decides on one of the reverse-chronological templates (Appendix A - Sample 5) and begins using the step-by-step procedures and guidelines in writing his resume (Appendix B - Sample 9). Notice how the reverse - chronological resume allowed Mark to highlight his level of responsibility in regards to work experience, the ability to manage many activities, and the necessary skills the employer of the marketing agency would like to see.

Exhibit 3.2 Reverse Chronological Resume Template
NAME
Address, City, State, Zip ■ Phone ■ Email Address
OBJECTIVE: Write objective here
EDUCATION
Degree – Expected Graduation
Name of school – city, state
GPA or Academic honors/awards (if applicable)
■ Thesis or special projects (if applicable)
■ Scholarship/fellowship (if applicable)

RELEVANT EXPERIENCE (most recent first)

Employers name, Employers city, state, zip   Employment Dates

   Position title

- ■ Duties and accomplishments
- ■ Duties and accomplishments
- ■ Duties and accomplishments

Employers name, Employers city, state, zip   Employment Dates

   Position title

- ■ Duties and accomplishments
- ■ Duties and accomplishments

Employers name, Employers city, state, zip   Employment Dates

   Position title

- ■ Duties and accomplishments
- ■ Duties and accomplishments
- ■ Duties and accomplishments

Combination Resume

The combination resume is a combination of the skills and reverse-chronological format. This resume may be used when you have some work experience related to the position, yet you also have acquired skills through unrelated or non-work experiences. The combination resume is a good strategy when your experience is limited but the employer wants to see a chronological listing of your work history. You may begin the resume by highlighting your qualifications, personal attributes, transferable skills, extracurricular activities, professional memberships, and/or achievements that showcase your work history. The scenario of Stephanie provides a good example of a student with work experience not related to a position within health and fitness, but who may showcase other attributes of extracurricular activities, professional memberships, and achievements. Stephanie has several combination resume templates to choose from including the one in Exhibit 3.3 and additional options in Appendix A. Stephanie finally decides on one of the combination resume templates (Appendix A – Sample 9) and begins using the step-by-step procedures and guidelines in writing her resume (Appendix B – Sample 17). Notice how the combination resume allowed Stephanie to highlight her transferable skills, solid work ethic, academic accomplishments, extensive honors, professional development training, and her prior experience in the health and fitness industry.

Exhibit 3.3 Combination Resume Template

NAME	**Address**
	Phone Number
OBJECTIVE:	**Email Address**

HIGHLIGHTS OF QUALIFICATIONS

- Qualifications
- Qualifications
- Qualifications

SKILLS

List by name (specifics to field)   List by name (Specifics to field)

List by name (Specifics to field)   List by name (Specifics to field)

EDUCATION   **EXTRACURICULAR ACTIVTIES**

Degree, Name of School   • Activity

    Anticipated graduation Date   • Activity

    GPA or academic honors   • Activity

Research project/Academic Honors   • Activity

RELATED EXPERIENCE

Position title

    Employers name, Employers city, state, zip - Employment dates

    Duties and accomplishments (paragraph form)

Position title

    Employers name, Employers city, state, zip - Employment dates

    Duties and accomplishments (paragraph form)

PROFESSIONAL MEMBERSHIPS **PERSONAL ACHIEVEMENTS**

- Organization
- Organization

• Personal achievement

• Personal achievement

Curriculum Vita

The Curriculum Vita (CV) is similar to the resume and is considered to be the standard by some specialized professional groups, including college professors, researchers, physicians, attorneys, and various other professions. If you plan to go to graduate school, you will probably need to develop a CV. The CV provides the employer with a comprehensive record of accomplishments emphasizing education and professional qualifications (Pierce & Snyder, 2006). It is inclusive and displays qualifications in a substantive way; does not have a standard length and, like all resumes, is usually more effective when targeted to the position and institution applying for (Doyle, 2013).

Step-by-Step Procedures and Guidelines in Writing a Resume

Andrea, Mark, and Stephanie did not create their resume overnight. The resume takes time to develop. Andrea, Stephanie, and Mark followed simple guidelines and exercises located throughout this chapter for constructing each section of their resume. The steps are summarized in Exhibit 3.4 and exercises are located throughout the chapter to keep you organized while making sure important information is not omitted from your resume.

Exhibit 3.4 Step-by-step Procedures and Guidelines in Writing a Resume

1. Develop content sections of resume

   a. Contact information

   b. Career objectives

   c. Skills section (soft and hard)

   d. Combine objective with skills summary or profile (optional)

   e. Education and/or military experience

   f. Work experience

   g. Professional certifications

   h. Professional and university club memberships and/or awards

   j. Extracurricular activities or personal information

2. Use the content sections and presentation guidelines to write the resume

   a. Choose a resume format

   b. Develop an appropriate resume template

---

c. Place content into template

d. Finalize the length

e. Proofread and correct the resume

3. Determine transmission of the resume (internet, email, faxed, scanned, paper)

4. Determine follow-up procedures after submitting resume

Step 1 – Develop Content Sections of Resume

Since the sections of the skills, reverse-chronological, and combination resumes are very similar you can begin the process of writing the resume by developing the content sections.

Contact Information

The contact information consists of your name, mailing address (s), phone numbers, fax number, and email address. Although this section seems quite simple to develop on a resume, Exhibit 3.5 provides some general guidelines about issues that may not have occurred to you (Betrus, 2011; Kursmark, 2011; Kursmark, 2012).

Exhibit 3.5 General Guidelines for Content Information

NAME

1. Do not use a nickname

2. Do not use "Jr." or "II" following the name — readers may think you are defining yourself

3. Avoid using the academic degree after the name (displayed in education section)

MAILING ADDRESS

1. Do not abbreviate "Street" or "Avenue"

2. Do not spell out the state – use the accepted two-letter abbreviations

3. Use the nine-digit zip code from www.usps.com or local post office

4. If you live in an apartment make sure to include the number

5. Avoid using a post office box if at all possible (reflects instability)

6. If you are moving make sure to ask someone you know for a temporary address

---

PHONE NUMBERS

1. Do not include current employer's phone number (use of current employer's resources)

2. Always include area code

3. Make sure an appropriate voicemail is set-up for the phone numbers provided

4. Be careful about providing cell phone numbers. You must consider whether you will be able to talk whenever the prospective employer calls and you answer.

FAX NUMBER

1. Using your fax number is optional

2. Do not include fax number of employer (use of current employer's resources)

3. If you list a fax number make sure to check it often.

EMAIL ADDRESS

1. Using your email address is optional

2. Use one email address specifically to send and receive information about positions. Free email accounts - gmail/yahoo/hotmail

3. You do not need to include the email in the heading. Place this information on the signature line of the email

4. If you use an email address make sure to check it often

Now complete Exercise 3.1 to prepare your contact information.

Exercise 3.1 Contact Information

NAME _____

CURRENT ADDRESS _____

_____

CELLULAR PHONE _____

CURRENT TELEPHONE _____

CELLULAR PHONE _____

EMAIL ADDRESS _____

FAX _____

Exhibit 3.6 contains samples of how Andrea, Stephanie, and Mark utilized their contract information in the resume.

Exhibit 3.6 Contact Information Samples
ANDREA MARTIN
1345 Clairview Drive * Ithaca, NY * 34567
Home: (432)567-8965
Cell Phone: (342)546-4356
Email: Amartin@netcom.net
MARK O'REILLY
15 North 1234 East
Salt Lake City, UT
(988)434-5687 Morelly@aol.com
STEPHANIE MCCULLOUGH
2345 Deed Street, #15
864-456-9876
Maiden, NC
Jane.McC@wiscon.edu

Objective

Although an objective is not a requirement of a resume you can benefit quickly and easily by focusing the employer's attention to your areas of interest. In writing the objective, do not make the mistake of focusing on "your wants" instead emphasize what you can do and how your skills can be used to benefit the position. The objective should be direct, specific, and brief while avoiding irrelevant statements, such as "Desire a position in a health and fitness facility" (Kursmark, 2011). Instead provide an example like Stephanie's (Exhibit 3.7), "Seeking a practicum that requires personal training skills and business skills." Stephanie is specific in stating she is looking for a practicum specifically in the personal training area while learning about the business side. Before developing your own objective, there are four basic questions Andrea, Mark, and Stephanie used in constructing an effective and accurate objective statement for their resume (Kursmark, 2012).

- **What type of position do you want to apply for? What is the title of that position? (if applicable)**

  - Andrea – field experience within campus recreation

  - Stephanie – personal trainer with a specialization in sport management

  - Mark – sport advertising associate for a professional baseball team

- **What type of responsibility would you like to have within this position?**

  - Andrea – exposure to intramurals

  - Stephanie – personal training and management skills

  - Mark – advertising, public service announcements, press releases, flyers, banners, and obtaining local radio stations for advertisements and entertainment

- **What specific areas of expertise would you like to use in this position?**

  - Andrea – self-motivated college students, perseverance with projects and accomplishing goals (limited or no experience so Andrea needs to use personal attributes)

  - Stephanie – personal training skills such as sales, initial consultations, fitness assessments, program designs, and orientations

  - Mark – solid understanding of sport marketing and advertising strategies

- **What additional information would you like to include in your job objective?**

  - Andrea – strong work ethic

  - Stephanie – unique blend of personal training, sport, and physical activity

  - Mark – team-oriented environment

By completing this exercise, Andrea, Stephanie, and Mark were able to develop objectives as illustrated in Exhibit 3.7.

Exhibit 3.7 Objective Samples

Scenario #1 – Andrea/Sophomore/20 hour field experience

Objective   Self-motivated college student with a strong work ethic, evident through perseverance to finish projects and accomplish objectives. Seeking a field experience with a **recreational sports** facility where I can utilize my knowledge of intramurals.

Scenario #2 – Stephanie/Junior/150 hour practicum

Objective: Seeking a practicum where I can improve my **personal training** skills (sales, initial consultation, fitness assessment, program design, orientations) and gain valuable **business** knowledge. Qualified by a unique blend of personal training, sport and physical activity skills.

Scenario #3 – Mark/Senior/450 hour internship

Objective: To obtain a Sport Advertising Internship for a minor league baseball team, where I can have the opportunity to utilize my solid understanding of sport marketing and advertising strategies in providing public service announcements, press releases, flyers, banners, and obtaining local radio stations for advertising and entertainment.

Skills Section

You need to identify core qualifications of your resume by developing a combination of personal attributes "soft" and transferable "hard" skills. Personal attributes or soft skills are part of the "skills" (sometimes called profile, qualifications, or summary) resume providing the employer with an idea of the person behind the resume. The National Association of Colleges and Employers (NACE, 2013) provided a list of top soft skills employers highly value:

- Communication skills (listening verbal, written)
- Honesty
- Teamwork skills
- Motivation/initiative
- Strong work ethic

Now you are ready to develop your own objective using Exercise 3.2.

Exercise 3.2 Objective

What type of position do you want to apply for? What is the title of the position (if applicable)

_____

_____

What type of responsibilities would you like to use in this position?

_____

_____

What specific areas of expertise would you like to use in this position?

_____

_____

_____

What additional information would you like to include in your objective?

_____

_____

_____

Write your objective from the information obtained from Exercise 3.2.

_____

_____

_____

_____

_____

Identifying your positive personal characteristics is extremely useful in preparing your resume (Kursmark, 2011). For example, personal attributes may be all that Andrea has to highlight on her resume due to her lack of experience. Andrea does not develop her personal attributes by simply choosing from Exhibit 3.8, but she focuses on asking herself the following question, **"What really makes me a good worker?"** **"What may employers like about me?"** Andrea may choose to highlight being a highly motivated team player because of her willingness to take on additional responsibilities during class projects, her "strong work ethic" because of working part-time while being a full-time student, and/or her ability to be reliable because of maintaining a perfect employment attendance record for all of her summer Sports Camp Counselor positions. Notice in Exhibit 3.9 how Andrea highlighted her personal attributes.

Exhibit 3.8 Salvador's Modified Personal Attributes Relevant to Sport and Physical Activity

1. Able to show good judgment	21. Innovative
2. Able to show initiative	22. Intelligent
3. Action-driven leader	23. Leader
4. Balanced	24. Motivator
5. Client focused	25. Multitalented or skilled
6. Collaborative	26. Optimistic
7. Communicative	27. Organized
8. Creative	28. Outside-the-box thinker
9. Customer service oriented	29. Passionate
10. Dedicated	30. People-oriented
11. Dependable	31. Professional
12. Educated	32. Respected by others
13. Energetic	33. Role model
14. Ethical	34. Self-confidence
15. Genuine	35. Self-disciplined
16. Goal-driven	36. Success-driven
17. Good listener	37. Team player
18. Hardworking	38. Trusting
19. Honest	39. Visionary
20. Independent	40. Willing to learn

Exhibit 3.9 Personal Attribute Sample Andrea - Sophomore - Field Experience - 20 hours

Objective	Self-motivated college student with a strong work ethic evident through perseverance to finish projects and accomplish objectives. Seeking a field experience within a Recreational Sports Department where I can be exposed to intramurals, special events, extramurals, fitness, and outdoor adventure programs.
Profile	Highly motivated team player, willing to take on additional responsibilities as I have done with group projects in my sport and physical activity courses.
	Strong work ethic illustrated through my determination of working part-time while being enrolled in 16 credit hours a semester. Employers consider me a reliable employee because of my impeccable attendance record as a summer Recreational Sports Camp Counselor.

Exercise 3.3 allows you to list your personal attributes and a supportive example.

Exercise 3.3 Personal Attributes

What really makes you a good worker? What may employers like about you?

1. _____

2. _____

3. _____

4. _____

Examples

1. _____

2. _____

3. _____

4. _____

Transferable skills or hard skills (innate, learned, function-related) are ones that can be transferred to the job (Kursmark, 2011). Transferable skills are the ones learned from a previous position, college, or another part of life that are applicable to the position being sought. Exhibit 3.10 provides a partial list of transferable skills relevant to jobs in sport and physical activity. Mark does not simply choose transferable skills from Exhibit 3.10, but asks himself **"What skills have I obtained through my previous or current volunteer or work experience?"** Mark immediately thinks about his current Marketing Liason for the Annual Golf Tournament at the University of Louisville. Through this experience Mark is able to demonstrate transferable skills because of his responsibility in developing strategies (press releases, electronic media, radio media) to communicate and market the annual faculty golf tournament to faculty, students, and the community. Notice in Exhibit 3.11 how Mark highlighted transferable skills of marketing strategies from the Marketing Liason position.

Exhibit 3.10 Transferable Skills for Jobs in Sport and Physical Activity

1. Advertising
2. Event management
3. Budgeting or managing money
4. Obtaining sponsors
5. Organizing or managing projects
6. Web-based marketing
7. Media/client relations
8. Computer skills (be specific)
9. Exercise recommendation
10. Exercise testing
11. Client needs assessment (consultation)
12. Program planning and implementation
13. Public-relations
14. Scheduling
15. Sales
16. Incentive programs
17. Electronic media
18. Marketing strategies
19. Sport camp development
20. Coaching and motivation
21. Equipment maintenance
22. Training & development programs
23. Network (build relationships)
24. Intramural Sports
25. Group exercise instructor
26. Personal trainer
27. Public speaking
28. Equipment selection
29. Leadership
30. Website development
31. Research and analysis
32. Tournament coordinator
33. Referee
34. Customer service
35. Branding
36. Safety and risk management
37. Special events
38. Extraintramurals
39. Sport clubs
40. Press releases

Exhibit 3.11 Transferable Skills – Mark – Senior - Internship - 450 hours

Objective: To obtain an internship as a Sport Advertising Associate for a professional baseball team, where I can have the opportunity to utilize my solid understanding of sport marketing and advertising strategies in providing public service announcements, press releases, flyers, banners, and obtaining local radio stations for advertising and entertainment. Wish to work in a team oriented environment.

Competencies: Advertising Communications * Press Releases * Electronic Media * Radio Media * Media Interviewing * Web page Development and Design * Proficient in Computer Skills of Adobe Photoshop, PageMaker, and Microsoft Office.

Once Mark has obtained his Bachelor's degree he will use his education experience as a transferable skill as well. Now, think about the skills that you have developed in previous or current volunteer or work experience to the future job for which you would like to apply and complete Exercise 3.4.

Exercise 3.4 Transferable Skills

What skills have you obtained through my previous or current volunteer or work experience? List the position (s)

1. _____
2. _____
3. _____
4. _____

List the skills or responsibilities you obtained from this position

1. _____
2. _____
3. _____
4. _____

Another common strategy in developing the skills section of the resume is to include both personal attributes and transferable skills on the resume. Stephanie decides to use the combination approach because she does have some experience but not enough to highlight all transferable skills. Exhibit 3.12 provides a sample of Stephanie's skills section.

Exhibit 3.12 Personable/Transferable Skills – Stephanie – Junior - Practicum - 150 hours

OBJECTIVE

Seeking a practicum where I can improve my **personal training** skills (sales, initial consultation, fitness assessment, program design, orientation) and gain valuable **business** knowledge. Qualified by a unique blend of personal training, sport and physical activity skills.

HIGHLIGHTS OF QUALIFICATIONS

- Recipient of "Outstanding Group Leader Award"·
- Good communicator in group exercise classes and monthly nutrition seminars
- Advanced personal training seminar in developing my skills
- Interact with clients and employees in a professional manner

---

Education and/or Military Experience

The education and/or military experience is the next section of the resume. The tactic of listing the education and/or military experience after the skills section helps to de-emphasize limited work experience when you first begin applying for jobs. For example, we have already established that Andrea lacks work experience, however she does have military experience and follows these guidelines in preparing the education portion of her resume:

- Begin the education section by listing the degree first (BS, BA).

- List the minor, specialization, or concentration (if applicable).

- List year of graduation (do not list year you began the major).

- List school's name and location (city and state).

- Include GPA if 3.0 and above.

- Include honors.

- Do not include any school except the ones granting the degree.

- Use "projected" or "anticipated" graduation date.

- Use relevant coursework only if you have additional space.

- Do not include high school information unless you received impressive honors and/or awards.

- If you have an associate degree, include graduation dates.

Exhibit 3.13 provides a sample of Andrea's education and military experience.

Exhibit 3.13 Education and Military Experience Sample Andrea-Sophomore – Field Experience - 20 hours

EDUCATION/MILITARY EXPERIENCE

Pursuing a **Bachelor of Science in Recreation and Leisure Services** from Ithaca College in Ithaca, NY. My projected graduation is May of 2015. I have completed introductory courses in Recreation, Parks, and Tourism. I maintain a GPA of 3.4/4.0.

Reserve Officers Training Corps (ROTC), 2013 to present

Instruction and training provided both in the classroom and at Army installations range from strategic studies to tactical exercises – air-land battle doctrine, rappelling, and marksmanship.

Now complete Exercise 3.5 to compile the information for the education and military experience (if applicable) of the resume.

Exercise 3.5 Education and Military Experience

Education

Name the degree (s) obtained or anticipated to obtain (include minor/specialization/concentration)

Name of university (s) (include city and state)

Degree, (expected graduation or degree obtained – month/year)

GPA (3.0 or higher – include scale – i.e., 3.8/4.0)

Major coursework (if needed only use for filler space)

Academic

Honors/Awards

Research (oral and poster presentations)

Military Experience

Military Base

Specific courses or programs and relate to your job objective

Related awards, achievements, and extracurricular activities

Scholarly Work

Another area appearing under the education section is scholarly work. During your college years, you may have the opportunity to participate in a research project, give an oral presentation at a conference, and/or contribute to a poster session. For example, Stephanie completed a research class the prior semester before entering her internship. During the research course Stephanie had to complete a research project under the direction of her professor. Stephanie decides to focus on an aspect of personal training that was of interest – core stability. The professor guided Stephanie through the research project and encouraged her to submit a poster session to the American College of Sports Medicine (ACSM) annual conference. Exhibit 3.14 provides a sample of Stephanie's scholarly work.

Exhibit 3.14 Scholarly Work Sample – Stephanie – Junior - Practicum - 150 hours

---

EDUCATION

Major: Exercise Science, (NASPE accredited)-with a specialization in sport management
Bachelor of Science degree anticipated May 2015.
Cum GPA 3.9/4.0

University of Wisconsin, Madison, WI.

SCHOLARLY WORK

Binh, N. X., McCue, C., & O'Brien, K. (2014, April). *An integrated approach to training core stability.* Poster session presented at the American College of Sports Medicine Annual Conference, Indianapolis, Indiana.

Since Mark is a senior, and he has been involved with prior research projects, he was not only encouraged to present his work at the North American Society for Sport Management (NASSM) conference, but also to submit a paper for publication to the *Journal of Sport Management*. Exhibit 3.15 is a sample of Mark's scholarly work with the focus on an oral presentation and the manuscript that followed.

Exhibit 3.15 Scholarly Work Sample – Mark – Senior - Internship - 450 hours

---

EDUCATION

University of Wisconsin, Madison, WI 54308 **B.S. Sport Management -** projected completion December 2015

SCHOLARLY WORK

O'Reilly, M. & Thomas, B. (May, 2013). *Take me out to the ballgame: Satisfying the season ticket holder.* Presented at the North American Society for Sport Management, Clearwater, FL.

Thomas, B., Martin, S., & **O'Reilly, M**. (2014). Factors affecting baseball club season ticket holders' satisfaction. *Journal of Sport Management, 24*(5), 246-252.

Now complete Exercise 3.6 to compile the information of your scholarly work experience. Depending on your work in this area, you may complete the first, second, and/or third sample or you may be like Andrea and do not have this section on your resume.

Exercise 3.6 Scholarly Work Exercise

POSTER PRESENTATION

Last Name _____

First Initial _____

Year/Month of Presentation _____

Title of Poster _____

Name of Conference _____

City, State where Conference was held _____

PRESENTATION

Last Name _____

First Initial _____

Year/Month of Presentation _____

Title of Presentation _____

Name of Conference _____

City, State where Conference was held _____

PUBLICATION

Last Name _____

First Initial _____

Year of Publication _____

Title of article _____

_____

Journal or Book Title _____

Volume _____ Issue_____ Page Numbers _____

Work Experience

All relevant work experience, both paid and unpaid, should be included on the resume. Trying to obtain your first job can be overwhelming and difficult at times, so you might begin with obtaining a position on-campus. During the summer you could work summer camps or find a job at a local gym. There are always opportunities throughout the school year to volunteer to coach a youth team at a YMCA or work a 5k run. Your field experiences also show what you have learned and achieved. The often overlooked non-paid positions can demonstrate to a prospective employer your skills relevant to the current job for which you are applying.

You may opt to include additional work experience that is not relevant to the career objective. If you have more than one "additional" work experience you want to add another section entitled, "Additional Work Experience" to the resume. Mark and Stephanie followed the work experience guidelines below in developing this section of the resume:

- List most recent positions first.

- Include the job title, dates of employment, and the name and location of the company where you worked.

Exhibit 3.16 Non-Action and Action Statement Samples	
Effective communication and marketing skills	Student liason for sport management annual golf tournament – communicate and market the benefits of participating in the annual faculty golf tournament to faculty, students, and the community.
Initial consultation skills	Experience with initial consultations including fitness assessment, exercise prescription, and orientation
Aware of responsibilities of a student manager for a sport team	Assisted with the pre-season conditioning and regular season practice by timing the players, setting up equipment, running copies of the workout routine, and all practices and team meetings.
Motivating individual	Motivated a variety of populations (ages 18-55) through their workouts.
Networking experience within intercollegiate athletics	Networked with Varsity Club to increase membership and help improve on the support of the athletic program.
Management experience	Supervised 25 student employees: Welcome Greeters and Fitness Consultants.

- List duties, skills, and achievement obtained from the position. The skills and achievements are beneficial in allowing the employer to realize any unique contributions you may bring to the company.

- Use well thought out action statements that will provide quick and powerful evidence to support your skills and achievements for each work experience (Kursmark, 2012). Exhibit 3.16 provides samples of non-action and action statements.

Exhibit 3.17 presents a sample of Mark's work experience in obtaining a Sport Advertising internship position for a minor league baseball team.

Exhibit 3.17 Relevant Work Experience Sample – Mark – Senior - Internship - 450 hours

RELEVANT WORK EXPERIENCE

University of Louisville Sport Management Department, Louisville, KY

Marketing Liason   **October 2013-Present**

- Student liason for sport management annual golf tournament – communicate and market the benefits of participating in the annual faculty golf tournament to faculty, students, and the community.

- Develop marketing strategies and communications to student body and U of L constituents in promoting the event.

- Develop and maintained Web pages for the annual golf tournament.

    University of Louisville Athletic Department, Louisville, KY

Student Worker in Marketing Department   **August 2012-Present**

- Work with Athletic Department in developing brochures for athleticTeams.

- Monitor media interviewing schedule with basketball personalities

- Relay information from leader board to media continuously throughout basketball tournaments.

University of Utah Athletic Department, Salt Lake City, Utah

Media Relations Runner   **Summer 2011**

- Relayed information from leader board to media continuously throughout Utah Baseball Tournament.

- Monitored media interviewing schedule with baseball personalities.

Complete Exercise 3.7 matching your previous work experiences to the job you identified in Chapter 1.

Exercise 3.7 Work Experience

Position #1

Employers Name _____

City, State _____

Position Title_____

Employment Dates (month/year): from _____ to _____

Duties, Skills, and/or Achievements _____

_____

_____

Position #2

Employers Name _____

City, State _____

Position Title _____

Employment Dates (month/year): from _____ to _____

Duties, Skills, and/or Achievements _____

_____

_____

Position#3

Employers Name _____

City, State_____

Position Title_____

Employment Dates (month/year): from _____ to_____

Duties, Skills, and/or Achievements _____

_____

_____

Professional Certifications

The professional certification section may be an option. Professional certification options for sport and physical activity are discussed in Chapter 5. All these certifications require continuing education credits showing the employer a commitment to the field. Also note any certification exams you may have registered to take in the future. This is a very similar technique as used with education, "anticipated graduation date May 2015." You simply state, "signed-up for personal training certification exam in December 2014." You may opt to place this information with the education category as Stephanie illustrates in Exhibit 3.18 or develop a new "certification" category following the work experience section.

Exhibit 3.18 Professional Certification Sample – Stephanie – Junior – Practicum - 150 hours

Education

    Major: Exercise Science (NASSM/NASPE accredited)
    Bachelor of Science degrees anticipated May 2014
    GPA 3.9/4.0
    University of Wisconsin, Madison, WI, 2011 to Present

Scholarly Work

    Binh, N. X., McCue, C., & O'Brien, K. (2012, April). *An integrated approach to training core stability* Poster session presented at the American College of Sports Medicine Annual Conference, Indianapolis, Indiana.

Professional Certifications:

    ACE Group Exercise Instructor, August 2008
    NSCA Strength and Conditioning Personal Trainer, May 2014

Use Exercise 3.8 to list any relevant certifications you have or are seeking.

Exercise 3.8 Professional Certification Exercise

List professional certifications

Certification organization _____

Certification _____

Date (month/year) of Certification _____

Certification organization _____

Certification _____

Date (month/year) of Certification _____

Certification organization _____

Certification _____

Date (month/year) of Certification _____

Are you going to include in the Education section or develop a separate category following work experience? _____

Professional and University Club Memberships and/or Awards

The professional membership section helps you showcase relevant skills obtained through a university club or state, regional, or national professional organizations (see Exhibit 3.15). University clubs are an excellent place for you to begin building a resume. You can gain leadership experience and be an "active" member in a club before moving to professional organizations. Professional organization options for sport and physical activity are discussed in Chapter 5.

You may also be the recipient of awards that support a career objective within these clubs and organizations. For example, Andrea was the recipient of the Student Government Association young student award. This award provided her with funds to attend the National Intramural Recreational Sports Association (NIRSA) annual conference. Mark was the recipient of the ACSM student research award for his presentation and paper on *Factors Affecting Baseball Clubs Season Ticket Holders' Satisfaction.* Stephanie is a member of the Sport Management club at the University of Louisville and received an annual award that paid for all of her expenses to attend the International Health, Racquet, and Sportsclub Association (IHRSA) annual conference. Exhibit 3.19 provides samples of Andrea's professional memberships and/or awards section. You may opt to place the awards under "education" depending on the amount of organization and award activities.

Exhibit 3.19 Professional Memberships and/or Awards Andrea – Sophomore – Field Experience - 20 hours

Objective: To obtain a position with a community campus recreation department

Professional Memberships and/or Awards

North American Society for Sport Managers

    Active student member since August 2013

    Acted as proctor for National conference 2011, 2012, 2013, 2014

    Volunteer for registration booth for National Conference 2011, 2012

Recipient of the Ithaca College Student Government Award

Use Exercise 3.9 to list professional and university organizations to which you belong and any awards received.

Exercise 3.9 Professional and University Club Memberships and/or Awards

List professional and university club membership and/or awards (make sure to include dates)

Organizational membership _____Dates _____

Organizational membership _____Dates _____

Organizational membership _____Dates _____

Organization/Award_____Dates _____

Organization/Award_____Dates _____

Extracurricular Activities or Personal Information

You may participate in extracurricular activities or have personal information which provides a personal touch to the resume (see Exhibit 3.20). As with Andrea's lack of work experience, the extracurricular activities or personal information is a good way to demonstrate her interests related to the field experience she is pursuing. The extracurricular activities may include being involved in intramurals, physical activity (running, biking, swimming, lifting), reading, writing, and other highlights you want the employer to know. The activities related to the position you are seeking are of most interest to prospective employers.

Exhibit 3.20 Extracurricular Activity Sample – Andrea – Sophomore – Field Experience - 20 hours
EXTRACURRICULAR ACTIVITIES
Team captain of the bike club on campus. Enjoy participating in all intramural events held at our university, leading my basketball, softball, flag football, and soccer teams to two consecutive tournament wins.

Note any extracurricular activities or interests or hobbies especially those related to the position you are interested in obtaining in Exercise 3.10.

Exercise 3.10 Extracurricular Activities

List extracurricular activities_____

_____

You have completed the hard part of developing a resume, now it is time to put the exercises you just completed into motion.

Step 2 – Use the Content Sections and Presentation Guidelines to Write the Resume

Step 2 requires you to use the content sections and presentation guidelines in writing the resume. Whether you intend to post the resume for an online job or submit the resume electronically, fax, or mail you need to follow these steps.

1. *Choose the Resume Format.* Choose the appropriate format for your resume, a reverse-chronological, skills, or combination, depending on the work experiences.

2. *Develop an Appropriate Resume Template.* In typing your document in a word processing program, you want to decide and follow a design for your resume's appearance. Refer to the samples at the beginning of this chapter and those in Appendix A for additional examples of resume templates. Although resume writing software programs and pre-formatted templates are available, they often limit the creativity of the resume writer. You are strongly encouraged to develop your own "template" to personalize your resume using a word processing software program. Use the following presentation guidelines to develop your resume template.

    ■ **Appearance** - The appearance of the resume includes appropriate spacing, italics, small caps, all caps, underlining), paper color, paper and envelope selection.

    ■ **Spacing** - a lot of valuable space can be saved by just pressing the space or tab button once instead of twice.

    ■ **Margins** - use a consistent margin (left, right, top, bottom), ideally one inch, throughout the entire resume. The temptation to deviate from this standard is often done to help you add more to the resume. Another and perhaps better solution would be to make the font size slightly smaller while selecting words carefully (Enelow & Kursmark, 2010).

    ■ **Font Selection** - although there are many fonts to choose from you need to pick one that has been proven to be easier to read, and virtually any employer can download a resume you prepared with the "Times New Roman" font (Enelow & Kursmark, 2010). In the early 1990's research conducted by print advertising experts found "Times New Roman" was easier to read than any other. This research is still used by many of the print advertising agencies today.

    ■ **Font Size** - it is recommended to use no more than two font sizes. One font size can be used for your name (16 or 18 point), and the other for the rest of the resume (11 or 12 point) (Enelow & Kursmark, 2010).

    ■ **Type Enhancements** - use boldface and italics sparingly by accenting those areas that provide the employer with an easy pathway to read. For example, boldface only the name and the categories and use italics for publications (APA style). Caps and underlining should be used sparingly if at all throughout a resume. All caps maybe construed negatively and be interpreted as rudeness by an employer. The underlining may take the employer's eye away from important parts of the resume (Kursmark, 2012).

- **Paper Color** – regular white, ivory, or light gray are colors that you want to consider for your resume. Avoid bright, flashy colors such as brown, tan, orange or other distinctive colors. These colors may be appropriate for graphic artists, but not for a student applying for a position in sport and physical activity.

- **Type of Paper** - invest in 8 ½ x 11, 24 pound, 100% bond, linen, cotton, or parchment paper. Be consistent and use the same color and type of paper as the resume (Kursmark, 2011; 2012).

- **Envelope Selection** - consider using a 9 x 12 envelope to mail your resume package because creasing and folding printed pages can lead to smudges.

3. *Place content into template.* Once you have chosen and developed a resume template in Microsoft Word or WordPerfect, take the content you wrote in each exercise to develop a draft of the resume. For your reference, various sport and physical activity resume samples are located in Appendix B.

4. *Finalize the length.* The general rule for resume length for undergraduates and college graduates (within the last five years), regardless of the field, is one page (Kursmark, 2012). If you are having problems placing the information on one page then kerning may be used. Kerning is a font technique to help with getting the lines back on one page of the resume by adjusting the space between letters. Kerning saves a considerable amount of space and is not usually noticeable to the employer if the spacing is not tightened excessively. As you acquire more work experience it is important to focus on keeping the resume to a maximum of three pages. Employers are busy people and do not have the time to read more than two to three pages (Kursmark, 2012).

5. *Proofread and correct the resume.* After writing the resume you need to proofread it for errors in spelling, punctuation, mistakes, and grammar. It is important to make sure your resume is error-free. Ninety-percent of employers have mentioned that quality and appearance, such as misspellings, typos, low-quality paper, and smudged print are the top reasons for immediately discarding the complete resume package (Enelow & Kursmark, 2010). Once you have checked the resume for errors you need to allow someone else to read the document. The more people who read the resume before the employer receives a copy, the better.

6. *Save the document.* You must not forget to save your resume. You can save the document in a traditional (Microsoft Word) document and make the appropriate conversions according to the employer's preference.

Step 3 – The Transmission

Often employers have a preference on resume transmission. You can post the resume on the internet, email, scan, fax, and/or mail it. With each of these transmissions you may need a text version, scannable version, PDF version, web version, or traditional (printed on paper) version (Kursmark, 2011). All of these transmission versions are discussed throughout this next section.

1. *Posting the resume on the internet.* Chapter 8 provides over 50 websites to help you find a field experience specific to sport and physical activity. However, the websites can also be used to sift through the job postings, apply for jobs, and make your resume available to employers. Sometimes job postings specify "no attachments," and you need to post your resume online. Posting your resume online using the traditional version does create some formatting problems. Instead you will need to convert your resume to a ASCII **text** file. A text resume does contain the same content of your traditional resume but does not include any formatting or graphics. A text version is not the prettiest document, but it is effective because any computer may access and read the resume without file-conversion or formatting problems that do occur with the traditional Microsoft word processing.

   When posting a resume online, make sure to use the following conversion guidelines:

   - Click on "Save As" and choose "Text Only" as the file format and rename your document. By using "Save As" you still have your traditional resume.

   - Once you have saved the document, the resume should convert to a Courier font and almost all of the formatting is stripped.

   - You need to review the resume in eliminating any formatting glitches, to add any extra blanks between sections, and to make sure the text is in the right location. This resume is not intended to be printed so do not worry about how long it is or if there are any breaks in pages

   Now you are ready to post the resume. Since there is not a university wide protocol for posting the resume, you need to follow the instructions provided by each individual site.

2. *Transmission via email.* In some cases you may transmit the resume via email. Email provides an instant response. When using email for transmission, make sure to follow a few guidelines:

   - You can often send the resume either by the **traditional** (Word file) or **PDF** (Portable Document Format) version as a file attachment. When converting the Word file to a PDF version you can purchase a copy of Adobe Acrobat or utilize the free online service (www.gobcl.com). The software and website have step-by-step instructions on converting the word document to PDF format. Once you have converted the document to a PDF format make sure to name the file in a way that is easy for employers to locate (resumelastnamefirstname).

- If a job posting specifies "no attachment" then you need to convert the resume to a **text** version. Following the conversion, cut and paste your cover letter and your resume into the body of the email.

- Before sending the resume you need to include the title of the position you applying for and your name. Exhibit 3.21 provides a sample of Mark's subject line for the email transmission.

Exhibit 3.21 Subject Line Sample - Mark - Senior – Internship – 450 hours
Sport Advertising Associate Internship – Resume of Mark O'Reilly

3. *Transmission via scanning or faxing.* Although scanning and faxing a resume may hurt its appearance, you may opt to take this route at the employer's request or with his/her permission. If scanning the document, you should follow the appropriate guidelines,

- In Mircrosoft Word save the resume using the "save as" feature under a different name.

- Make sure the entire document has one font, font size, and consistent category points.

- Put the following information of name, address, phone number, email address, and other contact information on its own line.

- All lines, boxes, graphics, and non-text elements need to be removed from the document.

- Do not include any shapes, stars, arrows or unusual shapes in the resume.

- The resume may go to two pages so include an appropriate header with the name, phone number, and email address.

4. *The traditional version – Mailing the resume.* If you are mailing your resume, it is best to print it using black ink for all pre-interview documents. Often, multi-color ink may put you at the risk of not being taken seriously. When sending by mail, choose the best paper is also important. Use top-quality paper as opposed to copy-machine paper. As mentioned above, you need to invest in a regular white, ivory, or gray 24 -pound, 100 percent cotton paper that can be purchased at any office store (Kursmark, 2011; 2012).

Finally, many photocopy machines and laser printers create a good quality image; however you need to check the copy quality when printing a resume. You should print enough copies for prospective jobs and a few extra for those unexpected opportunities.

Step 4 — Follow-Up Procedures

The final part of the transmission is the follow-up procedures. You need to follow-up via email or phone to confirm the organization has received the resume, to reiterate your interest in the position, and highlight your qualifications. This follow-up may influence the employer to offer you an interview because it shows your initiative and interest in the position. Chapter 4 provides guidelines on writing the follow-up letter and Chapter 8 provides guidelines on the follow-up call.

JIST Cards (Mini-Resumes)

You can create even greater exposure by creating a JIST card. A JIST card is a mini-resume highlighting key points of your resume (Kursmark, 2011). It provides essential information most employers want to know in a short format. JIST cards are best used when enclosed with a resume, application, or thank you letter. To develop a JIST card, there are some easy steps to follow (Kursmark, 2012):

■ Provide your name at the top of the card and at least two ways for the employer to contact you

■ Provide the objective you have already developed earlier in this chapter

■ List years of experience

■ Provide information on education

■ Provide information on transferable skills

■ Provide adaptive [term not used before] skill information

■ Provide availability information

Exhibit 3.22 and 3.23 provide examples of Mark's and Stephanie's JIST card.

Exhibit 3.22 JIST Card Sample – Mark – Senior - Internship - 450 hours

Mark O'Reilly   Home: (988)434-5687
                                                          Message: (735)-657-0689
                                                          Email: Morelly@aol.com
Objective: Seeking a **Sports Advertising Associate** internship with a minor league baseball team where I can utilize my skills and experience in marketing, management, and information systems.
 	
Currently working for the University of Louisville Sport Management Department as a Marketing Liason May 2015. Experience with advertising communications,

press releases, electronic media, radio media, media interviewing, and web page development.

Senior year completing a Bachelor of Science Degree in Sport Management from the University of Louisville. Anticipated graduation May of 2014.

Proficient in computer skills of Adobe Photoshop, PageMaker, Microsoft Word, PowerPoint, and Excel

Dedicated, organized, hardworking, and reliable

Availability: August 2015

Exhibit 3.23 JIST Card Sample - Stephanie – Junior - Practicum - 150 hours

Stephanie McCullough

Home: (864)456-9876
Message: (435)-657-0689
Email: SmCull@yahoo.com

Objective: Seeking a practicum where I can improve my **personal training** skills (sales, initial consultation, fitness assessment, program design, orientation) and gain valuable business knowledge.

Currently work for the University of North Carolina Human Performance Department as a fitness consultant and group exercise instructor. Experience with initial consultations including fitness assessment, exercise prescription, and orientation. Instructor of Kickboxing, Spinning, Circuit Training, Body Sculpt, and Six Pack.

Junior year completing a Bachelor of Science Degree in Exercise Science and Administration from the University of North Carolina, Raleigh. Anticipated graduation May 2015. Specialization in Sports Management.

Based on the resume you created, create a JIST card using Exercise 3.11.

Exercise 3.11 JIST Card

Name _____

At least two ways employers can contact you _____

_____

Objective _____

Experience _____

Education _____

Transferable Skills_____

Availability_____

Summary

Andrea, Stephanie, and Mark followed procedures and guidelines in developing their resume (Appendix B). By completing the exercises with Andrea, Mark, and Stephanie you have also developed an effective resume. You are able to prove your value to employers, see how your college and part-time work experiences have prepared you for the "real world," discovered and communicated your core knowledge and abilities, and matched your qualifications to the job you have been working towards.

Frequently Asked Questions

Should you list the community college attended prior to transferring to the current university?

Students should only list the granting university unless there is a specific reason for listing others. If a student attended Yale the experience may need to be listed.

Should you include coursework?

The "relevant coursework" can be important for interns because it allows employers to see what coursework has been completed in the major. Coursework is also important if you took unusual or advanced classes that are not as well known.

Should you include high school information?

In the majority of cases the high school information is omitted. If an impressive honor or award was received during high school then you may want to consider adding high school information.

Student Learning Activities

Complete the Resume Exercises listed throughout this chapter.

Bring a draft of your resume to class and exchange with a partner. Have your partner use the resume critiquing checklist below to make sure you have completed all the necessary components of the resume.

After your partner has provided you with feedback, make changes and re-submit the revised draft of your resume to your instructor.

Determine the resume transmission and submit your resume for a job.

Choose a follow-up technique and make contact with the employer.

➤ Resume Critiquing Checklist

- ❑ Did you include your content information of your name, mailing address, phone number (s), fax number (if applicable), and email address?
- ❑ Did you include your objective emphasizing what you can do and how your skills can be used to benefit the position?
- ❑ Did you include personal attributes and transferable skills you want to highlight?
- ❑ Did you include your education background?
- ❑ Did you include your military experience (if applicable)?
- ❑ Did you include your scholarly material (paper, poster or oral presentation – if applicable)?
- ❑ Did you include relevant or other work experience?
- ❑ Did you include professional certifications (if applicable)?
- ❑ Did you include university club memberships and/or awards (if applicable)?
- ❑ Did you choose an appropriate resume format?
- ❑ Did you choose an appropriate resume template?
- ❑ Did you follow the presentation guidelines to make your letter, neat, clean, well-presented, and error-free (spacing, margins, font selection, font size, type enhancements, paper color, type of paper, and envelope)?
- ❑ Did you place the content of the resume in the template?
- ❑ Did you finalize the length?
- ❑ Did you proofread and correct the resume?
- ❑ Did you save the document?
- ❑ Did you decide on the transmission of the document?
- ❑ Did you send the document
- ❑ Did you decide on with a follow-up?
- ❑ Did you follow-up?

CAREER HIGHLIGHT – MARKETING ASSISTANT (INTERN)

Beth Johnson

Marketing Assistant

Xavier University Athletic Department

Cincinnati, Ohio

Education And Certifications

Master of Education in Sport Administration from Xavier University (May 2008)

Bachelor of Science in Sport Management from the University of Dayton (2006)

Years In Position

3 years.

Previous Positions

From 2004 to when I graduated in 2006, I was a student marketing intern at the University of Dayton, where I did my undergrad in sport management. In 2006 I interned at the Sporting Goods Manufacturer's Association's "Super Show" for a week in Orlando, Fl. I was a marketing intern, and it was set up through my sport management program at UD. I was a marketing intern for the Cincinnati Mighty Ducks for a summer in 2004, between my sophomore and junior years of college, and I served as a teacher's assistant my sophomore year of college for my sport management professor's "Introduction to Sport Management" class.

Current Job Responsibilities And Hours

I have sole responsibility for the marketing, promotions, game day operations, sponsorships and group sales for men's and women's D-I soccer, volleyball, and baseball. I organize and run the "Junior Musketeers" kids club and the "Musketeer Reading Program" for youths. I am partially responsible for a $95,000 women's basketball ticket revenue goal for 07-08 (mostly group sales), and serve as the "timeout coordinator" at the scorer's table during women's basketball games. I also help plan the in-game events for women's basketball. I do game day operations for men's basketball, such as set-up and in-game promotions. I book and maintain contact with ball kids and national anthem singers for all sports. I receive the athletic department's donation requests for nonprofits and maintain the database of what is sent and to whom. I have 3-4 student workers each semester who I delegate jobs to. I also assist with any other day-to-day duties of the marketing department, or whatever my bosses need help with!

I'm *supposed* to be limited to 37.5 hours per week (I'm capped at 1,950 for the year), but I usually work an average 45-50 hours per week. Occasionally I work more than that when we have a lot of games that week.

Greatest Challenges

I am a 27-year-old female who tends to be cheerful and energetic at work. I have an easy time talking to fans, customers, parents and other outsiders, but I fear that because of my age, sex and personality, some of the males in my department don't take me as seriously as I deserve. My greatest challenge at work is to constantly show that I am serious, competent, hard-working, and determined. In a field this competitive, I understand the importance of always selling myself to everyone I meet.

My other main challenge is selling. As I stated before, I have a women's basketball ticket revenue goal to meet, and quite honestly, it's difficult to sell a product that is so greatly overshadowed by men's basketball. This challenge goes hand-in-hand with the development of my reputation – the more I can sell, the more I am taken seriously.

On a personal level, I am working on thickening my skin. In a field that is so fast-paced, typically male-dominated, and occasionally stressful, I have to learn to not take things so personally. In any job, people's personalities will differ and clash, and if I'm going to survive in sports, I need to be able to deal with a wide variety of people and the different ways they express themselves.

Career Advice

My first piece of advice would be to know what you're getting into. Jobs in sports are hard to find, hours are usually long, and pay is usually low – but you meet great people and the work is often fun and exciting.

If you're set on the industry, then my best advice would be to get experience any way you can. Sport is a difficult field to break into, partially because it's so appealing to so many. Start early, vary your experiences, and meet as many people in the industry as possible. Use your experiences and your contacts to set yourself apart. Don't be afraid to ask someone make a phone call on your behalf. Jobs often come because of who you know.

Once you've found a door to put your foot in, keep it there, even though it'll be tough at the beginning. Suck it up, be patient, and wait out the low pay and intern status. It *will* get better!

TO VICE PRESIDENT OF BUSINESS OPERATIONS – MINOR LEAGUE BASEBALL

James Breeding

Director of Sales

Louisville Riverbats

Louisville, KY

Education And Certifications

Bachelor of Science in Sport Administration. University of Louisville, 1998.

Years In Position

4 years

Previous Positions

Intern, Account Executive, Director of Group Sales, Director of Ticket Sales for Louisville Riverbats

Coordinate the team's activities

Ensures team operates within its budget and all fees (the field booking fee and training facility fee) are paid for in time.

Works closely with the director of baseball operations and comes up with the schedule of activities for the team.

Ensures that the team schedule is implemented.

Facilitates communication between the team and event organizers, media and fans.

Ensures that travel arrangements are made and that the team's needs are catered for when the team is traveling.

Assists and coordinates other departments in baseball operations such as the merchandising department and ticket sales department.

Greatest Challenges

Keeping sales staff motivated to make sales calls and appointments. Handling customer service issues during the season.

Career Advice

Work to get as much experience possible in the field that you wish to pursue long term. Develop exceptional verbal and written communication skills as this is the area in which most applicants are lacking. Understand customer service and develop the ability to turn problems into positive solutions whenever possible.

References

Betrus, M. (2011). *Perfect phrases for job seekers*. New York, NY: McGraw Hill.

Doyle, A. (2013). *Top 10 curriculum vitae (cv) writing tips*. Retrieved December 28, 2013, from, http://jobsearch.about.com/od/cvadvice/tp/cvtips.htm.

Enelow, W., & Kursmark, L. M. (2010). *Cover letter magic: Trade secrets of professional resume writers*. Indianapolis, IN: JIST Works.

Kursmark, L. M. (2011). *Best resumes for college students and new grads: Jump-start your career!* Indianapolis, IN: JIST Publishing, Inc.

Kursmark, L. M. (2012). *Same day resume, third edition*. Indianapolis, IN: JIST Works.

National Association of Colleges and Employers. (2013). The skills and qualities employers want in their class of 2013 recruits. Retrieved December 28, 2013 from, http://www.ask.com/web?q=national+association+of+colleges+and+employers&qsrc=0&o=0&l=dir&ad=dirN&ap=ask.com

Pierce, P. A., & Snyder, J. F. (2006). *Resume for health/fitness students and professionals. ACSM's Health & Fitness Journal, 10*(2), 19-27.

Salvador, E. U. (2010). *Step-by-step resumes, second edition: Build an outstanding resume in 10 easy steps!* Indianapolis, IN: JIST Works.

4

JOB SEARCH CORRESPONDENCE

SCENARIO #1 — FIELD EXPERIENCE/OBSERVATION - SOPHOMORE

Patty

Patty is a sophomore and currently enrolled in a sport and physical activity field observation course (20 hours - 1 credit hour). Patty is a student-athlete and has only worked sports camps during the summer. Patty is interested in high school coaching for girl's basketball. Patty has already completed a skills resume and she is ready to complement her resume with a cover letter. Patty decides she wants to complete her field experience at a local high school. Patty completed her skills resume and is ready to write the cover letter.

SCENARIO #2 — PRACTICUM - JUNIOR

Jane

Jane is a junior enrolled in a practicum course (200 hours — 4 credit hours). Jane has obtained experience through volunteer and field observations in sports retail. Jane has also has experience in sales outside of sport, and she discovers several positions available in sport retailing. This practicum allows Jane to gain practical experience while expanding her network. Jane has completed her combination resume and she is ready to write her cover letter.

SCENARIO #3 – INTERNSHIP - SENIOR

Jim

> *Jim is a senior enrolled in an internship course (450 hours – 9 credit hours). Jim has accumulated two years of work-related experience by taking advantage of his part-time positions, his field experiences and volunteer work-related experiences within sport and physical activity. Jim has a desire to work in Athletic Training and Physical Therapy, and is inspired by career highlights of Dan Baumann (end of chapter). Janda Crosby is currently a Head Athletic Trainer for the Chicago Steel Hockey Team and certified licensed Physical Therapist. Dan is currently an Athletic Trainer at a local high school and a Partner of ProRehab PC in Evansville, Indiana. Jim has been applying for internships similar to Dan's positions which allows Jim to gain valuable experience with an individual that has already accomplished an Athletic Training/Physical Therapy career. Jim has already completed his reverse-chronological resume and is ready to write the cover letter.*

Writing job search correspondence such as the cover letter, follow-up letter, thank you letter, electronic (email) letter, networking letters, and JIST cards is perhaps the greatest stumbling block for an efficient job search. Being able to write a cover letter to either accompany a resume, to follow-up on a resume sent to an employer, or to thank a perspective employer can be an important marketing tool. To optimize the impact of your job search correspondence you must be willing to invest the time and energy to create customized letters that may lead to job opportunities. Anything less reduces your chances of capturing your reader's attention and being offered an interview or position.

The purpose of this chapter is to help you identify the strategies for writing effective job search correspondence. The chapter also introduces step-by-step procedures, guidelines, and exercises to successfully guide you in writing job search correspondence for obtaining sport and physical activity positions.

The Cover Letter

You have the resume written and you are ready to begin writing the cover letter. The cover letter, often referred to as the letter of application, is submitted with the resume and allows the employer to know why you are contacting them (Salvador, 2010). Writing a cover letter is an essential component for any job search. A successful cover letter is important for a number of reasons (Salvador, 2010):

- The cover letter is the first opportunity to make a first impression on an extremely influential employer making the decision to hire you.

- Entices the reader to want to read the resume.

- Provides a personal touch so the employer can get a feel for you, which absolutely cannot be done through a resume alone.

- You can tell the reader why you are interested in a particular position.

- You can link your skills, work experiences, talents, and interest highlighted in the resume with a job opportunity.

- Illustrates to the employer how you can be an asset to their company.

- Compels the employer to call you for an interview. Well-written cover letters may have the employer calling you without looking at the resume.

- An effective cover letter may be the difference in an employer examining your materials or following-up with you in the future.

Although the cover letter is important for several reasons, the thought of writing an individual cover letter for each potential position can be overwhelming and a challenge. You search for the right words, tone, and information trying to match your qualifications for the position. You want to be able to convey the "right" message in the right tone to the perspective employer.

Types of Cover Letters

The two basic types of cover letters you may consider writing include paragraph and bullet style. Both of these cover letters are acceptable, and it is your personal preference of which one you choose to use (Enelow &Kursmark, 2010).

Paragraph Style

The paragraph style also referred to as the block-style, cover letter, allows you to communicate who you are and what value you bring to the company in a "story" format. The paragraph letter is flush with the left margin with all components (introductory material, opening/middle/closing paragraphs, and the signature line), except for the contact information of the cover letter. The paragraph cover letter may also be indented. With the indented-paragraph style cover letter you simply indent the opening line of each paragraph four inches from the left margin.

Patty decided to utilize the paragraph style format for her cover letter. Patty has several paragraph style templates to choose from including the one in Exhibit 4.1 and additional options in Appendix C. Patty finally decides on one of the paragraph style templates to begin writing her cover letter as shown in Appendix D (sample 1).

Exhibit 4.1 Paragraph Style Format Cover Letter Template

Your Name	**Home Phone**	**Cellular Phone**
Email address	**Home address**	

Date

Name of Company

Address

Dear Mr. or Ms. Last name here

Opening paragraph – focus on thanking the individual for the interview

Bullet points of relevant skills and experience focused on the needs of the employer

- Bullet point 1
- Bullet point 2
- Bullet point 3

Closing paragraph – assertive not aggressive

Sincerely,

Your Name

enclosure: resume

Jane decides to use the indented-paragraph style format for her cover letter. Jane also has several indented- paragraph style templates to choose from including the one in Exhibit 4.2 and additional options in Appendix C. Jane finally decides on one of the indented paragraph style templates and begins writing her cover letter as shown in Appendix D (sample 5).

Bullet-Style

The bullet-style cover letter is a combination between paragraphs and bullets. The bullet-style cover letter begins with the paragraph format, followed by the bullet-style, and ends with paragraph format again. The bullet-style cover letter is flush with the left margin (introductory material, opening/middle/closing paragraphs, and the signature line), except for the contact information. The bullet-style format can be one of the most powerful cover letters providing the employer with a bulleted list of your previous work experience and skills, and how they relate to the position. Therefore, Jim decides to develop a bullet-style cover letter because of his work experience. Jim has several bullet-style templates to choose from including the one in Exhibit 4.3 and additional options in Appendix C. Jim finally decides on one of the bullet-style templates and begins writing his cover letter as shown in Appendix D (sample 9).

Exhibit 4.2 Indented-Paragraph Style Format Cover Letter Template

Address   Phone

Name

Date

Name of Company

Address

Dear Mr. or Ms. Last name here

    Opening paragraph – my resume outlines or I am enclosing my resume for your review or I saw your advertisement

    2nd paragraph – reinforce your skills and experience that you can bring to the company

    Closing paragraph – assertive NOT aggressive

Sincerely,

Your Name

enclosure: resume

Exhibit 4.3 Bullet-Style Cover Letter Template

Date

Your Name

Name of Company

Address

Dear Mr. or Ms. Last name here

Opening paragraph – Thank you for taking the time to meet with me

Bullet points of relevant skills and experience focused on the needs of the employer

- Bullet point 1

- Bullet point 2

- Bullet point 3

Closing paragraph – assertive not aggressive

Sincerely,

Your Name

enclosure: resume

Your Name

Address

Phone

Email address

Step-by-Step Procedures and Guidelines in Writing the Cover Letter

Since the cover letter is not an easy task to accomplish, Patty, Jane, and Jim use the steps summarized in Exhibit 4.4 and the exercises throughout this chapter to organize and make sure important information is not omitted.

Exhibit 4.4 Step-by-Step Procedures and Guidelines in Writing a Cover Letter

1. Develop the content sections of cover letter

   a. Contact information

   b. Introductory material

   c. Opening paragraph

   d. Middle paragraph (content/main body of the letter)

2. Use the content sections and presentation guidelines to write the cover letter

   a. Choose a cover letter format

   b. Develop an appropriate cover letter template

   c. Place content into template

   d. Finalize length

   e. Proofread and correct the resume

   f. Save the document

3. Determine transmission of the cover letter (email, faxed, scanned, mail).

4. Determine follow-up procedures after submitting cover letter.

Step 1 - Content Organization

You can begin the process of developing a cover letter by addressing the following areas:

- Contact information

- Introductory material

- Opening paragraph

- Middle paragraph

- Closing paragraph

- The signature line

Contact Information

The contact information consists of the name, mailing address, phone numbers, fax number, and e-mail address. Although this section seems quite simple to develop Exhibit 4.5 provides some general guidelines explained throughout this chapter for each piece of the contact information (Betrus, 2011; Kursmark, 2011; Kursmark, 2012). Exhibit 4.6 contains samples of how Patty, Jane, and Jim utilized their contact information within the cover letter.

Exhibit 4.5 General Guidelines for Content Information
Name
1. Do not use a nickname
2. Do not use "Jr." or "II" following the name – reader may think you are defining yourself
3. Avoid using the academic degree after the name (displayed in education section)
Mailing Address
1. Do not abbreviate "Street" or "Avenue"
2. Do not spell out the state – use the accepted two-letter abbreviations
3. Use the nine-digit Zip code from www.usps.com or local post office
4. If you live in an apartment make sure to include the number
5. Avoid using a post office box if at all possible (reflects instability)
6. If you are moving make sure to ask someone you know for a temporary address

Phone Numbers

1. Do not include current employer's phone number (use of current employer's resources)

2. Always include area code

3. Make sure an appropriate voicemail is set-up for the phone numbers provided

4. Be careful about providing cell phone numbers. You must consider whether you will be able to talk whenever the prospective employer calls and you answer

Fax Number

1. Using your fax number is optional

2. Do not include fax number of employer (use of current employer's resources)

3. If you list a fax number make sure to check it often

Email Address

1. Using your email address is optional

2. You should have one email address specifically to send and receive information about positions. Free email accounts – gmail/yahoo/hotmail

3. You do not need to include the email in the heading if you send it via email Place this information on the signature line of the email

4. If you use an email address make sure to check it often

Exhibit 4.6 Contact Information Sample

Patty Thomas

3245 Dover Parkway	Home 324-897-9086
Bloomington, IN 32456	pattyhom@earthlink.net Mobile 543-908-9543

Jim Royce

School Addres	Permanent Address
3456 University Blvd	854 WillowDrive
Iowa City, Iowa 43567	Atlanta City,GA43567
(584)456-9044	Jroyce@att.net (435)243-0976

Jane G. Dove

2345 Mile Lane Rd, Tampa, FL 43567 * 743-908-7546 * jdove@verizon.net

Now complete Exercise 4.1 to prepare your contact information.

Exercise 4.1 Contact Information Exercise

Name _____

Current Address _____

_____

Alternative Address _____

_____

_____

Phone _____

E-mail Address _____

Fax _____

Introductory Material

The introductory material follows the contact information. The introductory material includes information such as the date, employer's information, the reference line (optional), and the formal salutation. Exhibit 4.7 provides general guidelines to follow when writing the introductory material for the cover letter.

Exhibit 4.7 Introductory Material Guidelines
1. Leave three spaces between the contact information and the date
2. Leave three spaces between the employer's information and the date
3. Always call the company requesting information if you do not know the name, title, or address of the employer you are sending the cover letter to. Do not address the letter "To Whom It May Concern."
4. Leave one space between the formal salutation "Dear Ms. Martin" and the Employers information.
5. Use Mr. and Ms. for the salutation. Include a colon following the salutation.

Exhibit 4.8 provides a sample of how Patty combined her content information with the introductory material in the cover letter.

Exhibit 4.8 Introductory Material Sample

Patty Thomas

3245 Dover Parkway
Bloomington, IN 32456
324-897-9086 Home
543-908-9543 Mobile
pattyhom@earthlink.net

November 5, 2015

Ms. Cathy Martin
Head Basketball Coach
Lincoln High School
1324 Dame Kate
Bloomington, IN 32456

Re: Field Experience (optional)

Dear Ms. Martin:

Now you are ready to complete Exercise 4.2 to complete your introductory material.

Exercise 4.2 Introductory Material Exercise

Employer Information

Name _____

Title _____

Current Address _____

_____

Formal Salutation

Determine what formal salutation you are going to use. Do you need to make a phone call to the company in order to find out this information? Please check one of the following

Ms. _____   Mr. _____   Dr. _____   Professor _____

Opening paragraph

The opening paragraph is often the section of the cover letter that takes the longest to write. You are writing the opening paragraph to entice the employer to continue reading the letter in its entirety and to closely review your resume. In essence the opening paragraph may address <u>some or all</u> of the following:

■ **Introduce yourself to the employer** – include your degree and the month/year you anticipate graduating. Highlight your academic achievements and experiences (if applicable) indicating your intelligence, competitiveness, and evidence of potential. For example, Jim is currently pursuing a Bachelor of Science degree in Exercise Science at the University of Southern Indiana. He anticipates graduating in May of 2014. His academic experience coupled with his work experience makes him a viable candidate for the organization. He has worked important team projects while at school and he knows how to get results in a team environment.

■ **What field experience, internship, or practicum are you applying for?** For example, Patty is interested in applying for a field experience coaching position at Lincoln High School during the December 2015.

Exhibit 4.9 Opening Paragraph Samples

Patty – Sophomore – Field Experience (20 hours) – Coaching
I am interested in applying for a field experience coaching position at Lincoln High School during the December 2014. I am a student-athlete (women's basketball) at Indiana University Purdue University at Indianapolis (IUPUI) pursuing a Bachelor of Science Degree in Kinesiology with a specialization in coaching. My coach speaks highly of you and your team.

Jane – Junior – Practicum (200 hours) – Sport Retailing
I am an energetic, motivated, assertive individual pursuing a Bachelor of Science degree in Sport Management with an emphasis in Marketing from the University of Florida. I anticipate graduating in May of 2016. My career goal is to become a manufacture representative selling products to sport teams and sporting good stores. I definitely want to be a part of this booming business and that is why I am extremely interested in the sport retailing practicum you advertised through the University of Florida Career Services Center. This position would complement my career goal to become a Manufacture Representative.

Jim – Senior – Internship (450 hours) – Athletic Training/Physical Therapy
I am extremely interested in an internship with the Rehabilitation Institute in Michigan. I am currently pursuing a Bachelor of Science degree in Exercise Science at the University of California at Berkeley. I anticipate graduating in May of 2015 My field experience, practicum, and volunteer work with the University of California at Berkeley and local high schools have provided me valuable experience in physical therapy. My academic experience coupled with my work experience makes me a viable candidate for your organization.

Now you can complete your opening paragraph by completing Exercise 4.3.

■ **Why would you be an asset to the company?** Highlight experiences, transferable skills, coursework, and/or personal attributes. For example, Jane's career goal is to become a Manufacture Representative selling products to sport teams and sporting good stores. She defiantly wants to be a part of this booming business and that is why she is extremely interested in receiving a sport retailing practicum. This position would complements her career goal to become a Manufacture Representative.

- **You could also communicate how you found out about the position.** For example, Patty indicates her coach speaks highly of Lincoln High School's coach and the team.

As illustrated Patty, Jane, and Jim answered some of these questions in developing their opening paragraph. Exhibit 4.9 provides samples of Patty's, Jim's, and Jane's opening paragraphs.

Exercise 4.3 Opening Paragraph Exercise

How will you introduce yourself?_____

Academic experience _____

Anticipated Graduation Date/Year _____

Are you an athlete? _____

What specific position are you applying for? _____

_____

How did you find out about the position?(optional)_____

_____

Write an opening paragraph _____

_____

_____

_____

_____

Middle Paragraph (Content/main body of the letter)

The middle paragraph is the heart of the letter. This paragraph is the substance of the cover letter communicating to the employer what you can bring to the organization. Patty, Jane, and Jim began the process of writing the middle paragraph by obtaining a copy of their job description and determined how they met the needs of the position by answering four questions and providing supporting evidence through examples from their academic preparation, previous work experience, strengths, skills, and/or relevant training:

- What are your key qualifications?

- What have you accomplished?

- How have you been successful?

- What other information may entice the employer to closely review your resume?

Exhibit 4.10 provides samples of Patty, Jane, and Jim's middle paragraph.

Exhibit 4.10 Middle Paragraph Sample

Patty – Sophomore – Field Experience (20 hours) - Coaching

While I have not had much experience in the area of coaching, I feel as though my background as a student-athlete coupled with my academic achievements makes me an excellent candidate for the field experience position.

Jane – Junior – Practicum (200 hours) - Sport Retailing

The majority of my previous work experience has been with local department stores. Although these positions have been outside the sport industry they have provided me with valuable interpersonal skills and the ability to identify individual needs. Both of these attributes are beneficial to this position. Recently, I accepted a position with Dick's Sporting Goods. I am responsible for selling exercise equipment. This position is a good match because of my knowledge in knowing the brands and specifications for the equipment. In addition to my work experience I have also completed courses in sport financing and sport business.

Jim – Senior – Internship (450 hours) – Athletic Training/Physical Therapy

My education, experience, and extracurricular activities are all indicators of a successful career as a physical therapist. I have been working within the University of California at Berkeley Athletic Training Department as a volunteer for the past three years. This experience has allowed me to gain valuable skills that complement athletic training/physical therapy:

- Prevention of athletic injuries

- Recognition and evaluation of athletic injuries

- Rehabilitation of athletic injuries

- Educational counseling of student athletes

Complete Exercise 4.4 in developing your own middle paragraph.

Exercise 4.4 Middle Paragraph Exercise

Obtain a copy of the job description

What are your key qualifications specific to the job description? _____

_____

Match specific job points to the following:

Academic Preparation _____

_____

Previous Work Experience _____

_____

Strengths/Skills (chapter 3) _____

_____

_____

Relevant Training _____

_____

_____

Write a middle paragraph _____

_____

_____

Closing Paragraph (Call to Action)

The closing paragraph is your action plan. Your action plan consists of providing valuable follow-up information the employer needs in order to contact you, shows a desire in the position, and gratitude for their time and consideration. Here are the key points to the action plan Patty, Jane, and Jim followed in developing their closing paragraph:

- Provided a reason to why you would be an ideal candidate

- Asked for a follow-up interview

- Provided a phone number (s) and available times to call OR told the employer when they may be calling to inquire about obtaining the position

- Provided an email address

- Thanked the employer for his or her time and consideration

Exhibit 4.11 provides samples of Patty's, Jim's, and Jane's closing paragraph.

Exhibit 4.11 Closing Paragraph Sample

Patty – Sophomore – Field Experience (20 hours) - Coaching

I would like to learn more about the current field experience position. I am confident my skills would enable me to make an immediate contribution to your organization. I can be reached at (812)564-8790 after 5 pm or pattyhom@earthlink.net. Thank you for your time, and I look forward to hearing from you soon.

Jane – Junior – Practicum (200 hours) – Sport Retailing

I would like to meet with you, at your convenience, to discuss the sport retailing practicum positon in further detail. You can reach me at my home telephone number in the morning and evening at (743)908-7456 or through my email jdove@verizon.net. Thank you for your consideration. I look forward to hearing from you.

Jim – Senior – Internship (450 hours) – Athletic Trainer/Physical Therapist

In summary, I hope my past coursework and additional skills described in my resume illustrates that I can make a direct contribution to ProRehab. I would like to further discuss my qualifications in relation to this internship opportunity. You may reach me at (324-897-9086) from 2:15 p.m. until 4:00 p.m. any day of the week or via email at Jroyce@att.net. I look forward to speaking with you soon. Thank you for your time and consideration.

Now it is time for you to complete Exercise 4.5 in developing your closing paragraph.

Exercise 4.5 Closing Paragraph Exercise

Provide a reason(s) of why you are an ideal candidate _____

Ask for an interview _____

_____

Time (s) available to call _____

Phone number (s) to call _____

Email address _____

Thank the employer _____

_____

Write closing paragraph _____

_____

The Signature Line. The signature line is often referred to as the "complimentary close." The cover letter should always be personally signed and begin two lines below the closing paragraph. Complimentary closing words include the following.

- Sincerely

- Sincerely Yours

- Yours

- Yours Truly

- Best Regards

- Thank You

Following the complimentary close, you need to space down four lines and type your name exactly as it appears on the top of the cover letter and resume. Two spaces below your name should include a notation of "enclosure" or "attachment." Exhibit 4.12 provides a signature line sample for Patty.

Exhibit 4.12 Signature Line Samples – Patty – Sophomore Field Experience (20 hrs)
Sincerely,
Patty Thomas
Patty
Thomas enclosure: resume

Complete exercise 4.6 in developing a signature line for your cover letter.

Exercise 4.6 Signature Line

Choose complimentary closing word (s)_____

Practice your signature _____

Print your name _____

What are you going to place on the enclosure line? _____

Write Signature Line _____

_____

_____

Step 2 – Use the Content Sections and Presentation Guidelines to Write the Cover letter

Step 2 requires the use of content sections and presentation guidelines in writing the cover letter. Whether you intend to post the cover letter for an online job or submit the resume electronically, by fax, or mail, you need to follow these steps (Enelow & Kursmark, 2010; Kursmark, 2012)

1. *Choose a cover letter format.* Choose the appropriate format for your cover letter, a paragraph style, comparison-list style, or bullet style, depending on who you are writing, why you are writing, and the type and amount of information you want to include.

2. *Develop an appropriate cover letter template.* Software programs and templates are available but often limit the creativity of the letter writer. You are strongly encouraged to develop a personalized cover letter using a word processing software program such as Word or WordPerfect. Refer to the samples at the beginning of this chapter and those in Appendix C for additional samples of templates. Use the following presentation guidelines to develop your cover letter template.

   ■ **Appearance** - the appearance of the cover letter includes appropriate margins, selection of font and font size, type enhancements (boldface, italics, small caps, all caps, underlining), paper color, paper and envelope selection.

   ■ **Margins** - the temptation to deviate from using a one inch margin (left, right, top, bottom) is often used to help add more to the cover letter. Instead of changing the margins consider making the font size slightly smaller while selecting words carefully.

   ■ **Font Selection** - the Times New Roman font is the most widely used font because it is highly readable and anyone can download a cover letter file with this typestyle.

   ■ **Font Size** - use a font size of either 11 or 12 point for the cover letter.

   ■ **Type Enhancements** – type enhancements are utilized in developing the resume on a consistent basis. However, the cover letter should be a conservative business document and should not use type enhancements.

   ■ **Paper Color** - avoid colored paper such as green, blue, pink, yellow, gold, or any of a number of flashy colors. Although these colors may be appropriate for graphic artists, you are applying for a position in sport and physical activity and you should use safe paper colors such as white, ivory, or light gray. These papers are always appropriate for any position in sport and physical activity.

- **Type of Paper** - purchase 8 ½ x 11 bond, linen, cotton, or parchment paper. Make sure you are consistent in using the same color and type of paper as the resume.

- **Envelope Selection** - consider using a 9 x 12 envelope to mail your resume package because creasing and folding printed pages sometimes cause smudges.

3. *Place content into cover letter template.* Once you have developed a cover letter template in Microsoft Word or WordPerfect, take the content reference in each exercise to develop a cover letter draft. For your reference, various sport and physical activity cover letter samples are located in Appendix C.

4. *Finalize length.* The general rule of the cover letter length for undergraduates and college graduates (within the last five years), regardless of the field, is one page. If you are having problems placing the resume on one page then kerning may be used. Kerning is introduced in Chapter 3.

5. *Proofread and correct the cover letter.* The cover letter is the first document the employer may read and the quality and accuracy of this document is extremely important. As mentioned in Chapter 3, ninety-percent of employers have mentioned quality and appearance, such as misspellings, typos, low-quality paper, and smudged print are the top reasons for immediately discarding the complete resume package (cover letter, resume, references). Therefore, check for errors and make sure the cover letter reads well, moves smoothly from one paragraph to the next, has a consistent writing style, and is professional. Once you have followed the presentation guidelines for these areas you need to allow someone else to read the document. The more people who read the cover letter before the employer receives a copy, the better.

6. *Save the document.* Do not forget to save your resume. You can save the form in a traditional form (Microsoft Word) and make the appropriate conversions according to the employer's preference.

Step 3 – The Transmission

Communication has been altered in recent years and employers are relying more on email and other online means of transmitting job correspondence. The transmission of the cover letter is similar to the resume and can refer to Chapter 3 for guidelines and procedures in sending the cover letter via email, scan, fax, or mail. However, there are some unique characteristics to be aware of when formatting a cover letter to transmit in the body of an email (Kursmark, 2011),

- Brief and to the point. The goal is to communicate the value you can bring to the organization. This letter is not written in depth as the conventional cover letter.

- Do not include the traditional contact information. Include the same subject line you used to send shown in Chapter 3, Exhibit 3.16. The first line of email should include a formal salutation, such as Mr. Thomas.

- Use brevity when writing your opening paragraph. Use bullet points to match your skills and abilities to the job requirements. You should reference your attached resume or hyperlink to your online version (if the document is an attachment). In the final paragraph you need to provide follow-up information. Exhibit 4.13 provides a sample of Jane's cover letter that she is going to transmit via the body of the email.

Exhibit 4.13 Transmission of Cover Letter via Body of the Email Sample Jane – Junior – Practicum 150 hours

Ms. Brook:

Dr. Radcliff suggested that I contact you regarding a practicum in your athletic apparel department. Some of my key qualifications for this practicum include:

- Pursuing a Bachelor's degree in Sport Management plus 3 years of sales experience as a Sales Associate for athletic equipment.

- Solid understanding of marketing fundamentals, qualitative/quantitative research, and marketing strategies

- Passion for sports

- Excellent customer service skills

I believe I can be a valuable asset to your company, and I would love the opportunity to speak with you further about the practicum experience. Please feel free to contact me at 843-678-9843 after 3 pm. I look forward to hearing from you soon.

Sincerely,

Jane Sampson

Jane Thompson

attachment

One final thought when it comes to attaching the cover letter and resume is to provide a brief statement in the body of the email. Exhibit 4.14 provides a sample of Patty's brief statement she used when attaching her cover letter and resume.

> **Exhibit 4.14 Brief Statement Sample – Patty – Sophomore – Field Experience 20 hrs**
>
> Please see attached cover letter and resume highlighting my skills and athletic experience qualifying me for a field experience as a student assistant.

Step 4 – Follow-Up Procedures

The final part of the transmission is the follow-up procedures. Follow-up via email or phone to confirm the organization has received the cover letter and resume, to reinforce your interest in the position, and to highlight additional qualifications you did not mention during the first correspondence. This follow-up could be the difference in the employer hiring you over another candidate. The follow-up via email is the focus of this chapter while guidelines for the follow-up call are located in Chapter 8.

The follow-up letter via email should include an introductory, middle, and final paragraph. The following information should be included for each paragraph,

- Introductory paragraph – the reason why you are writing and communication that you contacted the employer before

- Middle paragraph – show that your skills or experience match the employers position requirements. Highlight different skills other than the ones you provided in the original cover letter.

- Final paragraph – contact information in order to be contacted by the employer

Exhibit 4.15 provides a sample of Jim's follow-up email letter after applying for one of his athletic internship positions.

Thank You Letter or Thank You Note

Now that you have learned how to develop a cover letter, you can use similar steps in writing additional job search correspondence such as the thank you letter or thank you note.

Thank You Letters and Thank You Notes

It is proper job search etiquette to send a thank you letter or thank you note following an interview. The thank you letter or thank you note may provide an advantage over other candidates in this extremely competitive job search market. By sending a thank you letter or thank you note following an interview, you are conveying the following (Kursmark, 2011).

Exhibit 4.15 Follow-up Letter via Email Sample – Jim – Senior – Internship 450 hrs

Mr. Tyler:

One week ago I applied for an internship with your athletic department via email. I am contacting you to see if you received the resume package.

In brief, my qualifications include:

- Competing as a Division I intercollegiate basketball player where I was exposed to athletic training techniques.

- Completion of an athletic training field experience at a Division I university where I observed rehabilitation of knee, ankle, and shoulder injuries.

- Volunteer for the athletic training department during summer basketball camps.

- Pursuing a Bachelor of Science degree in Exercise Science with a Pre-Physical Therapy emphasis.

I can easily be reached at 875-908-4573 or at Jrosen@yahoo.com. I am confident of my skills and my intangible qualities of dedication, energy, enthusiasm, and intellectual curiosity. Thank you for your time.

Best Regards,

Jim Rosen

Jim Rosen

- You appreciate their time and consideration for the interview while building a relationship with the employer (s).

- You have an additional opportunity to detail what was discussed during the interview by highlighting your skills, qualifications, and experience related to the current position. You may also share new information that was not mentioned during the initial interview. All of these details and new information reinforces that you are the right person for the job.

- You can use the thank you letter or thank you note as a marketing tool that may advance your candidacy.

- You provided yourself with an additional opportunity to touch base with the employer again which may distinguish you from other candidates.

Each thank you letter or thank you note should be written specifically to the person you interviewed with. You can decide the format, style, and length of the thank you letter or thank you note. For example, as shown in Exhibit 4.16, Patty chose a brief (one paragraph) thank you note following her field experience interview.

Patty follows these guidelines in writing the thank you note:

- Begin the note by thanking the employer for an opportunity to interview for the position.

- Mention something about learning more about the program or what interested you in the position. What were you impressed with during the interview?

- Reinforces the fact that you are still interested in the position.

- The final statement provides information on your phone number and when you can be reached.

Patty sent this thank you note via email with a subject line, "Thank You Note – Patty Thomas".

Exhibit 4.16 Brief Thank You Note – Patty – Sophomore – Field Experience 20 hrs

Mr. Franklin:

Thank you for providing an opportunity to interview for the student coaching assistant. I enjoyed the opportunity to learn more about your team and coaching philosophy. I am quite interested in the position and would love to have the opportunity to work with you and your team. If you have any further question, please do not hesitate to call me at 765-895-0974 after 4 pm Monday-Friday.

Complete Exercise 4.7 in developing a thank you note you could use in a situation where you need a brief, to the point, quick turnaround form of appreciation for allowing you to interview.

Exercise 4.7 Thank You Note

Provide an opening statement thanking the employer _____

_____

_____

Provide a statement about what you learned about the program, what interested you the most about the organization _____

_____

_____

_____

Provide a statement that you are still interested in the position _____

_____

_____

Final statement of where and when you can be reached _____

_____

_____

Since Jim is completing an internship as a student physical therapy assistant, he decides to lengthen his letter to the three paragraph format. For this thank you letter make minor modification to the cover letter content guidelines mentioned earlier in the chapter. Simply modify the material to relate to a thank you letter. Exhibit 4.17 provides a sample of Jim's content information and introductory paragraph thanking the employer for the interview and including information about what he liked about the facility.

Exhibit 4.17 Thank you Letter Contact Information/Introductory ParagraphJim – Senior - Internship 450 hrs

June 26, 2014

762 University Blvd
Evansville, IN 47712
(812)435-6789

ProRehab PC 543
Mr. Dan Baumann
W. Burnet Street, Suite 234
Evansville, IN 47712

Mr. Dan Baumann:

I wanted to thank you for meeting with me about the student Physical Therapy Assistant position this past week. I found ProRehab to have a team approach with a variety of physical therapy techniques that I could learn from and utilize for my future career as a Physical Therapist.

Sincerely,

Jim Royce

Jim Royce

Complete exercise 4.8 in developing your contact information and introductory paragraph of the thank you letter.

Exercise 4.8 Thank You Letter Contact Information/Introductory Paragraph Exercise

Choose introductory wording thanking the employer for the interview

_____

_____

List the position you are applying for _____

_____

Add information that may trigger the employer of who you are and your qualifications _____

_____

Tell the employer what you liked about the organization and/or facility

_____

_____

Jim continues by writing his middle paragraph that pertains to his skills and qualifications for the position. Exhibit 4.18 provides a sample of Jim's middle paragraph. Notice how Jim uses a bullet point approach to highlight his skills and qualifications.

Exhibit 4.18 Thank you Letter Middle Paragraph- Jim – Senior - Internship 450 hrs
I believe my academic preparation and athletic training experience makes me a valuable asset to your team at several reasons: ■ Exercise Science major   ■ Background working at a university athletic training facility   ■ Knowledge and exposure to the prevention, evaluation, and rehabilitation of athletic injuries   ■ Exposure to educational counseling of student athletes

Complete Exercise 4.9 in writing your middle paragraph of the thank you letter.

Exercise 4.9 Thank You Letter Middle Paragraph Exercise

List your skills that relate to the position_____
_____

List your experience that directly or indirectly relate to this position_____
_____

List your personal attributes that relate to this position_____
_____

Jim concludes his letter with the final paragraph and signature line. The final paragraph should illustrate your appreciation and opportunity to meet with the employer. Exhibit 4.19 provides a sample of Jim's final paragraph and signature line.

Exhibit 4.19 Thank You Letter Final Paragraph/Signature Line – Jim – Senior –Internship 450 hrs

I look forward to hearing from you soon to discuss the possibilities of completing my internship at your facility. In the interim, I thank you for your time and consideration.

Sincerely,

Jim Royce

Jim Royce

Complete Exercise 4.10 in developing your final paragraph of the thank you letter.

Exercise 4.10 Thank You Letter Final Paragraph Exercise

Reiterate your appreciation for the interview
_____

Provide your contact information and number for any follow-up questions that may need to be answered (optional) _____
_____

Choose how you would like to write the signature line _____
_____
_____

Unlike Patty, Jim decides to send his letter via mail because he has time and he likes the formality of the letter.

Summary

The information presented in this chapter introduced step-by-step procedures, guidelines, and exercises in writing effective job search correspondence. Patty, Jane, and Jim used these same procedures and guidelines in developing their cover letter (Appendix D) and thank you letters. By completing the exercises with Patty, Jane, and Jim, you have also developed effective job search correspondence important to moving one step forward towards achieving your career in sport and physical activity.

Frequently Asked Questions

How long should the cover letter be?

The cover letter should not be longer than one page. Choose the most important information that will highlight what you have to offer the organization.

Should you include a list of references with the cover letter and resume?

Employers may want to contact some references if they get serious about you as a candidate. Provide the employer with a list of people to contact and include information such as name, title, organization, address, e-mail, and phone number.

How many pages should the thank you letter be?

The thank you letter should be one page depending on the amount of information you want to communicate the employer.

How soon should the thank you letter be sent following the interview?

Send the thank you letter within 24 hours of your interview. Have the thank you letter ready to mail once you receive the appropriate name (s). If you know the employer is going to make a decision within the day send the thank you letter via email.

Student Learning Activities

Complete the Cover Letter Exercises listed throughout this chapter.

Bring a draft of your cover letter to class and exchange with a partner. Have your partner use the cover letter Critiquing Checklist to make sure you have completed all the necessary components of the cover letter.

After your partner has provided feedback, make changes and submit the revised draft of your cover letter to your instructor.

Determine the cover letter transmission and submit your cover letter for a job.

Bring a draft of the "Thank You" Letter to class and exchange with a partner. Have your partner use the "Thank You" Letter Critiquing Checklist below to make sure you have completed all to necessary components. After your partner has provided feedback, make changes and submit the revised draft to your instructor.

➤ Cover Letter Critiquing Checklist

Cover Letter Format
- ❑ Did you choose an appropriate cover letter according to your needs?
- ❑ Did you choose an appropriate template to begin writing the cover letter?

Contact Information
- ❑ Is your name a larger font and bold?
- ❑ Did you include your address, phone, and email address.
- ❑ If you used two addresses did you specify one as a school address and one as a home address?
- ❑ Did you include the date?
- ❑ Did you verify that you had the right employer to contact?

First Paragraph
- ❑ Did you convey immediate understanding of "who" you are?
- ❑ Did you provide information on how you found out about the position?
- ❑ Did you include information on what position you are applying for?
- ❑ Did you include information on what you know about the company?

Second Paragraph
- ❑ Did you highlight your most relevant qualifications?
- ❑ Did you highlight your relevant achievements?
- ❑ Did you highlight why you would like to work for this company?

Appearance
- ❑ Did you use the appropriate paper?
- ❑ Are there any smudges on your cover letter?
- ❑ Is your font size easy to read (Times New Roman)?
- ❑ Did you use the same font size and paper as you did for your resume?
- ❑ Is the cover letter succinct (one page)?

CAREER HIGHLIGHT - ATHLETIC TRAINER/ PHYSICAL THERAPIST

Janda Crosby, MS, ATC, LAT
Head Athletic Trainer for the Chicago Steel Hockey Team
(USHL)
ATI Physical Therapy Licensed Athletic Trainer

Education And Certifications

BS in Kinesiology (Human Movement Sciences)/ Athletic Training

MS in Sport Administration

NATA-BOC certification, Illinois State License for Athletic Trainers, CPR for the Professional Rescuer (American Red Cross), Instructor certified to teach community CPR and CPR for the Professional Rescuer (American Red Cross).

Years In Position

Sports Information Directors of America

1 year and 9 months. I am entering my 3rd season with the team (second full season)

Previous Positions

- Out reach Athletic Trainer for Kentucky Orthopedic Rehab Team (KORT) and Head Athletic Trainer for Christian Academy of Louisville (CAL)

- Graduate Assistant Athletic Trainer for Women's Soccer and Women's Tennis at the University of Louisville

Current Job Responsibilities And Hours

My current job responsibilities fall into two categories which overlap each other: I am employed by ATI Physical Therapy and am contracted out to the Chicago Steel. My main responsibility is to provide all athletic training services for the Steel including the prevention, recognition, evaluation, rehabilitation, and education of all athletic injuries. I also manage all supplies and inventory for the athletic training room, and assist the equipment manager in daily laundry and cleaning responsibilities as well as preparing water/sports drinks for practices and games. I travel with the team and am basically on call 24/7 through out the season. I manage all athlete medical files and keep notes on all injuries and well as coordinate all doctors appointments/surgeries for the team and its staff. I also arrange physical therapy appointments for the athletes with one of our clinic locations, if necessary, and coordinate treatments with the physical therapists and athletic trainers in the clinics. I have also become part of the marketing team at the Chicago Steel, helping to pursue and attain new sponsorship opportunities. I also serve as the bridge between the Steel and ATI. I negotiate the contract every year between the two, attempting to make our relationship mutually beneficial. I also assist in coordination of ATI sponsored events during Chicago Steel games. I am responsible for maintaining a relationship with our team physicians, which benefits the Steel as well as ATI. I must also maintain a current Emergency Action plan and coordinate responsibilities with coaches, doctors, game day staff, emergency response staff, and the visiting teams. In the off season, I work full time in one of our ATI Physical Therapy clinics providing patient care. I also cover any off season hockey activities such as selection camps, etc, as well as plan for the upcoming season and maintain contact with players and follow up on any off season injuries.

Greatest Challenges

One of the greatest challenges I face is being the only female athletic trainer in our league. It was difficult to gain the trust and respect of the coaches, players and other athletic trainers around the league. Fortunately, I have gained the respect and support of my team and staff as well as the other athletic trainers in the league; but continue to have to prove myself to others throughout the league.

Another challenge I face is balancing my time between work and the rest of my life. It is very difficult for me to maintain relationships outside of work, especially during the season. Fortunately, I have a fantastic family who understands the demands of my job (even if they don't always like it).

Career Advice

Know what you're getting into. This is a high stress job with a lot of required hours. Make sure you love what you do because it makes all the difference in the world. Also, learn new things outside your field. For example, my main "career" is as an athletic trainer, but my master's degree has enabled me to be more than that. By exploring a new (but related field) I was able to gain a better understanding of how the entire sports entity works. Also, make sure you stand up for yourself and fight for what you know is right. The road may not always be easy and people may try to change your mind for you, but never ever compromise what you stand for. I cannot stress that enough.

CAREER HIGHLIGHT – ATHLETIC TRAINER/PT

Daniel Baumann, DPT, ATC, CSCS
Athletic Trainer/Physical Therapist
Mater Dei High School/Partner of ProRehab, PC
Evansville, IN
Evansville, IN

Education And Certifications

BS in Exercise Science, Masters in PT, St. Louis University, Doctorate in PT – all from St. Louis University; I am working on a DScPT at Andrews University (Berrien Springs, MI) and a COMT (certified orthopedic manipulative therapist) through NAIOMT (North American Institute of Orthopedic Manual Therapy).

ATC (certified athletic trainer), CSCS (certified strength and conditioning specialist)

CPR/First Aid

Years In Position

Head ATC at Mater Dei = 9 yrs; PT = 9 yrs & certified ATC = 11 years; Partner 5 years

Previous Positions

Since graduation in late 2001, I have always worked as a PT/ATC. For 6 months I worked for another outpatient PT clinic.

Current Job Responsibilities And Hours

Athletic trainer at Mater Dei High School—working with all the student athletes, and occasionally coaches/teachers. Co-owner/partner of ProRehab, PC. Clinical manager of ProRehab's Pearl Drive Clinic (West side)—in charge of staffing, ordering, day to day operations, etc. Staff Physical Therapist at the same clinic—treating patients.

I am salaried. Officially I am work 40 hours/week, but where and how long varies. However, I actually works many more hours while covering events at the school and doing the things that ownership requires (ie meetings, events, etc.). During the summer, I work 40 hours/week seeing patients in the clinic only. During high school football and wrestling/basketball seasons I am in the clinic 45 hour/days and 1 full 8 hour/day, while I am at the school approx 4+ hours each of the 5-hour-workdays. The nights of events (i.e. football, basketball, wrestling events) I can be there until 9 or 10 at night and on weekends. Obviously that adds the total hours/week dramatically.

Greatest Challenges

Time management with wearing so many hats, including husband and father of 2 (soon to be 3). Patients/athletes who want you to cure them without putting forth any effort of their own. Keeping employees working efficiently and happily at the same time.

Career Advice

The field of ATC: make certain you truly love working with sports and athletes. With the hours (both the quantity and the times of the day) they practice and play, you want to make certain you truly enjoy doing it. It is definitely not an 8-5, 40 hour/week job. If you become an ATC for all the right reasons, it is truly a unique and rewarding career.

References

Betrus, M. (2011). *Perfect phrases for job seekers*. New York, NY: McGraw Hill.

Enelow, W., & Kursmark, L. M. (2010). *Cover letter magic: Trade secrets of professional resume writers*. Indianapolis, IN: JIST Works.

Kursmark, L. M. (2011). *Best resumes for college students and new grads: Jump-start your career!* Indianapolis, IN: JIST Publishing, Inc.

Kursmark, L. M. (2012). *Same day resume, third edition*. Indianapolis, IN: JIST Works.

Salvador, E. U. (2010). *Step-by-step resumes, second edition: Build an outstanding resume in 10 easy steps!* Indianapolis, IN: JIST Works.

THE STUDENT PORTFOLIO

SCENARIO #1 – FIELD OBSERVATION - SOPHOMORE

Sabrina

*Sabrina is a sophomore and currently enrolled in a sport and physical activity field experience course (20 hours - 1 credit hour). Sabrina is an active student interested in cardiac rehabilitation. Her interest in cardiac rehab was heightened when her grandmother was diagnosed with heart disease. Sabrina believes she would like to help heart disease victims regain their health and develop a fit lifestyle. Sabrina developed a four-year plan to help her focus on a career in cardiac rehab. Her professor also encouraged to develop a **working portfolio**.*

SCENARIO #2 – PRACTICUM - JUNIOR

Lacey

*Lacey is a junior enrolled in a practicum course (250 hours – 5 credit hours). Lacey desires to become an Intramural Recreational Sports Director. Lacey currently has a part-time job as a Sports Official for basketball. Lacey developed a four-year plan around opportunities presented to her through her Intramural Recreational Sports program. Lacey was able to gain valuable experience as an official for basketball and volleyball and supervisor experience. She was able to attend the National Intramural Recreational Sports Association (NIRSA) conference and become a member. Lacey was able to utilize all of her experiences and coursework to develop a **showcase portfolio**.*

SCENARIO #3 – INTERNSHIP - SENIOR

Patrick

*Patrick is a senior enrolled in an internship course (450 hours – 12 credit hours). Patrick developed a four-year plan career to become a high school athletic director after reading the career highlight of Pete Huse (end of chapter). Pete has been a high school athletic director for 11 years and has also taught and coached. Therefore, Patrick developed his four-year plan with a focus on experience in teaching and coaching as well as athletic director. Patrick had already developed a working portfolio his sophomore year which accumulated into a **showcase portfolio** he can use to market himself.*

In addition to the resume and cover letter, you can benefit from developing a student portfolio. The student portfolio assists when applying for a field experience, a job, or preparing for a career in sport and physical activity. The portfolio is a personal marketing tool, and a branding tool for potential jobs. The portfolio demonstrates what you have accomplished and what you can offer employers (Foster & Dollar, 2010). For decades, artists, architects, photographers, and writers have been using portfolios to highlight their abilities. Academics (teacher education, business, applied health professions, health education) soon began to introduce the student portfolio when a group of researchers from Northwest Regional Educational Laboratory in Oregon provided a definition in the early 1990s. They defined a portfolio as "a purposeful collection of student work that tells a story of the student's efforts, progress, or achievement in a given area" (Arter & Spandel, 1992, p. 36).

To assemble the student portfolio focus on goals, documented skills, academic work, volunteer efforts, education, work experience, awards, clubs and organizations, and certifications. The organization of the portfolio helps to focus on your strengths and weaknesses, and highlights your learning and growth within the respective sport and physical activity program. The portfolio shows who you are and your capabilities. With this type of personalized information in hand you can go into interview settings with perspective employer with confidence and "proof" of your capabilities. Instead of just talking about what you can do during an interview you can show the potential employer evidence of skills by highlighting your student portfolio. This may provide an edge if you are trying to find new ways to distinguish yourself from the rest of the competition. Although portfolios can be developed in either electronic or hardcopy format, you may find it useful to collect the materials and organize the hardcopy version first and then convert it to electronic form.

Student Portfolio Types

Not knowing the difference between types of portfolios and their purpose can be a problem. For instance, you could mistakenly carry a 5-inch-thick notebook full of class projects to an interview thinking your only goal is to prove you have learned something. This type of student portfolio is commonly known as a working or learning portfolio (Foster & Dallas, 2010). You may want to consider carrying a more distinct collection of your best work into an interview showing evidence of your skills for a particular job. This type of student portfolio is commonly known as a showcase portfolio (Melograno, 2006).

Working Portfolio

The working portfolio contains cumulative work collected from many courses while you are in school and focuses on achieving specific standards or goals (Foster & Dallas, 2010). The goal is to collect sport and physical activity samples (Exhibit 5.1) focused on the specific content areas of the programs standards set forth by the Commission on Sport Management Accreditation (COSMA) (COSMA, 2013), the American College of Sports Medicine (ACSM, 2009), and/ or the American Society of Exercise Physiologist (ASEP, 2013) as illustrated in Exhibit 5.1.

Exhibit 5.1 Content Areas for Sport and Physical Activity

Commission on Sport Management Accreditation Common Professional Components

I.   Social, psychological, and international foundations of sport

II.   Ethics in sport management

III.   Sport marketing & Communication

IV.   Finance & accounting/economics

V.   Legal aspects of sport

VI.   Integrative experience

American College of Sports Medicine (ACSM)

I.   Anatomy and Biomechanics

II.   Exercise Physiology

III.   Human Development and Aging

IV.   Pathophysiology and Risk Factors

V.   Human Behavior and Psychology

VI.   Health Appraisal and Fitness Testing

VII.   Safety and Injury Prevention

VIII.   Exercise Programming

IX.   Nutrition and Weight Management

X.   Program and Administration/Management

XI.   Electrocardiography

American Society of Exercise Physiologist (ASEP)

I.   Basic Science Core (Math, Biology Chemistry, Physics, Computer Science)

II.   Exercise Physiology Core

III.   Lifetime/Personal Fitness

IV.   First Aid and CPR

V.   Movement Anatomy/Kinesiology

VI.   Biomechanics

VII.   Exercise Physiology

VIII. Exercise Biochemistry

IX.   Sports Nutrition

X.   ECG Interpretation & Exercise Testing

XI.   Statistics and Research Design

XII   Internship

XIII. Laboratory Skills

You need to develop a sport and physical activity working portfolio early in the academic career when assignments are being completed, and certifications, memberships, and other items are being sought for the respective standard areas. For example, Sabrina began to develop her working portfolio during her field experience course. One of her first assignments was to develop a notebook with academic samples. Sabrina had a few academic samples but not too many since she was a second semester sophomore. Sabrina's academic samples included assignments from the following courses:

- Field experience

- Foundations of Sport and Physical Activity

- First Aid

- Fitness and Wellness Appraisal

- Motor behavior

- Nutrition for Fitness and Sport

- Exercise Leadership

- Human Anatomy and Physiology I and II

Sabrina easily compiled her academic samples and electronically organized them according to Standards or ASEP Guidelines:

- Health Appraisal and Fitness Testing

- Safety and Injury Prevention

- Exercise Programming

- Nutrition and Weight Management

- Movement Anatomy and Biomechanics

Sabrina also developed a tab for the resume and cover letter since she developed these in her field experience course. The files/binder should organize academic work into areas for future use. Later, the working portfolio may be used to develop a future showcase or career portfolio in electronic or hard copy form (Foster & Dallas, 2010).

The Showcase Portfolio

The showcase portfolio is used if you are seeking a job interview. The showcase portfolio is a selection of your best works including other documents providing proof of skills and abilities to an employer. A showcase portfolio may include the following tabbed sections:

- Cover Letter and Resume

- Self-Statement, Career Plan, and Academic Plan

- Sample of your Work and/or Service Materials

- Professional Development Materials

- Letters of Recommendation (at least 3)

- Support Materials

The working portfolio begins to develop into a showcase portfolio during your junior or senior year. For example, Patrick and Lacey kept all of their academic work and documentation of other relevant information in a working portfolio until they had enough to develop the showcase portfolio. The organization and contents the showcase portfolios are presented in Exhibit 5.2.

Exhibit 5.2 Showcase Portfolio Sample

I.   Cover letter and resume

II.   Self-Statement, Career Plan, and Academic Plan

III. Sample of Work Related and/or Service Materials

- Academic

- Employment

- Volunteer

- Field experience

IV.   Professional Development Materials

- Memberships to university and professional clubs and/or organizations

- Certifications (i.e., first aid, CPR, personal training)

- Continuing Education

- Scholarship

- Awards

- Research Presentations

- Research Publications

V.   Support Materials - Letters of Recommendation (at least 3)

- Professor

- Advisor

- Professional or employer in the field

- Include faculty/employer biography for each letter of recommendation

---

Organization of the Showcase Portfolio – Eleven Steps to Success

The time and effort you put into the development of the portfolio is a career investment. Assembling and organizing your portfolio can be overwhelming but does not have to be a headache if you complete the 11 steps to success in Exhibit 5.3 and the exercises as Sabrina, Patrick and Lacey did to create their portfolio.

Exhibit 5.3 Eleven Steps to Success in Creating a Portfolio

1. Purchase supplies for the hardcopy version of the portfolio.

2. Include your cover letter (Chapter 4) and resume (Chapter 3).

3. Develop a self-statement for the introduction of section 2. Include your 4-year academic plan of study.

4. Gather sample of work-related and/or service materials - academic, employment, volunteer, and field experience work. Additional academic samples if they highlight your talents.

5. Gather professional development materials – memberships, certifications, continuing education, scholarships, awards, research presentations, publications.

6. Gather support materials – letters of recommendation from professors, advisors, professionals or employers in the field. Include biography for each letter of recommendation.

7. Consider audio and video.

8. Organize and assemble the portfolio.

9. Convert the portfolio to an electronic format.

10. Use the portfolio in a simulated interview.

11. Use the portfolio in a real interview situation.

Step 1 – Purchase Supplies for the Portfolio

The first step to develop a portfolio, regardless of the type, is to purchase the supplies. Patrick chose to purchase his supplies from the university bookstore while Sabrina and Lacey purchased from an office supply store (www.officedepot.com; www.staples.com; www.officemax.com). Sabrina, Lacey, and Patrick purchased the same materials:

- 3-ring padfolio
- Clear page protectors (1 box of 50)
- Plastic photo sheet protectors (if applicable)
- Dividers with tabs (at least 5)
- Plastic stick-on business card holder for front of portfolio (if not included with 3-ring padfolio)
- High quality paper (1 package)

- Extra ink cartridge (if using inkjet printer)

- Picture holders (if applicable)

Use the checklist in Exercise 5.1 to purchase your supplies for the portfolio.

Exercise 5.1 Supplies for Portfolio

❑ 3-ring padfolio

❑ Clear page protectors (1 box of 50)

❑ Plastic photo sheet protectors (if applicable)

❑ Dividers with tabs (at least 5)

❑ Plastic stick-on business card holder for front of portfolio (if not included with 3-ring padfolio)

❑ High quality paper (1 package)

❑ Extra ink cartridge (if using inkjet printer)

❑ Picture holders (if applicable)

Step 2 — Include your Cover Letter and Resume

The second step to assemble the portfolio is to update or develop a cover letter and resume. The cover letter is an essential component for any job search. The thought of writing an individual cover letter for each potential position can be overwhelming and a challenge. The cover letter is the first opportunity to make a first impression on an extremely influential employer making the decision to hire you. It is important to customize your cover letter according to the employer organization. If you do not have a cover letter refer to Chapter 4. The resume highlights your skills, education, and experiences. Keeping the resume up-to-date is a good way to save time and energy. Sabrina, Lacey, and Patrick made sure their resume was accurate and updated. If you do not have a resume refer to Chapter 3 and complete the exercises.

Step 3 — Include a Self-Statement and Include a 4-Year Academic Plan

You need to customize the portfolio for the sport and physical industry segment you are interested in pursuing. For example, in chapter 2, Lacey discovered she wanted to pursue a career in recreational sports. Once she established recreational sports as her career choice she began to write a self-statement that would be the introduction to her 4-year Academic Plan.

Write a Self-Statement. A self-statement is a philosophy statement that answers the question, Why do you do what you do? The focus is on why you want to be in the career you are choosing to pursue. The philosophy statement is your description about your beliefs, values, and outlook about sport and physical activity industry. The philosophy statement is often used by employers to see if you fit into the company's corporate culture. For example, Patrick may find a philosophy statement useful when answering specific questions addressing athletics:

- Should student-athletes be required to maintain a certain GPA?

- Should coaches be a allowed to recruit student-athletes who have been dismissed from another university?

- Should the athletic trainer, coach, or athlete make the final decision when an injured player returns to competition?

- Should the coach have the right to have double practices in one day?

- Should the coach be allowed to dictate lifestyle choices (code of conduct, curfew)?

Patrick's philosophy statement guides him to critically think about what he ought to do in these situations. (Wuest & Fisette, 2012) developed a series of questions and guidelines the author modified to help Patrick develop his philosophy statement located in Exhibit 5.4. Those questions and guidelines included the following:

- **Identify past experiences. What are your most outstanding and disheartening experiences?** Patrick played high school sports including baseball, basketball, and football. His most outstanding experience was when his team won the Iowa basketball state championship in 2013. Through this experience he learned how to be a leader and team player. Winning did not mean success but wanting and working hard to win meant more. Finding a way to pick your teammates up after a loss was the true key to success.

   His most disheartening experience was when his teammate was benched due his grades. This was his friend's senior year and he was not able to be a part of the championship team and did not graduate. Patrick learned it was important to evaluate grades of his future players on a consistent basis and help the student-athlete get help before it is too late.

- **Think about other professionals in the field of interest. Research their philosophy to see if it is compatible with yours. Do you have a role model that helped you to enter the sport and physical activity field? What was his or her philosophy? Do you currently have a role model? What is your philosophy?** Patrick's first role model was his coach. His coach instilled values of fair play, sportsmanship, and the value all student-athletes input. Patrick's advisor was his current role model in that she provided him with the upmost respect.

- **Review the codes of conduct for your career? What are the expectations?** Patrick has chosen to abide to the NCAA codes of conduct. He wants to make sure he builds the best athletic program that he can without violating any code of ethics.

■ **Take all of the information above and express your philosophy. Patrick summarized the following information to develop his philosophy statement.**

• Leader, team player, winning is not everything, value your team and listen to their ideas, evaluate student grades to help athletics be role models on and off the court, fair play, sportsmanship, and follow NCAA codes of conduct.

Exhibit 5.4 provides an example of Patrick's philosophy statement.

Exhibit 5.4 Sport and Self-Statement Activity Philosophy Statement - Patrick 450 hours internship

I believe a leader should be a team player and the value of all people is important to success of an organization. I strive to make sure the athletic programs abide by the NCAA Codes of Conduct, and the student-athlete is respected by others as a role model on and off the court.

Complete Exercise 5.2 to develop your philosophy statement. The philosophy statement should be no more than one to four sentences in length. If you are having problems writing the philosophy statement in paragraph form, bullet points may be used to add clarity.

Exercise 5.2 Philosophy Statement

1. Identify past experiences. What are your most outstanding and disheartening experiences? _____

_____

_____

2. Do you have a role model that helped you to enter the sport and physical activity field? What was his or her philosophy? Do you currently have a role model? What is your philosophy _____

_____

_____

3. Think about other professionals in the field of interest. Research their philosophy to see if it is compatible with yours. _____

_____

_____

4. Review the codes of conduct for your career? What are the expectations?

    _____

    _____

    _____

5. Take all of the information above and express your philosophy.

    _____

    _____

    _____

Academic Plan of Study. Documenting an academic plan of study is a logical way to begin this section of the portfolio. You want to display your program and the academic plan defines the courses you took to complete the degree. This information may help current or potential employers distinguish between your background from others because each school, college, or university usually has distinct curricula. The school bulletin, catalog, or the department is the best way to obtain a copy of the academic plan of study. Lacey obtained her academic plan by going to her advisor and requesting a copy. Sabrina chose to go online and print a copy.

Step 4 — Gather Sample of Work-Related and/or Service materials - Academic, Employment, Volunteer, and Field Experience Work

The fourth step to assemble your portfolio is to gather sample of work-related and/or service materials - academic, employment, volunteer, and field experience work.

You also want to include any previous employment and/or field experience materials. This type of work provides the employer with an idea of what you can already do. Sabrina, Patrick, and Lacey simply referred to their resume for this information. Sabrina, Lacey, and Patrick gathered relevant work experience samples to highlight their skills specific to the position. For example, Lacey collected tournament bracket and special events organization material as artifacts from her intramural supervisor position with the University of Iowa Recreational Sports Department. Refer to your resume and determine what positions you can gather relevant artifacts to include in your portfolio. Complete Exercise 5.4 to gather your work experience artifacts.

Academic Samples and Skill-Sets from Working Portfolio. You need to have academic samples reflective of your "best work" and demonstrates your abilities to meet the job requirements. A new portfolio may be required for each submission. Consider using a variety of samples to include class projects, papers (writing samples), presentations, skill check-off sheets, and specific samples. These documents may be found in your working portfolio if completed early in your academic career. For example, Lacey completed the same steps as Sabrina mentioned earlier in this chapter. Lacey was able to complete a working portfolio early in the academic plan and did not have to sift through electronic files stored in multiple locations. Lacey was able to use "works in progress" to update her portfolio.

Skill sets are essential to develop a portfolio. A set of pre-existing checklists of critical skills from sport and physical activity standards mentioned in Exhibit 5.1 may be introduced in several of your classes. Exhibit 5.5 provides a modified sample skills set from a Sports Event Management course where she was the leader of a golf tournament. There are three levels Lacey needed to accomplish before the skill set was complete:

- Awareness – Lacey was aware and completed the skill at least once

- Practice - during the practice stage Lacey followed a guide to complete the skill

- Master – Lacey consistently performed a skill without any effort

Notice Lacey was able to master all of the skills listed according to level of assignment. The skills sets demonstrated Lacey's competency and ability to perform. The sets provide the employer with checklists of critical skills related to a special event that may be ran in intramural recreational sports. These skills sets may not be completed by all professors and therefore may not be an option for your portfolio.

Exhibit 5.5 Sport and Physical Activity Skills Sets – Lacey – Practicum 200 hours

Scenario 1

Awareness = A

Practicing = P

Mastering = M

1. Is able to develop a budget for a golf Tournament – A __x__ , P__x__ , M __x__ .

2. Is able to develop a marketing plan (includes advertising and sponsorship) for a golf tournament – A __x__ , P __x__ , M __x__ .

3. Is able to organize the day of events (registration check-in, tournament, awards, etc) for the golf tournament - A __x__ , P __x__ , M __x__ .

4. Is able to order the necessary awards for the golf tournament A __x__ , P __x__ , M __x__ .

You may often overlook a great source of service activities that could be added to your portfolio. Service shows you are willing to give back. Sometimes this service comes in the form of a field experience. You can provide a page of what you have accomplished in terms of university and community service by simply writing a summary report and including pictures of involvement in the event. If you have artifacts include those in the portfolio as well. For example, Exhibit 5.8 provides service activities Sabrina completed during her freshmen year.

Exhibit 5.6 Service Materials – Sabrina – 20 hours - Field Experience
1. Volunteered to be a group leader for a corporate fitness center "Breakfast Retiree Club"
2. Volunteered to serve meals to the Solarbron to Assisted Living residence
3. Volunteer to help at St. Mary's Cardiac Rehab

Complete Exercise 5.5 to make a list of service activities. If you have artifacts include those as well.

Exercise 5.3 Service Materials

Volunteer Experience _____

Artifacts _____

Pictures _____

Volunteer Experience _____

Artifacts _____

Pictures _____

Volunteer Experience _____

Artifacts _____

Pictures _____

Exercise 5.4 Work Experience, Volunteer, and/or field experience Artifacts

Employer _____

Position Responsibilities _____

Artifact to Gather _____

Employer _____

Position Responsibilities _____

Artifact to Gather _____

Employer _____

Position Responsibilities _____

Artifact to Gather _____

Step 5 — Gather professional Development Materials — Memberships, Certifications, Continue Education, Scholarships, Awards, Research Presentation, Publications

The academic work is important to the portfolio but the employers also want to see your professional development materials. Do you belong to any organizations of professional interest? Do you have any certifications relevant to the field? Have you attended workshops to help keep you up-to-date on new sport and physical activity trends?

Organization Memberships. Holding memberships in professional organizations shows you made a commitment to the profession. There are many opportunities for you to be "active" in organizations. Many of the professional organizations host conferences and provide you with the opportunity to preside over sessions, or give oral or poster presentations adding additional skills of communication, writing, and technology to your professional growth. The majority of these organizations keep the cost to a minimum. If you cannot afford the membership with a state, regional or national organization, a sport and physical activity club or campus organization may be the first step in helping support professional development. Research in sport and physical activity contend these clubs and organizations provide you with a valuable means of meeting other academic professionals (Bower, 2012). You should check with the department to see if there are any programs supporting the profession and if so when and where do the organizations meet.

A list of sport and physical activity organizations are found in Exhibit 5.6. You may develop a list of memberships by including the name of the organization including the date joined, any offices, boards or committees served and a copy of the membership card for proof. The most recent memberships should be listed first.

Exhibit 5.7 Sport and Physical Activity Organizations

1. Aerobics and Fitness Association of America (AFAA)

2. American Alliance for Health, Physical Education, Recreation and Dance (AAHPERD)

3. American College of Sports Medicine (ACSM)

4. American Council on Exercise (ACE)

5. American Physical Therapy Association (APTA)

6. Cooper Institute for Aerobic Research

7. European Association of Sport Management (EASM)

8. International Association of Physical Education and Sport for Girls and Women (IAPESPGW)

9. International Dance Exercise Association Foundation (IDEA)

10. National

11. National Association for Sport and Physical Education (NASPE)

12. National Athletic Trainers Association (NATA)

13. National Intramural Recreational Sports Association (NIRSA)

14. National Strength and Conditioning Association (NSCA)

15. North American Society for Sport History (NASSH)

16. North American Society for Sport Management (NASSM)

17. North American Society for the Sociology of Sport (NASSS)

18. Philosophic Society for the Study of Sport (PSSS)

19. Program for the Advancement of Girls and Women in Sport (PAGWS)

20. Reebok International

21. Sport Marketing Association (SMA)

22. Sport Marketing Association of Australia and New Zealand (SMAANZ)

23. Sports and Recreation Law Association (SRLA)

24. Academy of Sports Medicine (NASM)

Certifications and Continuing Education. Certifications and continuing education are another way to add credibility to your skills. Exhibit 5.7 provides a sample of certifications and continuing education opportunities if you are wishing to pursue a career sport and physical activity.

Exhibit 5.8 Sport and Physical Activity Certifications

1. National Intramural Recreational Sports Specialist

2. American Coaching Effectiveness Program (ACEP)
   - Level One – Basic Education
   - Level Two – Beyond the Basics
   - Bronze - Level Certification
   - Silver - Level Certification
   - Gold - Level Certification

3. Coaching Education within National Governing Bodies
   - USA Volleyball Coaching Accreditation Program (CAP) (5 Levels)

4. American College of Sports Medicine (ACSM)

   Health Fitness Certifications
   - Certified Personal Trainer (CPT)
   - Certified Health Fitness Specialist (HFS)
   - Certified Group Exercise Instructor (GEI)

   Clinical Certifications
   - Certified Clinical Exercise Specialist (CET)
   - Registered Clinical Exercise Physiologist (RCEP)

   Specialty Certifications
   - Certified Cancer Exercise Trainer (CET)
   - Certified Inclusive Fitness Trainer (CIFT)
   - Physical Activity in Public Health Specialist (PAPHS)

5. American Council on Exercise (ACE)

   Health Fitness Certifications
   - Personal Trainer
   - Group Fitness Instructor
   - Health Coach Certification
   - Advanced Fitness Specialist

Specialty Certifications

- Youth Fitness
- Fitness Nutrition
- Weight Management
- Sports Conditioning
- Functional Training
- Mind Body
- Group Exercise Leadership
- Therapeutic Exercise
- Senior Fitness

6. Aerobic Fitness Association of America (AFAA)

- Personal Trainer
- Primary Group Exercise

7. National Strength and Conditioning Association (NSCA)

- Strength & Conditioning Specialist
- Personal Trainer

8. National Athletic Training Association (NATA)

- Athletic Trainer

9. Young Men's Christian Association (YMCA)

- Basic Fitness Leader
- Fitness Specialist
- Advance Exercise Specialist

10. The Cooper Institute for Aerobic Research

- Physical Fitness Specialist
- Advance Physical Fitness
- Program Director Specialist
- Group Exercise Leadership

11. American Red Cross (ARC) or American Heart Association

- CPR

- First Aid

12. National Academy of Sports Medicine (NASM)

- Personal Trainer

- Performance Enhancement Specialist

- Corrective Exercise Specialist

13. National Exercise Trainer Association (NETA)

Health and Fitness Certifications

- Group Exercise

- Personal Trainer

- Mind/Body

Specialty Certifications

- Indoor Group Cycling

- Kettleball

- Pilates Mat

- Pilates Reformer

- Yoga

Honors and Awards. Any awards you may have earned may be used to strengthen the portfolio. Honors may include a member of the Dean's List or Academic All American while scholarships may include academic, sports, and others showing your hard work and determination. Place the original documents into your portfolio.

Patrick answered several questions to gather his professional development material. The question included:

- **Do you have memberships with any organization?** Patrick gathered his original membership card for the North American Society for Sport Management (NASSM)

- **Do you have an acceptance letter for presentations or publications?** Patrick included a copy of his acceptance letter for a poster session at the NASSM conference

- **Do you have a letter about your involvement with any committees?**
  Patrick included a letter stating his involvement with the State Student Leadership Committee for Sport. He requested the letter from the State organization's president.

- **Do you have a list of all conferences you attended?** Patrick kept track of all his conferences and sessions he attended. He also related how his experience at the conference related to his professional development.

- **Do you have any certifications?** Patrick included a copy of his First Aid/CPR and AED certification.

- **Do you have any honors and awards?** Patrick was the recipient of the young student award by state association.

Exercise 5.5 Professional Development Artifacts

1. Do you have memberships with any organization? _____

_____

_____

_____

2. Do you have an acceptance letter for presentations or publications?

_____

_____

_____

3. Do you have a letter about your involvement with any committees?

_____

_____

_____

4. Do you have a list of all conferences you attended? _____

_____

_____

5. Do you have any certifications? _____

_____

_____

_____

Step 6 – Gather Support Materials – Letters of Recommendation from Professor, Advisor, Professional or Employer in the Field. Include Faculty/Employer Biography for Each letter of Recommendation

You can obtain additional proof and support of abilities by asking faculty and/or employer letters of recommendations or references.

Letters of Recommendation. Letters of recommendation provide support from individuals who have seen you perform. Letters of recommendation are often relied upon when academic samples or professional development materials do not provide enough proof of abilities. For example, Patrick gathered letter of recommendations from his professors and supervisors of current and past employment. Patrick provided specifics on what the letter should address to help guide the person writing the letter. Patrick did not wait until the last minute to ask for a letter of recommendation from his professors and supervisors. He provided them with at least two weeks to complete the task. Patrick also checked the status of the letter one week after the request. Patrick proofed the letter before placing it in his portfolio.

References. References are an alternative method to the letter of recommendation. You may opt to include three to five references. The list of names may include an academic, employment, and character reference. Lacey reviewed and decided to update her current reference list. Lacey gathered references from her professors, counselors, and previous coaches who could attest to her academic and/or skill ability. Lacey had more academic references since she was still in school. Lacey's employment references included supervisors or managers who attested to her work ethic. Finally, Lacey did choose to include a character reference from her Intramural Sports Club. Lacey was cautious to use more than one character reference and, therefore did not use her roommate. Lacey asked her professor, employer, and character candidates' permission to include them as references in her portfolio.

Faculty and Employer Biographies. Patrick and Lacey realized the credibility of the letter of recommendation and references can be supported by including a faculty, employer, and/or character biography. The faculty, employer, or character biography provides the employer with background on the people writing the letter of recommendations and how you know them.

Complete Exercise 5.6 to gather your support material certain items require a check mark when completed.

Exercise 5.6 Support Material

Gather support material by referring to Chapter 4 _____

Do you have any updates? If so list them (include name, employer, title, phone number, email address)

Name _____

_____

Employer _____

Title _____

Phone Number _____

Email Address _____

Name _____

Employer _____

Title _____

Phone Number _____

Email Address _____

Gather Letters of Recommendation (1) ___ (2) ____ (3) ____

Ask permission to use references (if applicable) (1) ____ (2) ____ (3) _____

Ask for Faculty and/or Biography (1) ____ (2) ____ (3) _____

Step 7 – Consider Using Audio and Video

You may want to consider using audio and video to show examples of yourself in action. The videos should be short (no more than 3 minutes) and emphasize your skills related to the specific job. For example, Lacey provided video of her golf tournament. She provided footage from the registration to the awards ceremony. Lacey gave her video to the perspective employer at the end of her interview. Lacey labeled the video with her name, subject area (golf tournament), and the length of the video clip (10 minutes).

Step 8 – Organize and Assemble the Portfolio

Once you have completed steps one through eight you need to complete six additional steps to organize and assemble the portfolio.

- Place the dividers in the 3-ring padfolio

- Develop a table of contents

- Make tabs for each section of the portfolio. Use your exercises to organize the portfolio.

- Place a professional business card inside the padfolio. The professional business card may be used for marketing and networking purposes

- Place a professional card on the outside of the portfolio. The professional card may also be used for marketing and networking purposes. Exhibit 5.9 provides a sample of Patrick's professional business card. Business card paper may be found at any office supply store. A template is provided to help guide you through the process of developing a business card.

- Proofread everything at least three times. Have someone else read the documents in the portfolio as well.

Parts of the Business Card

Think of your business card as a miniature resume and as a sales instrument and a representation of you. Business card paper will need to be purchased if you are going to develop your own card. Business card paper may be found at any office supply store. A template is provided to help guide you through the process in developing your business card. You still need to organize yourself by determining what you would like to put on the business card. You want to consider both the front and reverse side of the card. Exhibit 5.10 provides items that you may want to consider when developing your business card.

Exhibit 5.9 Professional Business Card Items to Consider	
Name	Mission statement
Degree	Photograph or picture
Address	Endorsements
Phone numbers (office, home, cell, fax)	Items that you did not want to put on the front side
E-mail address	
Your website (if applicable)	
Social media accounts (Blog, LinkedIN, Twitter, Facebook) – see chapter 7 for additional information on social networking	

Exhibit 5.10 Professional Business Card – Patrick – Internship – 450 hours

Patrick Scott

B.S. Sport Management Candidate

University of Pennsylvania

(405)302-5554

Pscott@penn.edu

Complete Exercise 5.7 to develop your professional business card.

Exercise 5.7 Professional Business Card

Below Email Address add the follow

Website address (if applicable)

_____

_____

Social Media – Blogging Site (if applicable) _____

_____

Social Media – LinkedIN (if applicable)

_____

_____

Social Media – Twitter (if applicable)

_____

_____

Social Media – Facebook (if applicable)

_____

_____

Mission statement (if applicable)

_____

_____

_____

_____

_____

Photograph or picture _____
(check if applicable)

Endorsements _____ (list)

Post Picture Here

Name _____

Degree _____

University _____

Phone Number _____

Email Address _____

Step 9 – Convert the Portfolio to an Electronic Format

An alternative way to increase your marketability is to use electronic portfolios. The electronic portfolio is the same as the hardcopy portfolio but essentially is organized and accessed differently. Like its paper counterpart, the electronic portfolio provides you with the ability to showcase your work and skills but in an innovative way. You can use the electronic portfolio as a career-oriented website for pursing a job, show yourself in action by using voice or video clips, and easily follow-up an interview with a copy of the electronic portfolio to be reviewed at a later time instead of bringing a large binder to the interview (Carliner, 2005).

Steps in Designing an Electronic Portfolio

You may not be technologically savvy but an electronic portfolio is not out of the question. Instead of hiring someone to design the electronic portfolio you can follow the steps listed in this section. If you run into a problem then you may want to seek assistance from computer technician on campus. For example, Lacey followed the steps below to convert her hardcopy portfolio to an electronic format:

- Gathered and separated materials
- Designed website on the computer
- Saved the electronic portfolio
- Uploaded the electronic portfolio to the internet

Step 1 – Gather and Separate Portfolio Material

The first step to design an electronic portfolio is to gather all your material. This material should be gathered and stored on a USB, CD-ROM. If you have hard copy material from a scanner make sure to convert it to electronic format (see step 2). Next, you want to separate the portfolio material so you can begin to develop the web pages. It is best to develop an organization system by using a sheet of paper and pencil, chalk or white board to develop a map of the "big" picture of where and what you want the links to consist of. For example, Lacey organized her materials and developed a map on paper and pencil that included the following material:

- Name, university, department
- Picture or graphic (optional)
- Letters of recommendation
- Fitness philosophy and objectives
- Resume
- Academic samples and skills sets
- Professional development samples
- Service samples

Step 2 — Design Website on Computer

You want to create web pages from the sample material through the use of Microsoft PowerPoint. Although the steps to follow focus on developing the web pages in Microsoft Powerpoint, you may opt to use Microsoft Word, Microsoft Publisher, Microsoft FrontPage, Microsoft Works Portfolio and many more. However, Microsoft PowerPoint is a common software most individuals understand and are able to operate.

Exhibit 5.10 Microsoft PowerPoint Web Page Development

1. Open Microsoft PowerPoint
2. Go to Format "Slide Design" and choose a "Design Template" or "Blank Presentation
3. Go to Format "Slide Layout" and choose "Title Only" from "Text Layout"
4. Develop a homepage by creating "Action Buttons"
   - Go to "Slide Show" and click on "Action Buttons"
   - Click and drag the "Action Button" on the slide
   - Select the "Hyperlink To" option, and select "Other File" from the dropdown menu
   - Locate and double click on the desired file· Click OK
   - Right click on the button, and select "Add Text"
   - Enter the desired button label
   - Double click on the button, and select the desired "Fill and Line" properties (optional)
   - Click OK
   - Repeat steps to create additional buttons (letter of recommendation, resume, etc)
5. To add a picture go to insert "Picture" and click on "Clip Art" or "From File"
6. To add additional text (name, address, email, etc) go to insert "Text Box" and click and drag box to slide.
7. Save the presentation and prepare to "package for CD"

A sample of Lacey's electronic portfolio homepage developed from Microsoft Powerpoint is found in Exhibit 5.11. Additional pages are developed according to the "action buttons" (letter of recommendations, fitness philosophy and objectives, resume, academic samples and skills set, professional development samples, and service samples).

Exhibit 5.11 Electronic Portfolio Homepage Sample

Step 3 — Save the Electronic Portfolio and Proofread

Once you have developed all of the web pages, make sure you and someone else double-check for errors. Next, you want to save the electronic portfolio to your hard drive, CD-ROM and label with a date and instructions on opening the files. Finally, you need to make plenty of copies for future use.

Step 4 — Upload the Electronic Portfolio to the Internet

Besides taking your CD to interviews you should also place your electronic portfolio on the internet. This tactic provides you with a tremendous amount of exposure to perspective employers. There are four steps in placing the electronic portfolio on the internet:

- Obtain a host for the website. The college or university may provide free web space or you may need to check with an Internet Service Provider (ISP). You want to ask professor how to contact the ISP. An ISP may charge a small fee.

- Take the web pages and upload them or publish (FTP) the files to the internet site. The ISP provider will include directions and help you on how to upload or publish files to the internet.

- You want to include the web address on the hard copy of your portfolio.

- After the portfolio is active you need to keep the site updated. For example, if you achieve a goal, you need to remove this goal.

Step 10 – Use the Portfolio in a Simulated Interview

After completing the portfolio, plan for five to eight minutes maximum in sharing the portfolio during an interview. To help with the five to eight minute sharing use the portfolio in a "mock" interview. Begin by getting acquainted with the portfolio, knowing about all the content of each tabbed section. You should feel comfortable navigating through the portfolio. For example, you should be able to tell the employer about your philosophy and goals, without looking at them.

Step 11 – Use the Portfolio in a Real Situation

Before an interview, a good marketing tool is to promote your portfolio by placing *Portfolio Available upon Request* on the bottom of your resume, refer to the portfolio in the cover letter, and communicate to the employer that you have a portfolio during a interview. You need to customize the portfolio according to the needs of the potential employer. For example, customize the career objectives and resume for the company; tweak the career goals if necessary; and customize the academic and work samples based on the position in the company.

Since you completed several simulated interviews you should be comfortable with your portfolio and know the contents of each tabbed area. Once you have an interview it is important to make sure to let the employer know within the first 15 minutes a portfolio is available. Begin by reviewing the career plan, point out the resume, and describe what the employer will view in the pages to come. During the interview use the portfolio to answer questions from the interviewer. For example, if the employer asks about your ability to organize a sporting event you can show then an academic sample. This academic sample has a greater impact than just answering the question. You will complete a simulated interview in Chapter 8

Summary

The portfolio assignment does not end after graduation. You need to maintain a professional portfolio once you have a position in your respected area. The portfolio is essential to the growth and development of the individual who is in a key position within sport and physical activity.

Frequently Asked Questions

How do you incorporate the hardcopy portfolio into an interview?

You can incorporate the hardcopy portfolio three ways: (a) you can use the portfolio during an interview, (b) use the portfolio to answer a question, or (c) use the portfolio as a summary at the end of the interview.

Why should you create an electronic portfolio versus a hardcopy portfolio?

You may use the electronic portfolio during the pre-interview process noting that he or she has a paper portfolio available for review. You may also leave a copy of the portfolio in electronic form for an interviewer to review at a later time. Leaving a hardcopy of the portfolio may not be an option if you have more than one interview. The electronic portfolio also contains more work samples that could support the hardcopy.

What are some common items to keep in mind when developing an electronic portfolio?

You need to think about the following items: (a) make the electronic portfolio easy to navigate, (b) be sure to attach directions, and (c) use a common platform such as Microsoft PowerPoint slides.

Student Learning Activities

Use the eleven steps of success to develop a learning portfolio.

Use the showcase portfolio in a mock interview. A mock interview simulation may be found in Chapter 6. Focus on highlighting contents or specific sections in the portfolio in five to eight minutes during the simulation.

Use the hardcopy of your showcase portfolio and follow the five steps in developing an electronic portfolio. Place at least five copies of the portfolios on CD ROMS.

Upload your portfolio on the internet using the steps provided in this chapter.

➤ Student Portfolio Checklist

- ❑ Purchased supplies for the portfolio
- ❑ Updated or developed cover letter and resume
- ❑ Developed a self-statement for the introduction and creating a 4-year academic career plan
- ❑ Gathered samples or work-related and/or service materials and academic samples if applicable
- ❑ Gathered professional development material
- ❑ Gathered support materials
- ❑ Used audio and video (optional)
- ❑ Organized and assembled the portfolio (optional)
- ❑ Converted the portfolio to an electronic format (optional)
- ❑ Used the portfolio in a simulated interview (optional)
- ❑ Use the portfolio in a real interview situation (optional)

CAREER HIGHLIGHT – DIRECTOR OF HEALTH, PHYSICAL EDUCATION, ATHLETICS, SUBSTANCE ABUSE, VIOLENCE, AND SAFETY

Jeanna Cooper

Director of Health, Physical Education, Athletics, Substance Abuse, Violence, and Safety

Hamden Public Schools

Education And Certifications

Bachelors of Science in Physical Education

Masters Degree in Health and Physical Education and an Administration Degree in Educational Leadership.

I am a Certified Teacher and Administrator; I am a Certified Coach; I am Certified in First Aid and CPR; I am a certified Racquetball instructor; I am a certified LCD Instructor to teach Coaching Modules and I am a certified BEST Portfolio Trainer and Scorer.

Years In Position

10 years

Previous Positions

Director of Athletics/Administrative Aide for Hillhouse High School in New Haven, CT - nine years; lead physical education teacher Hillhouse High School; after-school tutorial program coordinator – Hillhouse High School; Head Volleyball Coach 14 years; Assistant Softball coach 6 years at Hillhouse High School; Health and Physical Education teacher Hillhouse High School; Physical Education teacher at Prince / Welch Annex Elementary Schools, New Haven; Various coaching positions to include: East/West All Star Volleyball Game for Connecticut; Middle School girls basketball coach in Woodbridge, CT; Assistant Volleyball coach at the University of Bridgeport; Certified Racquetball Coach for youth ages 5-12 and adult racquetball trainer for Women and Beginners; Coached the Special Olympics in New Haven; Coached a parochial girl's basketball team ages 10-12 in Milford, CT; and Assistant coach of a Women's Slow-pitch team in Milford, CT.

Current Job Responsibilities And Hours

For Health and Physical Education: I am responsible for staff evaluations for Elementary, Middle and High School teachers; I interview and recommend staff for hire; I coordinate and run all department meetings; I develop department budgets, purchase equipment and supplies; revise curriculums and plan summer curriculum workshops; I prepare, plan and run professional development workshops; I assist Cooperating Teachers in developing student teachers; I provide drug prevention fairs for all the elementary schools with our SADD (Students Against Destroying Dreams) I coordinate Drug Free week with a community organization in which we have Motivational Media Presentations and Drug Free Presenters for Middle and Elementary Schools; I am a member of Safety, Health District and Health and Physical Education local and state organizations and attend meetings and conferences, locally and nationally; I am the coordinator of the Wellness Policy for the district and organize meetings and implementation changes, and I am the Hamden Administrators Union President.

For Athletics: I evaluate all coaches; interview and recommend coaches for hire; I prepare all athletic budgets, purchase equipment, hire all game help, officials, athletic trainers, ambulance, security, police and essential staff to run athletic events; I coordinate ticket sales; field maintenance and repairs; provide pay for officials and all staff; coordinate fields with the town park and recreation program, rent high school and middle school gymnasiums and fields to the public, I schedule all sports at the high school and middle school as well as intra-murals; I am responsible for repair and maintenance of all equipment, weight rooms, and fitness centers; I supervise all home high school athletic contests and some high profile away contests as well as tournaments; I teach LCD coaching modules for my staff; I am the league secretary and attend all league meetings, as well as executive committee meetings; I am a regional representative on the state level and attend those meetings; I organize all seasonal award ceremonies, parent-coaches nights for each season, and attend local banquets and state awards ceremonies; I co-chair the Hamden Women's Sports Foundation and the Hamden Athletic Hall of Fame Committee; I host and attend all state playoff competition when necessary and I am the league chairperson for Girl's Lacrosse and provide pre- and post season meetings and host the championships.

My hours vary between 60-80 hours a week and weekends

Greatest Challenges

Time !!!

Career Advice

If you plan on becoming an athletic director, you need to coach! The more coaching experience the more prepared you will be. Be prepared to work all the time and if you have a family they must be very forgiving!!! Make sure that you establish good relationships with **everyone** and try to be as positive as you can be. People will remember you from how you treated them most of all so always try to treat people with respect.

CAREER HIGHLIGHT – INTERSCHOLASTIC ATHLETIC DIRECTOR

Pete Huse

Athletic Director

Greenwood High School

Greenwood, IN

Education And Certifications

B.P.E.-Physical Education/U.S. History

Coaching endorsement

Athletic Administration endorsement

Years In Position

1 years

Previous Positions

Physical Education Teacher, Basketball Coach and Baseball Coach

Current Job Responsibilities And Hours

Run athletic department-Financial, scheduling, transportation, supervision home & away, set-up for events, concessions, schedule labor, work w/ coaches, hiring staff. Typically works 70-75 hours per week.

Greatest Challenges

Poor coaches

Career Advice

Be willing to put in the time, learn from your mistakes, find ways to control stress, do not let parents get to you

References

American College of Sports Medicine. (2013). *ACSM's guidelines for exercise testing and prescription, 9th edition.* Baltimore, Maryland: Lippincott Williams &Wilkens.

Arter, J. A., &Spandel (1992).Using portfolios of student work in instruction and assessment. *Educational Measurement: Issues and Practices, 11(1),* 36-44.

ASEP. (2013). *American Society of Exercise Physiologist.* Retrieved from www.asep.org.

Bower, G. G. (2012). Experiential classroom learning: Developing a sport management club. *theIndiana Association for Health, Physical Education, Recreation, and Dance Journal,* 41(1), 12-16.

Commission on Sport Management Accreditation. (2013). *COSMA accreditation principles and self-study preparation,* June 2010. Retrieved December 28, 2013, from http://www.cosmaweb.org/accredmanuals

Foster, S. B., & Dollar, J. E. (2010). *Experiential learning in sport management: Internships and beyond.* Morgantown: WV: Fitness Information Technology.

Melograno, V. (2006). *Professional and student portfolios for physical education.* Champaign, IL: Human Kinetics.

Wuest, D. A., &Fisette, J. L. (2012). *Foundations of physical education, exercise Science, and sport.* New York: NY: McGraw-Hill.

SECTION III

NETWORKING

6

NETWORKING

SCENARIO #1 – FIELD EXPERIENCE/OBSERVATION - SOPHOMORE

Veronica

*Veronica is a sophomore and currently enrolled in a sport and physical activity field experience course (20 hour - 1 credit hours). Veronica attends the department's "Alumni in Residence" yearly program. Veronica was introduced to a former student (Henry) who is working for Sarasota County Government. The position requires Henry to work with a wide range of departments such as fire, police, and sheriff in assisting employees with medical and health problems. Veronica meets Henry following the event and explains she is interested in completing a field experience through his company. Henry is delighted to accommodate this need. Veronica is excited to know this **strategic network** plan worked in helping her obtain a field experience.*

SCENARIO #2 – PRACTICUM - JUNIOR

Elizabeth

*Elizabeth is a junior enrolled in a practicum course (250 hours – 5 credit hours). Elizabeth loves to golf and worked as a caddy every summer for Helfrich Golf Course. Elizabeth knew she wanted to manage a golf course someday but needed to get her "foot in the door." Her day came when she was caddying for Mr. John Perry. Mr. Perry was on a business trip and wanted some peace and relaxation. Mr. Perry decided to visit Helfrich Golf Course. Elizabeth was his caddy. Elizabeth soon found out that Mr. Perry was the owner of Perry Golf Foundation. Perry Golf Foundation is one of the largest companies in the world with over 200 golf courses. Mr. Perry was so impressed with Elizabeth that he offered a practicum for the Fall semester. With this **serendipity** networking, Elizabeth knew she was one step closer to her dream job.*

SCENARIO #3 – INTERNSHIP - SENIOR

Steve

*Steve is a senior enrolled in an internship course (450 hours – 9 credit hours). Steve has already completed a field experience with GE Plastics Lifestyle Center, a practicum with Ameritech and has his site set on Mead Johnson Nutritionals. All of these corporate positions have allowed Steve to build his network. He was referred to Lisa Clark, the Director of Mead Johnson Nutritionals, by the Assistant Director of Ameritech. Steve was able to learn more about Lisa before meeting her by reading her career highlight located at the end of this chapter. Steve's **strategic and serendipity** networking paid off in the long run and Steve was hired to intern at Mead Johnson Nutritionals.*

According to *The Society of Human Resource Management* (SHRM) 60-80% of jobs are filled by word-of-mouth (McFarland, 2006). How does one obtain a job by word-of-mouth? The most common way is through networking, which is a vital strategy for you to obtain a job. You interact with a group of people with similar goals or like interests in a social or professional setting, who in turn are linked to other people, all of whom could be potential contacts for a job opportunity (Foster & Dollar, 2010). The more important and influential these people are in the network, the better for you.

Types of Networks

As illustrated in the scenarios, you may come in contact with one of two common types of networking: strategic and serendipity. Strategic networking is planned and consists of identifying people you may want to meet at a conference, workshop, or university event for a specific reason (Darling, 2010). With strategic networking there is a stated purpose and a desired outcome. For example, Veronica attended the Alumni in Residence to specifically meet the representative (Henry) from the Sarasota County Government. The Alumni in Residence was a university event that Veronica planned on attending to meet one particular person. Serendipity networking is unplanned and consists of an encounter that could lead to a mutually beneficial relationship (Greene & Greene, 2010). For example, Elizabeth caddied for one of the premier golf club owners in the nation. She was able to land herself a practicum because of her interaction during this social event. Although both networking types are important strategic networking instills confidence to meet new people and explore relationships that prepare you for serendipitous moments. Thus, strategic networking is the focus of this particular chapter.

Network Purposes

Networking serves several purposes when searching for a job. Networks may help to increase your knowledge about a particular career, find potential employers, and discover hidden job opportunities (Greene & Greene, 2010). Networks also serve several purposes for the employer searching for a potential intern. Employers respect and use networks to hire because they cannot afford to make mistakes during the hiring process. In other words employers trust networks because they take the "unknown" out of who the employer is hiring. Networks make the employer aware of you and your career goals while opening additional communication lines (Greene & Greene, 2010). Yet, most of you do not consider yourself to have a strong network and need to take advantage of situations in building your network. Once you show up to a networking event it is important to be "active" by participating in the conversation, lending a hand, or sharing an idea that could lead to a networking relationship. This chapter helps you to discover or add to an existing network while providing strategies on how to network effectively in sport and physical activity. Veronica, Elizabeth, and Steve used step-by-step procedures and guidelines in Exhibit 6.1 to develop their network.

Exhibit 6.1 Step-by-Step Procedure and Guidelines to Networking
1. Complete a network inventory
a. Known entity
b. Job fairs
c. Professional associations
d. Professional conferences and workshops
e. Past and present employers
f. Friends and fellow students
g. Talk to strangers
h. Additional opportunities for women
2. Decide on network strategies
a. Professional networking kit
b. Initial interaction with potential network contact
3. Decide on follow-up technique
a. Phone call
b. Email
c. Mail

Step 1 – Complete a Network Inventory

It is never too early or too late to begin building a network. You need to keep in mind everyone could potentially hold the key to your future (professors, other students, past and present employers, relatives, friends' relatives, neighbors) and most jobs are filled by a person the employer meets before the position formally opens (Kursmark, 2009). Veronica, Elizabeth, and Steve began to inventory their network by considering the following:

- Known entity on a university or college campus

- Job fairs

- Professional organizations

- Professional conferences and workshops

- University clubs and organizations on campus

- Talk to strangers

- Alumni

Known Entity on a University or College Campus

One of the first places you can begin to inventory a network for a career in sport and physical activity is to look on campus. The early college years are a good time to develop relationships with advisors, faculty and other administration (especially career services) on campus which could lead to a potential job opportunity. These contacts could also lead to relationships where someone genuinely wants to see you succeed and has the interest and time to mentor. You can begin to develop a known entity on a university or college campus by requesting a one-on-one meeting through a phone call or by emailing.

Job Fairs

Job fairs not only provide an excellent opportunity for obtaining information about possible jobs, but you can network and learn more about various areas within sport and physical activity. Before Veronica, Steve, or Elizabeth ever attended a job fair, they considered the following items:

- Appearance (Chapter 8 – Exhibit 7.4)

- Research the employers you want to visit at the job fair (Chapter 8 – Exercise 8.1)

- Come to the job fair prepared by developing a professional networking kit (pen, notebook, resume, business cards, portfolio, and name badge)

- Use your notebook to write down names and addresses. You can send thank-you cards to the employers where you would like to do a follow-up. You also want to collect as many business cards as you can (Chapter 8)

- Smile and be confident

Professional Associations

You need to consider joining a professional association. Professional associations are a good way to interact with other students who have the same industry goals. Although the majority of the associations do require annual dues, many take the college undergraduate pocketbook status into account. Once you have determined an association to join, it is important that you become an "active" member if at all possible. For example, Steve joined the American College of Sports Medicine (ACSM) during his sophomore year in college. Steve eventually joined the student committee and was able to help with ACSM conferences and workshops. Steve was also a presider for several speakers at these events. Steve's association with ACSM allowed him to interact with other students and professionals in the field. Chapter 5 (Exhibit 5.6) provided Steve with an initial list of professional organizations to consider joining. The next step Steve took was to become an "active" member within the organization by joining the student committee.

Professional Conferences and Workshops

Attending state, regional, national, or international conferences or workshops of the associations mentioned in Chapter 5 are excellent opportunities to maintain and continue to build a network. You need to develop a game plan of what events or sessions you want to attend during the event (s). You may want to meet with someone that will be at the conference and set-up an appointment ahead of time (strategic networking). During these events and sessions you need to plan on making quality contacts and gathering business cards. These business cards may be put in a rolodex or you may develop a list of e-mail addresses named "network".

University Clubs and Organizations on Campus

If you cannot "get your foot in the door" within a state, regional, national, or international association you may have a club or organization on campus that is relevant to the field. These clubs and organizations usually cost little or nothing to join and can provide you with a network on campus. You would get to know other students, faculty, and administration on campus that could be a potential contact for job in the future (Bower, 2012). For example, Veronica found out about the Alumni in Residence through the department's Health and Fitness club. A fellow student (Tom) knew Henry and introduced Veronica to Henry at the event. Tom essentially was the university contact that provided Veronica with a reference to Henry for a position because of her involvement in these clubs or organizations.

Past and Present Employers

A past or present employer makes an excellent candidate for your network. For example, Steve worked in the corporate scene since his sophomore year and established plenty of contacts. These connections provided Steve with an opportunity to obtain a position with another corporate facility.

Friends or Fellow Students

Friends or fellow students can be an addition to your network. Keeping in contact following graduation can lead to a valuable networking resource. These friends and fellow students have already gone through the job search process and may have contacts and advice. Find out if there is an alumni group or listserv by asking career services and make sure to keep involved. The alumni group was an excellent opportunity for Veronica to meet her contact for the position she was seeking.

Identifying and organizing existing or new contacts is a useful exercise that is the fundamental building block for a networking plan. Complete Exercise 6.1 to begin building your network.

Exercise 6.1 Building a Network

Known entity on a university or college campus_____

_____

_____

Job fairs _____

_____

Professional organizations _____

_____

Professional conferences and workshops _____

_____

University clubs and organizations on campus _____

_____

Alumni _____

_____

Networks for women _____

_____

Meet New People

It may seem awkward at first but meeting new people may open a door in the future. You should consider talking to people on the plane when traveling to a conference, in the shuttle to and from the airport, or in hotel elevators when conference name badges are apparent. In Elizabeth's case it was talking to a stranger which led to a position she was seeking. When attending an event do not hesitate to talk to the keynote speaker or others around. It may not be who the contact is but who the contact knows that could make a difference (Templeton, 2009).

Networking for Women

It is no secret that men have been networking for longer than women and therefore have more contacts (Bower & Bennett, 2012). However, women are making strides in developing "old girls networks" and this is illustrated by the number of networks listed in Exhibit 6.2 (Bower & Bennett, 2012). Along with this list of networks it is also important women continue to meet with men who want to facilitate introductions of talented women within sport and physical activity.

Exhibit 6.2 Networking for Women
Sports Industry
1. The Active Network – www.active.com
2. Advancing Women in Leadership – www.advancingwomen.com
3. International Association of Physical Education and Sport for Girls and Women (IAPESPGW) – www.iapespgw.org
4. Komen Race for the Cure – www.komen.org
5. Konnects – www.konnects.com
6. Networking Women – www.networkingwomen.com
7. Women in NASSM (WIN) - list serve
8. Womens in Sports Careers (WISC) – www. wiscnetworkfoundation.com
9. Womens National Basketball Association (WNBA) – www.wnba.com
10. WWWomen Reaching Women – www.wwwomen.com
11. Womens Sports Foundation – www.womensportsfoundation.org
12. Womens Sports Jobs – www.womensportsjob.com
13. Womens Sports Link – www.womenssportslink.com
14. Womens Sports Report – www.sportsreport.com
15. Womens Sports Services – www.womensportsservices

16. Womens Sports Wire – www.womensportswire.com

Outside the Sports Industry

1. www.publisher@advancingwomen.com

2. www.bellaonline.com

3. www.Grrls.org

4. www.ivillage.com

5. www.businesswomensnetwork.com

Step 2 – Determine Network Strategies

First impressions are everything. Regardless of where you are networking you need to realize there may only be a few seconds to make a first impression. You need to invest some time in preparing for the "little" things that can make a difference such as preparing a professional networking kit, learning initial interaction skills, and choosing the appropriate follow-up techniques.

Professional Networking Kit

Before you are ready to successfully navigate at a networking event you need to prepare. Being prepared means having everything you need for the networking event BEFORE you walk in the door. For example, Steve developed a professional networking kit which consisted of the following:

- A briefcase or handbag large enough to organize
- A legal pad
- Pen
- Business cards
- Resumes
- Portfolio
- Breath mints, mouth wash, and/or toothbrush
- Name Badge

Initial Interaction with Potential Network Contact

The initial interaction between you and the potential contact should relay a positive image of yourself, your abilities, and competencies. The goal is for the contact to remember your name or recognize you the next time a potential job opportunity may arise (Boothman, 2008). Items such as appearance and effective communication may play a role in how well the contact remembers you.

Effective Communication. Effective communication is important when it comes to networking (Boothman, 2008). The way you communicate with others also make a big difference when it comes to communication power. For example, communication consists of 55 percent body language, 38 percent voice, tone, and pitch, and only 7% words (Boothman, 2008). Knowing the impact that body language has on communication is important to consider and certain guidelines exist:

- Provide the potential network contact (s) with 18 inches of personal space.

- Face towards the potential network contact when speaking.

- Stand-up straight – watch the shoulders (slouching).

- Keep the hands out of the pocket and the arms uncrossed.

- Do not rattle change or other items in pockets.

The voice, tone, and pitch can also make an impact on effective communication. You should have energy, enthusiasm, a sense of purpose, and a smile when speaking to others in a networking situation. If you are talking to a potential network contact on the phone a smile should be heard through the phone. You should stand-up and make potential network contacts hear a content, calm and assured voice. You need to try and not mumble or talk too softly and assess the appropriate place for pitch and volume of each setting.

Although 93 percent of communication power is body language and voice, tone, and pitch, you still need to carefully choose quality words to help with effective communication. For instance what if you use email to network with potential contacts. You lose 93 percent of communication power from body language, voice, tone and pitch. You will only have words to rely upon and therefore should follow some guidelines:

- Select appropriate vocabulary for the audience

- User proper grammar

- Speak in complete sentences

- Do not use slang, vulgarities, or clichés

- Be cautious when using acronyms

- Use an "appropriate" email address (hotgirl1@yahool.com is not appropriate)

Conversation. The easiest way to meet people at networking events is to have someone else introduce you to the potential contact or by setting up an appointment before the event begins. For example, Veronica allowed her fellow classmate to set-up a time to meet Henry following the Alumni in Residence event. This type of networking provided Veronica with the time to plan for the initial meeting and conversation. You may be able to provide a firm handshake, while looking the person in the eye, and saying your name but you also need to know how to carry on a conversation. The key is to share stories, interests, and ideas that build rapport with the contact. When this type of connection is established, people want to listen and you begin building a network. During the conversation you need to consider following the guidelines:

- Listen

- Include others

- Do not control the conversation

- Find commonalities

- Do not interrupt

- Do not finish other people's sentences

- Be sincerely interested in others and respect the person's views

- Be aware of body language

- Remember "thank you" and "please" where appropriate

- Engage others around you

What if there are no people around to introduce you to others or you did not set-up an initial meeting? This is where you need to have a brief introduction in the event you would like to join a conversation. For example, Veronica may approach Henry smiling, offering a hand (right hand – badge is worn on right side), and saying,

- Hi, my name is Veronica O'Reilly, and I really enjoyed your presentation. I am interested in finding out more information about your company. I am currently in a field experience course, and I heard your company supports students by providing them with an opportunity to expand on their skills as an intern. Do you have time to talk with me during this event about the possibilities of completing the field experience at your site?

Steve may approach the situation in a different manner since he attends many conferences and does conduct research on the side.

- Hi, my name is Steve Simmons, and I am a student at the University of Southern Indiana. I attended your presentation on "Physical Activity and College Students," and I wanted your opinion on physical activity data I have collected for the past two years. Do you have time to talk or may I make contact with you outside the conference?

Develop your own initial introduction by completing Exercise 6.2.

Exercise 6.2 Initial Introduction

_____

_____

_____

_____

In both planned and spontaneous networking the ability to end these conversations is important. In most cases if the conversation has reached its plateau both parties probably want to move on. The exit may consist of the following:

- It has been a pleasure meeting you, and I hope that I will speak to you again in the near future. Do you have a card that I could take for my records?

- If there is food and drinks suggest venturing to this area, especially if there are people you see that you know. For example, I think I may get some food. Would you like to join me? If there are friends around then you will be able to expand the conversation.

Develop your own exit by completing Exercise 6.3.

Exercise 6.3 Exit

_____

_____

_____

_____

Step 3 — Decide on Follow-up Technique

Follow-up with potential contacts makes the difference between successful and unsuccessful networking. It is a waste of time if you are not going to follow-up and use the networking contact for obtaining potential job opportunities. There are several follow-up techniques you may choose including phone, email, or mail. Simply ask the person the best way to contact him or her.

Phone. You need to be careful when deciding to use the phone as a means for networking. You need to feel confident and know what to say before the potential contact answers the phone. More than 75% of new contacts make a decision about you during the follow-up or initial phone call (Casperson, 2009). For example, Steve scripts what he was going to say and practiced it out loud! Steve said:

- Hello, this is Steve Simmons. I am completing a practicum at Ameritech through the Health Fitness Corporation. I understand that Mead Johnson Nutritional is also contracted through Health Fitness Corporation, and I noticed you have an opening for an internship during the Spring of 2014. I wanted to know if you could provide me with some additional information on this internship?

You should also script what you say when leaving a voicemail as well. For example,

- Hello, my name is Steve Simmons, and I am calling about the internship position you have advertised through Mead Johnson Nutritionals. I am currently working for Ameritech within Health Fitness Corporation. I would like to have the opportunity to speak further about the internship. I can be reached after 5:00 pm Monday through Friday at 564-432-7689. Thank-you and have a great day.

If by chance the networking contact is going to call you then make sure to be prepared to answer the phone in an appropriate manner. For example, "Hi this is Steve Simmons." Some additional guidelines to follow when answering include:

- Answer the phone by the third ring (do not seem too overanxious)

- Write down the callers name immediately (do not forget)

- Smile when answering the phone (this really does make a difference)

- Return all calls within 48 hours if a message is left

- Use please and thank-you throughout the conversation as needed

- Have a glass of water or drink nearby (if not a spontaneous call)

- Thank the person for calling

If by chance you do not get the phone call, the voicemail needs to be appropriate. For example,

- Hi, this is Steve Simmons. I am unable to take your phone call at this time but if you leave you name, number, and the best time to reach you, then I will get back with you as soon as possible. Thank you and have a great day.

Email. You need to make sure email is the best way to reach the person after an initial contact. If you are not good at expressing yourself via email the message could be misunderstood. In addition, the potential contacts may not check email on a daily, weekly, or monthly basis, and therefore this would not be the best way to communicate. On the other hand email may be the perfect way to send a follow-up message but with the following guidelines :

- Make sure to use a subject line

- Make sure to use a bullet format if at all possible (easier to read)

- Be cautious when using "!"

- Make sure to use a signature

Mail. Although email has taken over the typical way of mailing a follow-up letter, most people would appreciate getting a handwritten thank you note/letter. Handwritten mail is so rare that potential contacts are more than likely to pay attention to them. A simple follow-up such as a thank you note/letter shows the potential network contact that you acknowledge and appreciate the time, advice, and ideas shared during the meeting. A sample thank you letter can be found in Chapter 4 (Exhibit 4.17). In addition to the thank you note/letter include a business card as illustrated in Chapter 5 (Exhibit 5.9).

Summary

As discussed throughout this chapter networking can be a viable strategy for obtaining an a field experience. The personal contacts you develop with others can be an important source of information in choosing a career and obtaining a job. Do not discredit any opportunity to meet or interact with someone. This connection may be the beginning to a career in sport and physical activity.

Frequently Asked Questions

How do you know the best method of contacting and individual you met that could possibility be added to your network?

You can determine the best way to contact an individual by simply asking them the best way to reach them.

How do you keep your network list current?

You need to begin your network list by creating a database of names. You need to send an email to check on possible job opportunities about every month. By keeping in network with your contacts you can keep the list updated.

Should you rely solely on your network contact to secure a job?

Knowing someone is not the sole criteria for obtaining a job. You need to prepare yourself by utilizing the chapters in this book to prepare your resume, cover letter, and conduct yourself in a professional manner during an interview.

Student Learning Activities

Complete Exercise 6.1 in developing a network list. Take the network list and begin building a database of the network's email addresses.

Develop a networking development kit.

Develop a thank you script for the phone, email, and mail.

➤ Networking Checklist
❑   Build your network
❑   Job fairs
❑   Professional associations
❑   Professional conferences and workshops
❑   University clubs and organizations on campus
❑   Past and present employer
❑   Friends and fellow students
❑   Talk to strangers
❑   Determine your network strategies
❑   Developed a professional inventory kit
❑   Prepared for initial interaction with potential network contact
❑   Decide on follow-up technique
❑   Phone call
❑   Email
❑   Mail

CAREER HIGHLIGHT – CORPORATE FITNESS

Elisha Koch

Early Symptom Intervention Specialist

Gibson Southern Hospital

Evansville, IN

Education And Certifications

General Physical Education with a specialty in Teaching from the University of Southern Indiana

Years In Position

< 6 months

Previous Positions

This is my first job out of college. I have not held any previous positions.

Current Job Responsibilities And Hours

Responsibilities include instruction of 6- minute stretch, team meetings, ESI roll out presentation and work simulation programs. Employee must also apply injury prevention, injury tracking, ergonomic assessment methods and exercise/ stretch prescription, enter data specific to class/ floor incident interactions, and assure adherence to safety and health program policies. Job duties also involve floor coverage and injury prevention. Responsibility exists for oversight and completion of data entry activities, facility maintenance, upkeep and cleaning. Application and administration of basic self-care methods such as ice/heat application is required. An ability to communicate with people of all levels within an organization is required. Added duties include: laminating, sorting, filing, and making copies, literature review, research, and other duties as assigned.

40-50 hours depending on week's activities

Greatest Challenges

My biggest challenge seems to be excepting change. This is something that really hit me in the face, coming straight from the college atmosphere where your schedule is set for 16 weeks into an atmosphere where something may change 5 times a day. It is something that I deal with every day and is becoming easier, you learn how to use time management because you never know what you day is going to bring.

Career Advice

My career advice would be to take chances. You never know what something has to offer. Never in a million years did I think I would graduate college and find myself working in a manufacturing plant with a General Physical Education degree.

CAREER HIGHLIGHT – CORPORATE FITNESS

Lisa Clark

Supervisor, Health and Fitness (Corporate Fitness)

Mead Johnson Nutritonals

Evansville, IN

Education And Certifications

M.S. in Physical Education (non-teaching, corporate fitness focus) from Western Illinois University.

ACE Fitness Instructor; ACE Clinical Exercise Specialist; IM=X Pilates Instructor

CPR/First Aid

Years In Position

19 years

Previous Positions

Previously held a Fitness Director position at a Health Club in Champaign, Illinois. Other experiences came from YMCA and Physical Therapy settings.

Current Job Responsibilities And Hours

Supervise two Indiana based corporate fitness centers for Bristol-Myers Squibb; one in Evansville, one in Mt. Vernon. Position involves supervising fitness instructors, class scheduling, overseeing center operations that include equipment maintenance, purchasing, facility/building functions, monitoring budget. Other responsibilities include teaching various fitness classes, completing new member orientations, writing up exercise programs and assisting members with general equipment usage. Also supervise an on-site Personal Training program. Typically works 40 hours per week.

Greatest Challenges

Juggling the many different tasks and demands from the management side as well as the member service side. It is sometimes frustrating to act as a "manager" and quickly change hats to being a "fitness instructor." However, that keeps the job full of variety and challenging. There is rarely a boring moment in my role. The best part about this job is having the opportunity to make a difference in people's quality of life. It is the most rewarding career a person can have and quite enjoyable. Some days, I have so much fun that it doesn't seem right to get paid for what I do! I feel fortunate to work in the field of Corporate Fitness, in addition, being employed by Bristol-Myers Squibb. It is truly a great Company and they really care about the health and wellness of their employees.

Career Advice

I highly recommend getting fitness class teaching skills, because the skills required to be a fitness instructor will help in many other aspects of a fitness career. Take every career opportunity serious. Be professional in appearance and manner. Always be accountable. Always be on time for appointments and work shifts. There is nothing worse than having an instructor not show up for teaching a class. Reliability is of highest importance in any chosen career.

References

Boothman, N. (2008). *How to make people like you in 90 seconds or less.* New York, NY: Workman Publishing.

Bower, G. G. (2012). Experiential classroom learning: Developing a sport management club. *the Indiana Association for Health, Physical Education, Recreation, and Dance Journal,* 41(1), 12-16.

Bower, G. G., & Bennett, S. (2011). The examination of the mentoring relationship between the head coach and assistant coach of women's basketball teams. *Advancing Women in Leadership Journal,* 31(1), 1-7.

Casperson, D. M. (2009).Power etiquette: *What you don't know can kill your career.* New York: NY: AMACOM.

Darling, D. (2010).*The Networking Survival Guide, Second Edition: Practical Advice to Help You Gain Confidence, Approach People, and Get the Success You Want.* New York, NY: McGraw Hill.

Foster, S. B., & Dollar, J. E. (2010). *Experiential learning in sport management: Internships and beyond. Morgantown: WV: Fitness Information Technology.*

Greene, H. R., & Greene, M. W. (2010).*College grad seeks future: Turning your talents, strengths, and passions into the perfect career.* New York, NY: St. Martin's Press.

Kursmark, L. M. (2009). *15-minute cover letter.* Indianapolis, IN: JIST Publishing, Inc.

McFarland, B. (2013). *Tapping the hidden job market. Retrieved December 29, 2013, from,* http://www.shrm.org/Communities/StudentPrograms/Pages/CMS_019704.aspx

Paternostro-Bayles, M. (2009).Maximizing your professional preparation. *ACSM Health & Fitness Journal,* 13(2), 35-37.

Templeton, T. (2009).*The referral of a lifetime: The networking system that produces bottom-line results…every day!: Easyread edition. North Charleston, SC: BookSurge: LLC.*

7

SOCIAL NETWORKING

SCENARIO #1 – FIELD EXPERIENCE/OBSERVATION – SOPHOMORE - MILLIE

*Millie is a sophomore and currently enrolled in a sport and physical activity field experience courses (20 hours – 1 credit hour). Millie is interested in pursuing a career in sport communication. Millie was introduced to the Sports Information Director (SID) at a Sport Management Summit. She spoke to the SID and discovered that he was responsible for the **Facebook, Twitter**, and **blogging** pages promoting college athletics. Millie decided to complete her 20 hours within the athletic department under the supervision of the SID. She thought it would assist her in learning skills for a SID position but also learn more about adding to her **social network**.*

SCENARIO #2 – PRACTICUM – JUNIOR - JOSIE

*Josie is a junior enrolled in a practicum course (150 hours – 3 credit hours). Josie attended a Fitness and Wellness Career Fair. Josie was pursuing a Kinesiology degree and was searching for a practicum that would provide her with some experience to add to her resume. After speaking to many potential employers that were looking for interns, Josie decided a practicum that would focus on personal training was the route to pursue. She secured a practicum with a local health club. Josie was exposed to many areas of personal training but was extremely intrigued by how social media was used to recruit clients. The main focus of the personal trainers was to focus on developing a network of potential clients on **Facebook**. This **social media** technique allowed many of the personal trainers to increase their clientele.*

SCENARIO #3 – INTERNSHIP – SENIOR - LOLA

*Lola is a senior enrolled in an internship course (450 hours – 9 credit hours). Lola attended the Sport Management Summit hosted on her university campus and met an individual from a professional football team. The professional was responsible for promoting events through **social media**. This type of career sounded great for Lola as she always wanted to go into event management and the **social media** aspect of the professional's position was something that she wanted to learn more about. The professional would assist her on how to become a better **Tweeter**, the management of **Facebook**, and a **blog**. These **social media** techniques would assist Lola in becoming a well-rounded employee.*

In chapter 6 you learned how networking is a viable strategy for obtaining a field experience. It is crucial to develop personal contacts with others to provide additional ways to obtain sources of information in choosing a career. Chapter 6 focused on the traditional "face-to-face" networking that has assisted many in obtaining jobs. In addition to "face-to-face" networking, social networking is becoming more and more popular. Throughout this chapter, Millie, Josie, and Lola used the step-by-step procedures and guidelines to begin a Blog (Exhibit 7.1), setting up a Twitter account (Exhibit 7.4), setting up a LinkedIN account (Exhibit 7.5), and setting up a Facebook account (Exhibit 7.7).

What is Social Networking?

Social networking is the "process of using Web-based tools to connect with people for the purpose of reaching your career and business goals, and in turn, helping others reach their goals" (Crompton & Sautter, 2011, p. 2). This chapter will focus on three types of networking technologies which include the following:

- Blogs
- Microblogs -Twitter
- Social Networking Sites - LinkedIN and Facebook

Blogs

Blogging can be very beneficial in developing a social network. Networking is about building relationships and helping others while blogging is also building relationships and sharing your knowledge and ideas with others by discussing subjects you are truly passionate about such as sport and physical activity. According to blogging statistics more than 42,000,000 people are blogging. In addition, 329 million people view blogs, 25 billion pages are viewed monthly, 500,000 new posts and 400,000 daily comments are made on a daily basis Salpeter, 2011). Blogging is shorthand for web logs and is a series of short comments or essays that are entered on a daily basis by a blog owner to form a chronological log (Salpeter, 2011). Basically, it is an online journal of your thoughts.

There are several benefits to blogging which include the following (Crompton & Sauter, 2012):

- Increase visibility and credibility

- Build community with other sport and physical activity minded individuals

- Enlarge your personal and professional network

- Provide a mechanism for expressing yourself and reaching an audience

Step-by-Step Procedures and Guidelines to Begin a Blog

Millie, Josie, and Lola all decided to develop a blog as one of their social networking strategies to assist them in finding a field experience. All three of them followed simple guidelines and exercises to develop a blog. A summary of the step-by-step procedures and guidelines to begin a Blog may be found in Exhibit 7.1.

Exhibit 7.1 Step-by Step Procedures and Guidelines to Begin a Blog
Step 1 - Research blogs in the sport and physical activity fields
Step 2 - Choose a name for your blog
Step 3 - Select your blog platform or host
Step 4 - Generate your content
Step 5 - Manage your comments
Step 6 - Go live

Step 1 — Find out where your bloggers are in the sport and physical activity fields

To begin with Millie, Josie, and Lola decided to assist one another to complete a Google search to find potential Sport and Physical Activity Blogs that would assist them in finding a field experience. Exhibit 7.2 provides a list of the sport and physical activity blogs that Millie, Josie, and Lola found (ACE, 2013; Career Moxie, 2013; Jobs in Sport, 2013; Midwest ACSM, 2013; NSCA, 2013; NCSF, 2013; PTDC, 2013; SPARTA, 2013; Real Clear Sports, 2013; Sports Career Institute, 2013; Theravid,

2013). Millie, Josie, and Lola each chose a different blog to research according to their sport interests. For example, Millie chose to observe the Jobs in Sport blogging site. Josie was interested in personal training so she pursued the Personal Trainer Development Center (PTDC). Finally, Lola was interested in a mixture of sports and researched the Big Lead blogging site. Getting connected to those blogging websites will assist Millie, Josie, and Lola in beginning their own site but also in building a community that has the same interest as you do.

Exhibit 7.2 – Sport and Physical Activiy Blogs

SPORT

1. Jobs in Sport
2. Sports Career Institute
3. Puck Daddy
4. Eye on College Basketball
5. Big League Stew
6. The Big Lead
7. The Point Forward
8. Sport Biz
9. Ball Don't Lie
10. ED SBS
11. ProFootball Talk
12. WorkInSports.com Blog

FITNESS – PERSONAL TRAINING & STRENGTH AND CONDITIONING

13. NSCA Young Coaches Blog
14. ACE Blog
15. ACSM Midwest Blog
16. NSCF Blog
17. NCSF Personal Trainer
18. Personal Trainer Development Center (PTDC)
19. Personal Trainer Success Academy
20. Sport Performance and Resistance Training Association (SPARTA)
21. Sports Training
22. ACE Blog

PHYSICAL THERAPY

23. Body In Mind
24. MikeReinold.com
25. The Manual Therapist
26. PT Diagnosis
27. Allan Besselink
28. Forward Thinnking PT
29. Dr. Jarod Carter.com
30. PT Think Tank
31. In Touch PT
32. Evidence in Motion
33. Web PT Blog
34. PranaPT
35. PT Talker

OCCUPTIONAL THERAPY

36. (B)e(LO)n(G), OT
37. ABC Therapeutic
38. Kara's OT Blog
39. Chronic Pain blog
40. Your Therapy Source
41. Gosh, that's neat!
42. WiiHab
43. OT Notes
44. Meta-OT
45. Health Skills

Exercise 7.1 – Blogging Research

Visit one of the blogging sites in Table 7.1 and provide a summary of what you learned from the blogging site.

_____

_____

_____

_____

Step 2 – Choose a Name for Your Blog

After Millie, Josie, and Lola finished their research of blogging sites, it was time for them to begin setting up their own blog. The first item of business was for them to choose their blogging name. The name of your blog is extremely important. You want to catch the reader's eye. Once you have decided upon a blogging name make sure to test its uniqueness by using a search engine (i.e., Google, Bing, Yahoo) to type in the name to see what comes up. No matter what you want to keep the name short and to the point, identifiable with you and your niche, and easy to remember. Millie chose to name her blog *Millie's Magnificent Sports Blog."* Josie chose to name her blog *Get Fit with Josie."* Finally, Lola chose to name her blog *Lola's Lasting Sporting Events."*

Complete Exercise 7.2 in developing your name for the Blog.

Exercise 7.2 – Name your Blog

Decide upon a name for your blog and complete a search to see of its uniqueness. Remember to be short and to the point, identifiable with you and your niche, and easy to remember. Write down the name of your blog _____.

Step 3 – Choose a Blog Platform

Now that Millie, Josie, and Lola have named their Blog it is time for them to choose a blogging platform. A blogging software or platform is needed to run your blog. You can choose from *hosted* or *nonhosted* options. Some of the blogging software is free while others come with a fee. Hosted servers are ideal if you are not as computer savvy although you have limited control over the look and functionality of your site. If you want complete control over the site, more flexibility, and more design options you want to go with a nonhosted site. Exhibit 7.3 provides the top 10 free online blogging platforms (Six Revisions, 2013).

Hosted Services

If you decide to choose a hosted service platform you will simply access everything from the host's website. The host will provide easy-to-use text editors to help create yours posts without technical knowledge. Host services also provide templates to develop your layout and design of your blogging site. The hosted services are free.

Nonhosted Services

Nonhosted services are standalone or server-side platform. You must secure a domain name and subscribe to a hosting server and download a content management system. The most popular content management platforms are WordPress and Movable Type.

Exhibit 7.3 Blog Hosting Platforms	
Blogger (www.blogger.com)	SitePoint (www.sitepoint.com/blogs)
Wordpress (http://wordpress.com/)	Blog.com (www.blog.com)
Jux (www.jux.com)	Tumblr. (www.tumblr.com)
Posterous Spaces (www.posterous.com)	Blogetery (www.blogetery.com
Weebly (www.weebly.com)	Live Journal (www.livejournal.com)

Millie, Josie, and Lola decide to choose a hosted services blogging site such as the *blogger*. The hosted services website would be easier to use than the nonhosted services website. Complete Exercise 7.3 in choosing a blogging platform.

Exercise 7.3 – Choose a Blog Platform

Use Exhibit 7.3 to choose a blog hosting platform. Choose one of the blogging platforms to begin developing your blog. Write down the name of your blogging platform _____.

Step 4 – Generate the Content

Millie, Josie, and Lola have been successful in naming their site and choosing a blogging platform but the crucial part of the blog is *the message*. The message is the most important part of blogging. Consider the following when developing the blog:

- Introduce yourself – use the information from the first paragraph of the cover letter you developed in Chapter 4 to assist you with this.

- Focus on your goals and objectives.

- What are you trying to accomplish?

- Are you trying to secure an internship or job?

When developing the content keep in mind that you should keep your blog short and to the point. You can use bullet points or provide a well-organized paragraph. Typically 200 words or even less is best. Add images and videos if possible. In addition, you can share your own stories or news that might engage your readers from the very beginning. Exhibit 7.4 provides an example of the blog developed by Lola.

Exhibit 7.4 Blogging Example

Hi all! Welcome to my blog. My name is Lolo Gene, and I am a senior at the University of Southern Indiana in Evansville, IN. I am majoring in Sport Management with a track in Sport Communication. I developed this blog to search for an internship that would allow me to focus on learning more about social media and how it is used with a professional sports team. I really feel comfortable with Facebook and Twitter. If anyone knows of a potential professional team that needs an energetic person to assist with social media please let me know. I am very interested in sharing my talents but also learning more prior to entering the workforce.

Complete Exercise 7.4 to develop your first message that you will post on your blog.

Exercise 7.4 – Generate the Content for the Blog

Develop the first message that you will put on your blog. The message should focus on your goals or objectives in obtaining an internship or job.

_____

_____

_____

_____

_____

_____

_____

_____

After you generate you first post you will also want to develop a biography to post on the blogging site. Consider including the following when developing your biography:

- Education – major, minor, graduation date, honors
- Current and previous jobs related to sport or physical activity and related to your interest
- Certifications
- Professional memberships
- Awards that you have received (other than educational)

Exhibit 7.5 is an example of the biography Josie posted on her blog.

Exhibit 7.5 Biography Example

Josie Anne is a Junior at the University of Southern Indiana (USI) majoring in Kinesiology with a minor in Personal Training. Josie is a Presidential Scholar and has been on the honor roll for the past 4 semesters. Josie is scheduled to graduate during the spring of 2015. Josie is a certified personal trainer with the American Council on Exercise (ACE). She is also a member of the American College of Sports Medicine (ACSM). Josie has worked at the USI Recreation and Fitness Center for the past 2 years as a personal trainer. Her responsibilities including training individuals from ages 18-64 in providing them with exercise testing, prescription, and orientations. Josie also has experience with Facebook and Twitter. Josie received the most outstanding student award during her sophomore year. Josie may be reached at janne@yahoo.com, Get Fit with Josie Blog, or Twitter account.

One last suggestion is to make sure throughout the whole process of developing the blog is to make sure to put in the "practice" mode. This way you can begin to understand the blogging site prior to going live. Complete Exercise 7.5 in developing your biography for the blog.

Exercise 7.5 – Develop your Biography

Use the suggestions under step 4 to develop your Biography

_____

_____

_____

_____

_____

_____

_____

_____

Step 5 — Manage Your Comments

Prior to posting you will need to know how you will manage your blog. How will you moderate comments? Will you allow people to publish their comments directly or would you serve as a moderator. Next, you will need to determine how you will respond to your comments. You will need to keep the dialogue going once you have someone posting on your blog. It is best to blog at the same time every day. This is part of developing that social network. To assist you may decide to streamline the process and allow the blogger to comment and receive updates via email. Millie, Josie, and Lola decided to organize themselves and complete exercise 7.5. You may also want to complete Exercise 7.6 in deciding when you are going to manage your comments.

Exercise 7.6 – Manage Your Comments

List the days you will management your account _____

List times you will manage your account _____

How will you manage your followers so that you know when someone new has posted or you have continuous followers? _____

_____

_____

Step 6 — Go Live!

Once you have posted and included your biography on your blog it is time to begin getting people to join. One way to get people to join your blogging site is to utilize search engine techniques by using relevant keywords, utilizing other social media such as Twitter, and link to other blogs. Twitter is one of the best ways to build a following for your blog. You can also use LinkedIN, Facebook, and MySpace. These are additional social networks that provide "touch points" to engage your audience and can serve as pointers back to your blog. Another popular technique for getting people to join your blog is to send emails to people in your network with the URL. You want to encourage people to join your blog and why they should join. Millie,

Josie, and Lola used all of the techniques in this paragraph to begin encouraging people to join their blog. Complete Exercise 7.6 in developing a plan to get people to join your blog.

Microblogs "Twitter"

Microblogging is a smaller version of a traditional blog. The content contains text, pictures, and/or links to videos (Carlson, 2013). The first microblog began in 2006 with Twitter (Carlson, 2013) and provided a means for you to share your ideas, showcase your expertise, and meet people that are interested in sport and physical activity. Microblogs, such as Twitter, allows you to connect with others and create conversations and community.

There are several benefits to microblogging which includes:

- Visibility – provides an excellent vehicle for expression of personal brand and establishing a digital trail.

- You can greatly expand your networks, stay updated on trends, and easily connect to thought leaders in the sport and physical activity field.

- You have access to top minds in the field.

Since Twitter is one of the most popular microblogs, you need to focus on becoming more familiar on how to network on the site (Ebiz, 2013). Twitter is about communicating and gaining visibility with others within your field. Communicating through Twitter is a series of short posts that are called tweets. Millie, Josie, and Lola used the step-by-step procedure and guidelines in Exhibit 7.4 to set-up a Twitter account to begin marketing themselves in obtaining a field experience.

Exhibit 7.6 Step-by Step Procedures and Guidelines for Setting Up a Twitter Account
Step 1 - Set your objectives
Step 2 - Develop your Profile
Step 3 - Tweet

Step 1 – Set your Objectives

You can spend as much as 10 to 15 minutes a day to hours on Twitter depending on your objectives. No matter what you will need to be consistent in your Twitters in terms of usage throughout the week.

For the purposes of this book your objectives will revolve around obtaining a field experience. There are several questions to ask yourself as you begin to set-up your Twitter account:

- **Who is the target audience?** Consider your profession. Do you want to be in intercollegiate athletics, recreational sports, a fitness club, or some other career opportunities within sport and physical activity? Additional careers opportunities were discussed in Chapter 2 (Exhibit 2.2). Millie, Lola, and Josie all wanted to be in a career that focuses on social media but in different areas. For example, Millie was interested in Intercollegiate Athletics, Josie was interested in Health and Fitness facilities, and Lola was interested in professional sport.

- **What message do you want to send about yourself** that potential employers may want to see? You may choose specific skills or jobs from the resume you developed in Chapter 3 that may be related to your career aspirations. For example, Lola completed a practicum her junior year with the Evansville Icemen in their marketing department. At least once a week she was given the opportunity to Tweet fans about upcoming games. She was also an integral part of maintaining Facebook.

- **What do you want to accomplish?** For example, you should be focused on obtaining a field experience in sport and/or physical activity. You can refer to your objective that you developed for your resume. For example, Millie would like to obtain a field experience with an intercollegiate athletic department shadowing a Sports Information Director.

- **How can you make yourself unique?** Have you accomplished something that others may have not been able to do? For example, Josie is a certified American Council on Exercise trainer with two years of personal training experience. This certification and experience is not something that you see every day from a student wanting to obtain a practicum.

- **What key words are you going use to attract potential employees?** For example, Josie chose to highlight words related to becoming a personal trainer. The words included ACSM certified, a specific gym, or familiarity with equipment such as the Bod Pod or Gait System. These words may attract the attention of someone in the field.

Complete Exercise 7.7 to determine your objectives for the Twitter account.

Exercise 7.7- Set your Objectives

Prior to setting up your Twitter account you want to set your objectives. Answer the questions in step 1 to set those objectives based on obtaining an internship or job.

Who is the target audience? _____

What message do you want to send about yourself that potential employers may want to see? _____

What do you want to accomplish? _____

How can you make yourself unique? Have you accomplished something that others may have not been able to do? _____

_____

What key words are you going use to attract potential employees? _____

_____

Step 2 – Develop Your Profile

The preparation is complete and you are ready to begin developing your profile. First, you need to set-up a Twitter account by visiting www.twitter.com. Twitter will ask for your full name, a user name, a password, and an email address. Make special considerations when developing your Twitter username (Twitter handle) as this is how it will appear on your tweets, replies or direct messages. The key is to have a recognizable name. Second, you will need to set-up a user profile. You may want to consider the following information for your Twitter account:

- Picture – make sure the picture is appropriate and professional. Recommendations are to use a head shot.

- Name - enter your complete name

- Where you live and work – list where you live and work

- Add your blog or LinkedIn URL (talked about later in this chapter) – add your blogging link that was developed in Exercise 7.2

- Resume – add your resume that you developed in Chapter 3

- Biography – add the biography that you developed in Exercise 7.5

Finally, you want to make sure that your Twitter account matches up to other online profiles that you developed. Millie, Josie, and Lola all used Exercise 7.7 to organize their profile for their Twitter account. Complete Exercise 7.8 to begin developing your Twitter Profile.

Exercise 7.8 – Develop Your Profile

Once you have set-up a Twitter Account begin to develop your profile. Once you have completed a part of the profile check it off below.

- Picture _____

- Name _____

- Live/Work _____

- Blog or LinkedIn URL (developed in Exercise 7.2) _____

- Resume (Completed in Chapter 3) _____

- Biography (Completed in this Chapter - Exercise 7.5) _____

Step 3 – Tweet

Now it is time to begin tweeting. You want to go to your Twitter home page and type your Tweet into the "what's Happening"? field, and select the Tweet button. Your goal is to establish a Twitter stream. Remember to follow the steps discussed in this section to assist in getting others to follow. You want to consider the following topics when marketing yourself to a potential employer to obtain a field experience within sport and physical activity:

- Industry trends

- The type of work and job you are targeting

- Events related to the field

- Resources that may be helpful to others in the field

- A recent accomplishment

- Work-related stories the career that you want to pursue

Exhibit 7.7 provides an example of how Lola set-up her first Tweet.

Exhibit 7.7 – "First" Tweet Example
My name is Lola Gene and I am a senior at the University of Southern Indiana majoring in Sport Management. I have completed a field experience within the USI Intercollegiate Athletic Department, a practicum within USI Recreational Sports, and another practicum with the Evansville Icemen. Within all of these experiential learning experiences I was involved with event management and marketing specifically through social media techniques. I assisted with

Facebook and Twitter management. At each of these establishments I received excellent evaluations from my employers. I am not searching for an internship that is in professional sport and focused on event management and social media.

Complete Exercise 7.9 to develop your *first* Tweet.

Exercise 7.9 – Develop your first Tweet

Use the guidelines in Step 3 to develop your *first* Tweet. Make sure it is related to the objective of obtaining an internship or job in your sport or physical activity career.

_____

_____

_____

_____

Social Networking Sites "LinkedIn" and Facebook

There are several social networking sites that may be helpful in your field experience search. Social networking sites included LinkedIn, Facebook, Plaxo.com, Ecademy.com, Ryze.com, Ning.com, Hubpages.com, Squidoo.com, and Knol. The key is choosing a social networking site that is targeted towards professionals. Since LinkedIn is the world's largest online network dedicated specifically to professionals this section, will focus on assisting you in setting up an account and becoming more familiar with its features (Linked Strategies, 2013; Salpeter, 2013). The benefits of using LinkedIn include the following:

- To enhances your credibility and expertise

- The ability to search for jobs

- The ability to research companies that may be of interest

- To find contacts within target companies

- To join groups in finding others with common interests and/or backgrounds

- To ask and answer questions to showcase your expertise

- To provide updates to promote your brand

LinkedIn

LinkedIn is the forefront runner for any social networking site. LinkedIn has more than 259 million members from over 200 countries (Digital Marketing Rambling, 2013). LinkedIn should be your first choice when looking to seek to enhance your professional images. Millie, Josie, and Lola used the step-by-step procedures and guidelines in Exhibit 7.7 to set-up a LinkedIN account.

Exhibit 7.7 Step-by-Step Procedures and Guidelines in Setting up a LinkedIn Account
Step 1 – Join LinkedIn
Step 2 – Develop a LinkedIn profile
Step 3 – Grow your network
Step 4 – Search for internships and/or jobs

Step 1 — Join LinkedIN

Millie, Josie, and Lola joined LinkedIN to assist with developing their social network. To join LinkedIn you will need to go to the LinkedIn website at www.linkedin.com and click on the "Join LinkedIn today box". This link will allow you to sign up for a LinkedIn account. You may sign-up for a free or paid account. The paid account does have more features. You will be prompted to include the following information:

- Your first and last name
- Email address
- Password
- Status
- Company, Job Title, Country, Zip Code

Complete Exercise 7.9 to join LinkedIN.

Exercise 7.9 – Join LinkedIn

Join the LinkedIn website by going to www.linkedin.com. Be prepared to enter the information that is listed under step 1.

_____

_____

Step 2 – Develop Your Profile

LinkedIn will automatically develop a simple profile based on the information you provided in Step 1. However, to really market yourself to potential employers you want to build a more comprehensive profile. Note LinkedIn will provide you with the opportunity to "import your resume" but it is only to use the data from your resume to populate your LinkedIn profile. Instead of "importing your resume" you may gather the following information so you can develop a more complete profile:

- Include your photo – as mentioned in the Twitter section you want to make sure the picture is appropriate and professional. Recommendations are to use a head shot. Millie had a friend take an updated picture for her profile.

- Share a professional headline – the headline will appear on the line just below your name. You should include keywords that indicate your areas of expertise as opposed to focusing on your title. For example, Josie used personal trainer for her professional headline.

- Select a personalized Uniform Resource Locator (URL) – after signing up you will have a public profile that looks like the following: www.linkedin. com/pub/ followed by your name and a random combination of numbers and letters. Make sure to edit and remove the random numbers and letters but keep your name as if you were developed a new email account. Lola's personalized URL looked like this: www.linkedin.com/pub/lolagene

- Include your current position and two past positions – this will include volunteer jobs and/or internships that you completed within sport and physical activity. This information may come directly from your resume. Make sure to include job titles and your employers. Millie did not have a lot of jobs but volunteer work which included ticketing with the University of Southern Indiana (USI) Athletic Department, operations for the USI Screaming Eagles Running series, and intramural supervisor of the USI Recreation Sports Program.

- Fill out the education section –LinkedIn will prompt you to select a state and choose and institution from a drop down box. You will need to enter the dates you attended college. Josie used the prompts to fill out her education section and provided the University of Southern Indiana in Evansville, IN. She also provided information on her dates of attendance to be fall 2011 to present.

- Additional information – you want to add your websites, Twitter, interests, groups and associations, and honors and awards. Lola added her www. lolagene.com website, Twitter account, her interests which included biking and swimming, that she was a member of the Greater Evansville Runners and Walkers Club, and she received a Sport Management Scholarship at the beginning of her sophomore year in college.

- Display at least three letters of recommendations – the recommendations may come from professors, advisors, employers, colleagues, or other important constituents. Mille, Josie, and Lola requested letters of recommendation from one faculty member, one employer, and one advisor.

Exercise 7.10 – Develop Your Profile

Using Step 2 develop your profile and gather or include the information below. Place a check once you have all the information. You may want to use your reference to gather the information.

- Photo – choose a professional photo _____

- Choose professional headline _____

- Choose a personalized URL _____

- Include two current positions _____

  _____

- Include two past positions _____

  _____

- Education _____

- Additional Information (list) _____

- Three recommendation letters (list names) _____

  _____

Step 3 - Grow Your Network

Now you are ready to begin building your network that may lead to a field experience. Millie, Josie, and Lola used three ways to initiate contact to build your network on Linked and they are listed in Exhibit 7.6.

Exhibit 7.8 Grow Your Network
1. Invitation – inviting others to join your network or accepting their invitations.
2. Introduction – asking your contacts to introduce you to others.
3. InMail – sending an email-like communication directly to someone not in your network.

Invitations

To begin with you will need choose a mechanism for inviting professionals to join your network.

- Choose *Add Connections* at the top right hand corner of the home page

- Choose *Contacts* at the top left side of the home page and then select Add *Connections* from the pull-down menu.

Once you have competed one of the applications above you will be able to invite professionals to your website in four different ways:

- Enter one or multiple emails addresses to ask several professionals to join your network.

- Important professionals you already have in Outlook, AOL, Hotmail, Yahoo!, or Gmail.

- Select the Colleagues tab at the top of the screen and LinkedIN will automatically search the entire database for professionals or organizations that may be of interest in searching for a sport and physical activity internship or job.

- Select the Classmates tab at the top of the screen and LinkedIn will automatically search for members who attended your alma maters.

Introduction – The Invitation

Personalizing your invitation is much more personal and allows the professional to understand what you are trying to accomplish. A good way to develop your introduction is to consider looking at the first and second paragraph of your cover letter making sure you make it specific to the person that you are writing to. Be short and specific on what you would like to accomplish from inviting this person to your social network..

InMail

Now that you have an invitation you can send invitations to people in and outside your network. You want to be selective when growing your social network. You must choose on whether you want quantity or quality when selecting names to build your social network. There is no real solution on which way to go in terms of quantity or quality but use your best judgment and focus on your objectives of obtaining an internship and/or job.

Josie provides an example in Exhibit 7.9 of an invitation she used to develop her social network

---

Exhibit 7.9 – Invitation to Join Your LinkedIN Account

My name is Josie Anne, and I will be attending the American College of Sports Medicine (ACSM) Health and Fitness Summit and Exposition April 1-4 in Atlanta, GA. I noticed your company will be attending this event as well. I am really interested in hearing more about your company and the prospects of completing and internship during the summer. I would like to stop by your booth and introduce myself. I hope that we do connect during this event.

Best regards,

Josie Anne

Exercise 7.11 – Grow Your Network

List individuals that you would like to use to build your network. Begin with your friends and others that are in the industry that you think would provide a solid foundation for finding a field experience.

Network (list names) _____

_____

_____

_____

_____

Develop an introduction for your invitation using your cover letter to synthesize paragraphs one and two _____

_____

_____

_____

_____

_____

_____

Step 4 - Search for Field Experiences

Once you have begun building that network you can begin searching for field experiences. LinkedIN is definitely a place to promote and pursue positions online. LinkedIn pulls positions from other sites such as CareerBuilder, Yahoo!, HotJobs,

SimplyHired, Dice or Vault, and Craigslist (Slideshare, 2013). This makes it easy to you to go to once site and have many audiences review your materials. You can also search for positions that are similar to those that you are interested in by selecting the Advanced Search tab. Josie, Lola, and Millie used the Advanced Search table to search for field experience and/or job opportunities.

Exercise 7.12 – Search for Field Experiences and/or Jobs

Use your LinkedIN account to begin searching for field experiences. Keep a list or print the positions for future use.

_____

_____

_____

_____

Facebook

Facebook is the worlds largest personal/professional social networking site with 550 million actives users (Ebiz, 2013). Although Facebook is commonly associated as a personal site for college-age friends and family networking, it can also be a valuable tool for job search and professional networking if used in the proper manner. The platform for Facebook has changed tremendously over the last 15 years with the fastest-growing age group on Facebook is the over-55 segment (Ebiz, 2013). In addition, Facebook is now drawing the business crowd and provide a large audience for you to marketing yourself to in finding an internship or job. There are several advantages to using Facebook for developing your social network which include the following:

- Easy to search for people and contact them freely

- Unlimited friend requests

- Less formal

- Less time-consuming

- A hybrid of social and professional

- Profiles easy to set-up

Millie, Josie, and Lola followed three easy steps to allow them to begin building your social network through LinkdIn that is provided in Exhibit 7.9.

Exhibit 7.9 Step by Step Procedures and Guidelines in Developing a Facebook Page
Step 1 – Join Facebook
Step 2 – Create a Professional Profile
Step 3 – Build Your Network
Step 4 – Search for internships and/or job

Step 1 – Join Facebook

To join Facebook, go to www.facebook.com and register. Your registration will include the following information:

- Name
- Email address
- Password
- Gender
- Date of birth

Millie, Josie, and Lola joined Facebook. Use the information above to complete Exercise 7.13 in joining Facebook.

Exercise 7.13 – Join Facebook

Join the Facebook website by going to www.facebook.com. Be prepared to enter the information that is listed under step 1.

_____

_____

Step 2 – Create a Professional Profile

You will be prompted to create a profile. You want to focus on the development of a profile from a professional side as opposed to a personal side. The profile that will be asked for include the following:

- Current City
- Hometown
- Sex

- What are you looking for (say networking)
- Biography
- Profile picture
- Education and work history
- Contract information

The biography field is one that you really want to put some effort into. You may upload a short Biography or copy of the summary of your resume. Millie, Josie, and Lola followed the guidelines in this chapter and completed Exercise 7.5 to develop their Biography. If you have not developed your Biography you will need to revisit this section of the chapter. If you decide to post a picture make sure it is professional looking. Do not put up a profile photo of a pet, child, or you with someone else.

The profile also asks for the following and you should consider leaving out as it is the personal side of the profile that you should not include:

- Birthday
- Political views and religious beliefs
- Relationship interests
- Family member's name and email address to send an invitation
- Interests section (activities, interests, and favorite music, books, movies, and TV shows)

Exercise 7.14 – Creating a Professional Profile

Develop a professional profile when Facebook prompts you to do so. Answer the questions when prompted but consider leaving out birthday, political views and religious beliefs, relationship interests, family member's name and email address to send an invitation, and interests section. By leaving these areas out you will focus on developing a professional profile and not a personal profile.

Step 3 – Build your Network

In step 3, Millie, Josie, and Lola began to build their network. Building your network on Facebook is a two-step process. You must search for friends and then contact them to ask them to be a part of your network. You need to think in terms of field experience prospects. Do you already have a group of individuals in your sport and physical activity network. Begin with those individuals You can search for people by name and complete a friend request. Complete Exercise 7.12 to begin building your network.

Exercise 7.12 – Build Your Network

Begin making a list of all those individuals that you may want to add as a Facebook friend. List their name and affiliation. Consider professional contacts that may assist you in obtaining a field experience and/or job.

_____

_____

_____

_____

Step 4 – Search Field Experiences and/or Jobs

Finally, Millie, Josie, and Lola began to search for field experiences. You may want to begin by joining a group. Often times many jobs are posted in the discussion of Facebook groups. You will need to find those organizations that are most relevant to your field. You may want to join one of the organizations that were listed in Chapter 5 (Exhibit 5.6) (North American Society of Sport Management, National Strength and Conditioning Association, American College of Sport Medicine.) Once you join the organization you will be able to find and contact members of the group as well create wall posts (links, photos, articles, comments, questions, and so on). Complete Exercise 7.13 in searching for a field experience.

Exercise 7.14 – Joining Groups to Search for Field Experiences

Research potential organizations that you would like to join. You may begin by looking at the list in Chapter 5 (Exhibit 5.6). You only want to focus on those organizations that would best benefit you in seeking a job in a sport and physical activity setting. List at least four organizations that you would like to join and list them below. Once you have mad that list join the organization and begin building your network.

_____

_____

_____

_____

Summary

As learned in Chapter 6, Networking is one of the most effective means to obtain a field experience. Social networking is also powerful and is a more efficient way of marketing yourself when a face-to-face meeting is not a possibility. As this chapter has illustrated, social networking will allow you to connect with industry insiders across the country around the world. This connection provides a means to optimize your social network to research potential employers or clients and allows you to begin the process of obtaining a field experience and/or job.

Frequently Asked Questions

Why should you consider using social networking over the traditional face-to-face avenue?

Networking online is a great time-saver over the more traditional face-to-face avenue. Social networking allows you to get advice about search techniques, identify employers to target, connect with key decision makers, and become visible to recruiters.

What are the best social networking avenues to explore when seeking an internship and/or job?

The social networking avenues within this chapter provide you with the most often used social media avenues than any others. LinkedIn is the front-runner of the professional networking sites. Twitter has more than 90 million visitors worldwide and provides an opportunity to develop relationships with those individuals that could assist you in obtaining a field experience and/or job.

Is Facebook a good mechanism to build a social network?

Facebook can be more than a social site if you decide to use it in a professional manner. You need to set-up a professional profile and only accept individuals that focus on your goals and objectives for obtaining a field experience and/or job. This means no family or friends or personal pictures being posted.

Student Learning Activities

Complete the exercises throughout the chapter to begin developing your social network as a means of obtaining a field experience.

Ask your fellow classmates to join your Blog, Twitter, and LinkedIN site.

Develop a mechanism for keeping track of your followers from your Blog, Twitter, and LinkedIn site.

➤ Social Networking Checklist

BLOGGING CHECKLIST

- ❑ Research Sport and Physical Activity Blogs
- ❑ Choose a name for the your blog
- ❑ Select a blog platform or host
- ❑ Generate your content
- ❑ Manage your comments
- ❑ Go live

TWITTER CHECKLIST

- ❑ Objectives
- ❑ Profile
- ❑ Tweet

LinkedIN CHECKLIST

- ❑ Join LinkedIn
- ❑ Develop a LinkedIn profile
- ❑ Grow your network
- ❑ Search for field experiences and/or jobs

FACEBOOK

- ❑ Join Facebook
- ❑ Create a professional profile
- ❑ Build your network
- ❑ Search for field experiences and/or jobs

CAREER HIGHLIGHT – GROUP SALES ACCOUNT EXECUTIVE – SEMI-PROFESSIONAL SPORT

Sallie Jung

Group Sales Account Executive

Evansville Icemen

Evansville, IN

Education and/or Certifications

University of Southern Indiana

Degree in Kinesiology

Minor in Sports Management

Years in Position

3rd Season in position

July 6th, 2014 will mark my 3rd year in the organization

Previous Positions

Same within this organization

Current Job Responsibilities and Hours

Generate revenue under the ticket sales department by creating group nights for every home game along with some themed nights that will grow our target population.

Personal customer service to all my clients and to upcoming prospects.

Daily cold calls to qualify new prospects within our community.

Greatest Challenges

Adapting to change every day within our office and handling time management within the change.

Career Advice

Experience is not just people telling you what you need it is what you want. Never reject an offer to "help" do anything, even if it is a small or very large project. You will learn so much more about yourself when thrown into a challenge! Good Luck!

CAREER HIGHLIGHT – CONSUMER SALES EXECUTIVE – PROFESSIONAL SPORT

Michelle Harrell

Consumer Sales Executive

Indiana Pacers

Indianapolis, IN

Education and/or Certification

Bachelors of Science in Sport Management University of Southern Indiana

Years in Position

3 months

Previous Positions

Indiana Fever Consumer Sales Executive, 6 months

Indiana Fever Community and Player Relations Internship, 6 months

Current job Responsibilities and Hours

High volume out bound calls-80 per day

Meet and exceed sales goals including season tickets, group outings, and suite rentals

Service all clients as well as field in bound customer service needs

Greatest challenges

Developing new leads

Balancing new business work with customer service responsibilities with existing clients

Career advice

Be willing to take chances

Work hard and volunteer as much as possible to gain experience

References

ACE Blog. (2013). *ACE fitness blog. Retrieved from http://www.acefitness.org/blogs/*

Career Moxie. (2013). Top 50 occupational therapy blogs. Retrieved from http://mastersinoccupationaltherapy.org/2010/top-50-occupational-therapy-blogs/

Carlson, N. (2013). *The real history of Twitter.* Retrieved from http://www.businessinsider.com/how-twitter-was-founded-2011-4

Crompton, D. & Sautter, E. (2011). *Find a job through social networking. Use LinkedIn, Twitter, Facebook, Blogs, and more to advance your career, 2nd edition.* St. Paul, MN: JIST Works.

Digital Marketing Ramblings (DMR). (2013). By the number: 48 amazing LinkedIN statistics. Retrieved from http://expandedramblings.com/index.php/by-the-numbers-a-few-important-linkedin-stats/#.UrNHj7Hna70

Ebiz. (2013). *Social media marketing helps to promote your amazing content to the right audience.* Retrieved from http://ebizresults.com/drive-traffic/social-media-marketing/

Jobs in Sport. (2013). *Jobs in sport blog.* Retrieved from http://www.jobsinsports.com/blog/.Linked Strategies. (2013). About LinkedIN. Retrieved from http://www.linkedstrategies.com/about-linkedin/

Linked Strategies. (2013). *Linked strategies.* Retrieved from http://www.linkedstrategies.com/training/

Midwest ACSM Blog. (2013). *Midwest American College of Sports Medicine is blogging.* Retrieved from http://www.mwacsm.org/docs/MWACSMPostGuide.pdf.

NSCA Group Blogging. (2013). *National Strength and Condition Association Young Strength and Conditioning coaches association. http://yscca.groupsite.com/post/2013-nsca-coaches-conference.*

NCSF. (2013). *National Council on Strength and Fitness personal trainer blog.* Retrieved form http://www.ncsf.org/trainerblog/

PTDC Blog. (2013). *Professional training development center blog.* Retrieved from http://www.theptdc.com/blog-2/.

Real Clear Sports. *Top 10 sports blogs.* Retrieved from http://www.realclearsports.com/lists/blogs_2011/.

Salpeter, M. (2011). *Social networking for career success.* New York, NY: Learning Express

Six Revisions. (2013). *Top 10 free online blogging platforms.* Retrieved from http://sixrevisions.com/tools/top-free-online-blogging/.

Slideshare. (2013). *The new way to look for a job, job boards, networking, online social sites.* Retrieved from http://www.slideshare.net/TReedGary/online-job-boards-networking-and-social-sites-5041903

SPARTA. (2013). *Performance blog.* Retrieved from www.spartapoint.com.

Sports Career Institute. (2013). *Sport career institute: Sports jobs blogs.* Retrieved from http://sportscareersinstitute.com/sports-jobs-blog.html.

Theravid. (2013). *13 physical therapy blogs you should be reading.* Retrieved from http://blog.theravid.com/physical-therapy-2/13-physical-therapy-blogs-you-should-be-reading/.

THE INTERVIEW

SCENARIO #1 – FIELD EXPERIENCE/OBSERVATION - SOPHOMORE

Bill

*Bill is a sophomore and currently enrolled in a sport and physical activity field experience course (20 hours - 1 credit hour). Bill knows he is interested in working with youth but does not know for sure in what capacity. Bill attended a career fair on campus and met a representative (Tammy) from a public recreation facility. Bill introduced himself to Tammy and explained he was looking for a field experience. Tammy had an informal conversation which Bill realized was an **unstructured, one-on-one, in person interview**. By the end of the conversation Bill obtained a position at Tammy's facility. Bill realized he needed to be careful even in informal conversations to answer questions precise and in a professional manner.*

SCENARIO #2 – PRACTICUM - JUNIOR

Andrea

*Andrea is a junior enrolled in a practicum course (200 hours – 4 credit hours). Andrea is interested in health promotion but has so many opportunities to choose from. Andrea reads about a position that she is curious about. The position is working with the local healthcare team. The main responsibility is working with the Association's Employee Health Promotion Program. Andrea applies for the position and is called by a representative from the company. Andrea is asked to come for an onsite interview which consists of a **structured, one-on-one interview** with the Supervisor of American Health Association (AHA). Andrea was not intimidated about the interview because of her professional development courses that introduced her to many types of interviews.*

SCENARIO #3 – INTERNSHIP - SENIOR

Kristen

> *Kristen is a senior enrolled in an internship course (450 hours – 9 credit hours). – Kristen is intrigued by the career highlights of Josh Wildeman and Dustin Murray (end of chapter). Josh is the Strength and Conditioning Coach for Castle High School. Dustin is a Sport Conditioning Specialist and Manager of Sports Acceleration Center. Ty is a Sport Conditioning Specialist and a manager Sports Acceleration Center at the Metro Soccer Complex in Evansville Indiana. Kristen decides to apply for a Sport and Conditioning Specialist internship with Explosive Performance. Kristen receives a phone call from the Director (Tom) of Explosive Performance and is asked if he could ask her a few questions. Kristen realizes this **preliminary, structured, one-on-one, phone interview** was her first step to getting an **onsite interview**. Kristen received an **onsite interview** which consisted of a **group panel, who asked structured, reality questions**. Kristen was prepared for all of the formats and types of interviews in this scenario because of her professional development courses.*

You found a job, submitted your resume and cover letter, and now you need to prepare for an interview. Although the interview can be a complex interaction with the employer, the interview is the most important part of the job process. However, you are not quite sure where to begin and you want to be well-prepared.

Format and Types of Interviews

As the scenarios indicated there is not one specific format or type of interview you could encounter when seeking a job. Bill, Andrea, and Kristen all encountered at least one format and one type of interview depending on the organizations methods. Your interview may fall into one of the three formats and types as well:

- Format - Preliminary phone interview
- Format - One-on-one interview
- Format - Group or panel interview
- Skype interview
- Type – Structured
- Type – Unstructured
- Type - Reality

Preliminary Phone Interview

The most common type of interview is the preliminary phone interview and it occurs before the "in person" interview. If you applied for a competitive job this phone interview may eliminate you from the applicant pool if you are not prepared as if it were a one-on-one interview. For example, Kristen realized she have an on-the-spot phone interview. Kristen prepared herself for this interview by practicing the 18 most common asked questions in Exhibit 8.2.

One-on-One Interview

The one-on-one interview usually follows after the preliminary interview and is the first opportunity to meet with the supervisor and other employees. The interview may be structured or unstructured. Bill, Andrea, and Kristen all experienced a one-on-one interview.

Group or Panel Interview

Kristen interviewed with two or more people for the job. This type of interview is called a group or panel interview. In some cases several applicants meet with a group of employers at the same time.

Skye Interview

Skype interviews have some advantages as you get face-to-face time with the employer while cutting travel out of the equation. Mastering the interview is common practice, but etiquette surrounding a Skype interview is different from the phone and in-person interviews. Since Kristen was extended a Skype interview she decided to review Exhibit 7.5 to assist her through the process.

Structured

Kristen and Andrea experienced the most common type of interview - structured. The structured interview consists of a series of questions all applicants are asked to answer. These questions have specific goals for the interview and are detailed, before the interview begins. This interview allowing employers to compare specific job tasks with criteria (Doyle, 2013a).

Unstructured

The unstructured interview has no strict guidelines and allows the question to be open but concise (Creglow, 2013). For example,Tammy (representative) from the health fair carried on a conversation with Bill which was actually an unstructured interview.

Reality

The reality interview is a type of interview where you may be asked to provide examples for the answer you have provided. Kristen was asked "What are your greatest strengths?" Kristen answered, "My greatest strengths are applying the principles of overload, progression, individualism, reversibility, and specificity to athletes. For example, "I focused on power lifts and power jumps when training centers for the women's basketball team. This training represents the principle of specificity."

Step-By-Step Procedures and Guidelines for Interviewing

The interview is the most important part of the job search process. However, many students are not well-prepared for the interview process. Regardless of the format or type of interview you need some guidance on how to present yourself effectively. Exhibit 8.1 provides step-by-step procedures and guidelines for interviews based on research that have been field tested over the years by others (Farr, 2008). The key to these step-by-step procedures and guidelines are to help you substantially improve your interview skills in a short period of time, thereby providing you with an advantage over other students.

Exhibit 8.1 Step-by-Step Procedures and Guidelines to Interviewing

Step 1 -Preparation – Before the Interview

1.   Knowing what you can do

2.   Research perspective employer

3.   Practice answering and asking questions

4.   Appearance

Step 2 - Day of the Interview - Meeting the employer

7.   Arrive early

8.   Check appearance

9.   Give a firm handshake and maintain good eye contact

10.   Act interested

11.   Avoid annoying behavior (tapping hand on desk, frequent "ummm," etc)

12.   Use the employers formal name

13.   Answering questions

14.   Ask questions

> **Step 3 - The Follow-Up**
>
> 15. Thank you letter
>
> 16. JIST Card
>
> **Step 4 - The Job Offer**

Step 1 - Preparation — Before the Interview

What happens before the interview can be extremely important. You can begin to prepare for the interview by identifying your skills, researching the perspective employer, practice answering and asking questions, and thinking about appearance.

Knowing what you can do

Before walking into a job interview it is important to know the skills you can offer an organization. More importantly how can you convey those skills to the perspective employer in an effective way? Personal attributes or soft skills provide the employer about who you are as a person (Kursmark, 2011). For example, Andrea focused on her communicative, client focused personal attributes.

Transferable skills or hard skills (innate, learned, function-related) are ones that are needed to perform the job. For example, Kristen focused on her experience as a student athlete and how the knowledge of various training specific to athletes could be transferred to this position. Refer to Chapter 3 to review your personal attributes (Exercise 3.3) and transferable skills (Exercise 3.4).

Research Perspective Employer

You know what skills you can offer an organization but now you need to research the organization, the job, and the interviewer (s). You can begin to research the organization by going to their website or talking to an individual within the organization. For example, Kristen began by visiting Explosive Performance's (EP) website and answered a series of questions:

- **What is the mission and/or vision of the organization?** To be the best sport-specific fitness program in the nation.

- **Who does the organization cater to?** EP provides elite athletic training for youth, high school, college, and pro athletes.

- **What type of programs does the organization offer?** The programs include speed, agility, quickness, strength, vertical jump, flexibility training, and overall anaerobic conditioning. A series of programs are offered such as Adult (EP), EP Jump, and EP Coaches clinics

- **How long has the organization been in business?** Established in 1997 by Rob Rose

- **What are some highlights of the business? Any awards, newspaper articles highlighting them, etc.** EP has grown from training a few hundred athletes per year to training over 3,000 athletes per year. Specializing in first step and reaction training, Rob Rose had developed a professional performance staff with degrees in the field of Exercise Science and certifications from nationally recognized organizations that certify trainers to train athletes

- **What is the name (s) of the individual (s) who will be interviewing you?** Rob Rose, Director, Explosive Performance

- **What information can you find out about these individuals? (read the info sheet on the website and print out the pictures so you can remember them.** Kristen prints biographies listed on the website of Rob Rose and some of the other staff.

Complete Exercise 8.1 to research your perspective employer.

Exercise 8.1 Research Perspective Employer

What is the mission and/or vision of the organization? _____

_____

_____

_____

Who does the organization cater to? _____

_____

What type of programs does the organization offer? _____

_____

_____

How long has the organization been in business? _____

_____

_____

What are some highlights of the business? Any awards, newspaper articles _____ highlighting them, etc. _____

_____

_____

What is the name (s) of the individual (s) who will be interviewing you?

_____

What information can you find out about these individuals? (read the info sheet on the website and print out the pictures so you can remember them.

_____

_____

Practice Answering Questions

Practicing possible interview questions can help improve your performance during an interview. You do not want to be the one the employer remembers as being unprepared and having a terrible interview. For example, Andrea practiced answering some common interview questions located in Exhibit 8.2 (USI Office of Career Services and Internships, 2013) before her interview. Andrea practiced answering the questions by herself and then in a mock interview with her fellow classmates. The mock interview consisted of a student (the employer) asking Andrea a series of questions she developed and was prepared to answer during the mock interview. Of course the professor was involved and interrupted the mock interview to guide Andrea in making sure she was prepared for a reality interview. During the mock interview Andrea was asked "What do you consider to be your greatest weakness?" Andrea was taught to present her weakness in a way that could be perceived as a strength. For example, Andrea responded by saying, "People tend to say that I am a workaholic." The professor follows-up with a question by asking Andrea to provide a specific example (reality answer) of what she means by a workaholic. Andrea explained, "I have a tendency to arrive early to organize for the day and leave late to complete project." From this one question Andrea learned how she could provide a reality answer, "People tend to say that I am a workaholic. For example, I have a tendency to arrive early to organize for the day and leave late to complete project." In providing the example, Andrea provided detail where additional follow-up questions were not needed. The mock interview made an enormous difference when Andrea interviewed for her position.

Complete Exercise 8.2 to prepare for a mock interview

Exhibit 8.2 18 Most Commonly Asked Questions
1. Why did you choose to pursue a career in sport and physical activity?
2. What do you consider to be your greatest strengths and weaknesses?
3. How would you describe yourself?
4. What motivates you to put forth your greatest effort?
5. Why should I hire you for the job?
6. What qualifications do you have that makes you think that you will be successful?

7. How do you determine or evaluate success?

8. In what ways do you think you can make a contribution to our company?

9. Describe the relationship that should exist between supervisor and subordinates.

10. What two or three accomplishments have given you the most satisfaction? Why?

11. Describe your most rewarding College experience.

12. Why did you select your College or University?

13. What made you choose your field or major study?

14. In what kind of work environment are you most comfortable?

15. How do you work under pressure?

16. What do you know about our company?

17. What two or three things are most important to you for this position?

18. What major problem have you encountered? How did you deal with it?

Exercise 8.2 18 Most Frequently Asked Questions During Interviews

Why did you choose a career in sport and physical activity? _____

_____

What do you consider to be your greatest strengths and weaknesses? _____

_____

How would you describe yourself? _____

_____

What motivates you to put forth your greatest effort? _____

_____

Why should I hire you? _____

What qualifications do you have that makes you think that you will be successful?

_____

How do you determine or evaluate success? _____

In what ways do you think you can make a contribution to our company?

_____

Describe the relationship that should exist between supervisor and subordinates.

_____

What two or three accomplishments have given you the most satisfaction? Why?

_____

Describe your most rewarding College experience. _____

_____

Why did you select your College or University? _____

_____

What made you choose you field or major study? _____

_____

In what kind of work environment are you most comfortable? _____

_____

How do you work under pressure? _____

_____

What do you know about our company? _____

_____

What two or three things are most important to you in your job? _____

_____

What major problem have you encountered? How did you deal with it?

_____

Determine what Question you May Ask

Once you finished answering the questions you must also figure out questions you may want to ask the employer. Kristen began by reviewing the top 18 questions to ask an employer in Exhibit 8.3 (Doyle, 2013b). Kristen simply substituted the sport conditioning specialist for the job. For example, Kristen asked, "What are the day-to-day responsibilities of a sport conditioning specialist intern?

Exhibit 8.3 Top 8 Questions to Ask An Employer

1. What are the day-to-day responsibilities of this job? Provide the percentage of time spent for each responsibility.

2. What are some of the skills and abilities necessary for someone to succeed in this job?

3. Could you explain your organizational structure?

4. Can you describe an ideal employee?

5. What are the company's strengths and weaknesses?

6. Could you describe your company's management style and the type of employee who would fit well with it?

7. How much guidance or assistance is made available to individuals in developing career goals?

Complete Exercise 8.3 to determine what questions you would ask an employer if you were interviewing for a job.

Exercise 8.3 Questions to Ask and Employer?

Write 5 questions to ask an employer before being offered the job

1. _____

2. _____

3. _____

4. _____

5. _____

Appearance

What could be worse than meeting the employer and not being dressed appropriately? You not only need to wear something that makes you feel confident but something that makes you look professional because dress does reflect self-image. Bill used the appearance guidelines in Exhibit 8.4 to help address many other factors that can make a difference at the career fair (Bonander, 2013; Gottsman, 2013).

Exhibit 8.4 Appearance Guidelines

Men

1. Two-piece matching suit with a silk tie, white or light blue shirt, dark socks, leather shoes, and black leather belt

2. Conservative colors – navy, gray, black

3. Facial hair – if worn well-groomed

4. Wear a watch – no earrings

5. Make sure everything is clean and well-pressed

6. Use cologne sparingly

7. Clean fingernails

Women

1. Dress, skirt covering your thighs, or two-piece suit, blouse that matches the skirt or suit, and low heels, high heels, or closed-toe leather shoes.

2. Conservative colors – navy, dark gray, brown, black

3. Wear a watch

4. Keep make-up conservative

5. If you carry a purse make sure to keep it small and simple

6. Make sure everything is clean and well-pressed

7. Use perfume sparingly

8. Clean fingernails

Step 2 - Day of the Interview – Meeting the Employer

Employers are less likely to hire someone who makes a negative first impression. The first impression is not only with appearance but the way you present yourself to the perspective employer which may include the following (Farr, 2008):

- Includes arriving early
- Checking appearance (after arriving)
- Giving a firm handshake while making eye contact
- Acting interested, avoiding annoying behaviors
- Using formal names, answering questions
- Asking questions

Arrive early

You want to arrive at least 5 to 10 minutes before the interview begins. To prepare for this arrival you need to make sure you know where you are going. For example, Andrea was not for sure where American Heart Association was located and therefore referred to mapquest.com for directions. Andrea could have called the employer to ask for directions as well. If you are interviewing for more than one job on the same day make sure to allow enough time in between the interviews.

Check appearance

Once you arrive to the interview site make sure to find a bathroom and check your appearance. Check for wind-blown hair, smudged lipstick, or food in your teeth. Spray your mouth with breath spray or use a mint just before going to the receptionist to check-in.

Give a firm handshake and maintain good eye contact

When first meeting the employer, you want to look at the employer in the eye and give a firm handshake. This may be the time when "small talk" shows that you are feeling comfortable. For example, Kristen researched the EP website and discovers Rob (Director of EP) is an avid golfer. Kristen has the perfect opportunity to make "small talk" because the weather is so nice. Kristen simply points out the nice weather and how it would be nice to be golfing right now. Hopefully, Rob follows up with something to do with golf so a "small talk" conversation may take place.

Act interested

During the interview listen carefully to the interviewer (s). Pay close attention to what the employer is saying. You do not want to be caught daydreaming when you should be answering a question.

Avoid annoying behavior

What could be more annoying than tapping your fingers on a desk, saying "umm" every other sentence, playing with your hair, or knocking your knees together? These movements or mannerisms are distracting to perspective employers and therefore you need to become aware and correct these behaviors.

Use the employer's formal name

During the interview use their formal name when referring to the employer. For example, Kristen met Rob Rose and addressed him as "Mr. Rose." Only use the first name if the employer suggests that you do so.

Answering Questions

You want to learn how to guide the interview by the way you answer the questions. You have already answered the top 18 questions in Exercise 7.2, and you should be ready to go! Remember Andrea learned the hard way when answering a question but learned how to present an example following her first response to the question. This "follow-up" technique allowed Andrea to guide the interview where employers had no reason to ask additional questions.

Ask Questions

In Exercise 8.3 you prepared the questions to ask during your interview. You also want to make sure that you are prepared to write down the answers to the questions. For example, Bill made sure he had a notepad available during the interview where he could take notes which allowed the employer to see he was serious in finding out the answers to the questions.

Step 3 - The Follow-Up

An effective follow-up can make the difference in getting the job over another candidate. A follow-up can be in the way of a phone call, thank you letter, or a JIST card. Refer to Chapter 4 for additional follow-up techniques.

Step 4 - The Job Offer

Once you decide on an appropriate job it is important for you to ask the employer at least three questions:

- When do you begin?

- What do you need me to bring to work?

- What is your dress code?

The Skype Interview

As mentioned earlier in this chapter, etiquette surrounding the Skype interview is different than your phone or in-person interview. Kristen was asked by an employer to have a Skype interview due to expense of traveling. Kristen reviewed the guidelines in Exhibit 7.1 but realized she needed additional guidance for Skype interview. She found that guidance in Exhibit 8.5 (Simply Hired Blog, 2013; Whittaker, 2013).

Exhibit 8.5 Skype Interview Tips

1. Look at the camera and not the screen

   Looking directly at the video camera is the only way to maintain a direct contact with your employer.

2. Prepare your surroundings

   You need to have a quiet place to conduct the Skype interview. You will also want to have a neutral backdrop so you are the focal point of the Skype interview.

3. Close all windows on your computer

   Make sure that all windows are closed on your computer.

4. Use your resume or notes

   One advantages of a Skype interview is that you can have a "cheat sheet" in the form of a resume or notes. Be careful relying too heavily on your resume and/or notes.

5. Avoid interruptions

   If you are interviewing in the house let everyone know so you are not interrupted.

6. Keep your profile professional

   The first impression that you make during a Skype interview is the Skype username and picture. You should consider creating a professional Skype account.

7. Check your audio

   Tweek the Skype audio ahead of time to make sure you can both hear and be heard without difficulty.

8. Don't forget to log off

   Make sure to log off so the employer cannot keep watching you following the interview.

Summary

Preparing for the interview makes an enormous difference in rather a job is offered. You need the employers to know who you are and what you have to offer. You need to spend time creating a solid foundation by researching the perspective employer, by answering and asking interview questions, and doing an appearance check. With a little fine tuning the interview process can be fun and rewarding as you watch opportunities for employment unfold.

Frequently Asked Questions

Should you do a follow-up phone call?

A follow-up phone call may be impressive to the employer. To make an effective follow-up phone call, find out the best date and time to call the employer. Next, call the employer when you say you are going to call.

When doing a follow-up phone call should you e-mail employers to communicate?

There are a variety of advantages to email such as being convenient, fast, free, and can be forwarded easily to others.

When doing a follow-up should you phone the employer to communicate?

Phone calls can provide more attention and provide a different, more interactive approach. If you prepare the follow-up phone call can be more beneficial than you think.

Student Learning Activities

Complete Exercise 8.1 and research a perspective employer for the position you are seeking.

Complete Exercise 8.2 and find a partner and exchange questions. Practice answering those questions while your partner provides feedback. Take notes on potential changes you may make to your answers.

Complete Exercise 8.3 and get into groups of 4 or 5 and discuss the questions you would ask an employer. Write down additional questions you would like to ask the employer from the discussion in the group.

Complete a mock interview among students in your class

➤ Interview Checklist

❑ You know about yourself before entering the interview (skills, personal attributes).

❑ You practiced answering questions.

❑ You have selected your outfit, shaved, brushed your hair, etc

❑ You mapquested your destination so you will be on time.

❑ You practiced your handshake.

❑ You made sure that you were interested in the position before applying.

❑ You practiced the interview being conscious of annoying behavior.

❑ You know the employers formal name.

❑ You practiced answering questions for an interview.

❑ You practiced asking questions for an interview.

❑ You have the thank you letter prepared to send to the employer following the interview.

❑ You prepared a JIST Card to give employers following the interview.

CAREER HIGHLIGHT – HEAD STRENTH AND CONDITIONING COACH/ADVANCED PHYSICAL EDUCATION TEACHER

Josh Wildeman

Castle High School

Advanced Physical Education Teacher

Head Strength and Conditioning Coach

Education And Certifications

Ball State University

Master's of Arts in Physical Education (Coaching Specialization)

Indiana University

Bachelor's of Science in Education

National Strength and Conditioning Association Registered Strength and Conditioning Coach

(RSCC)

National Strength and Conditioning Association Certified Strength and Conditioning Specialist (CSCS)

USA Weightlifting Level I Sports Performance Coach (USAW)

Years in Position

7

Previous Positions

None in the Field

Current Job Description and Hours

Currently teach five sections of Advanced and Basic Strength and Conditioning at Castle High School in Newburgh, IN. Additionally, serve as the Head Strength and Conditioning Coach for all varsity sports at Castle High School. Oversee the program design and implementation of all off-season, pre-season, and in-season strength and conditioning programs. Hours vary by season and typically range from 50-60 hours per week.

Responsibilities

Currently responsible for the exercise prescription and sport-specific strength and conditioning program design of each varsity athletic program. Instruct exercise technique for strength training exercises, Olympic lifts, and speed and agility development programs. Instruct weight room safety protocols and spotting guidelines. Educate student-athletes on nutrition, safe supplementation, and dangers of performance enhancing drugs. Also, responsible for weight room equipment maintenance and purchasing of new equipment.

Greatest Challenge

The greatest challenge of this position at the high school level is developing and maintaining a positive relationship with the head coach of each athletic program. While many coaches embrace the opportunity to give their student-athletes the opportunity to achieve their athletic potential, others are skeptical because they are unfamiliar with the practice and have coached so many years without utilizing the weight room. In these situations, it is imperative that the strength coach acknowledges this trepidation and works to build a relationship of trust. This process begins by discussing with the athletic coach the specific abilities (strength, power, endurance, speed, and/or agility) that he or she would like to see developed and ask for their input on the program design. Collaborating with the athletic coach gives them a sense of control over the program, which they are used to having, and reduces the anxiety they have about starting a strength and conditioning program. Typically, the student-athletes' development and enjoyment of the program will convince the athletic coach of the benefits of participating in this type of program. Then, gradually the strength coach will be granted more flexibility with the program design and implementation. However, the most convincing aspect will be the team's enhanced performance and reduction in injuries during their upcoming season.

Career Advice

Most successful strength coaches develop their own individual strength and conditioning philosophy in regards to how they train their athletes. This philosophy can come in the form of specific exercises or drills they prefer to employ and/or a program design variable that they believe provides their athletes with a decisive edge to their training. While developing his or her own philosophy is important for a strength coach, it is important that young strength and conditioning coaches understand that this should not be a rapid and rigid process. Instead of pigeon holing themselves into one specific discipline (traditional strength training, weightlifting, kettleball, crossfit, etc.) their philosophical development should be a slow and continually evolving process. The strength coach should try to gain as much experience with as many different disciplines as he or she can and then mold their training philosophy from the various benefits to performance enhancement that all of these disciplines possess.

CAREER HIGHLIGHT– FACILITY DIRECTOR – STRENGTH AND CONDITIONING

Dustin Lee Murray

Facility Director

Sports Acceleration Center

Education And Certifications

University of Southern Indiana

Master of Science Liberal Studies

Wisconsin Parkside

Bachelor of Science/Bachelor of Arts Sport and Fitness Management Wisconsin Parkside

CPT National Academy of Sports Medicine

Level II Athletic Republic Speed Certification

Years in Position

5 years

Previous Positions

Performance Coach - University Wisconsin Parkside and the University of Southern Indiana

Personal Trainer - University Wisconsin Parkside and the University of Southern Indiana

Assistant Baseball Coach - University Wisconsin Parkside and the University of Southern Indiana

Current Job Description and Hours

Oversee all Sales and marketing efforts, Budget planning, facility management (equipment maintenance etc), director of performance training and program development. Hiring and staff recruitment.

50-60 hours per week. Hours are unpredictable.

Responsibilities

Lead hitting instructor for Sports Accelerations Elite Baseball/Softball Academy

Greatest Challenge

Long hours, Small operating budget, competition, advancing field, recruiting qualified trainers (education, experience, self motivation, work ethic etc)

Career Advice

Career Advice: Higher education, find a mentor in the field, wide range of certifications, volunteer, network, self motivate, and Stand Out!!

References

Bonander, R. (2013). *Job interview etiquette: The secret to getting the job you want.* Retrieved December 29, 2013 from http://www.askmen.com/grooming/project/8_job-interviewetiquette.html.

Creglow, A. (2013). *Using structured interviews for selecting and developing employees.* Retrieved December 29, 2013 from http://www.kenexa.com/Portals/0/Downloads/Using%20 Structured%20Interviews%20for%20Selecting%20and%20Developing%20Employees. pdf

Doyle, A. (2013a). *Unstructured job interview.* Retrieved December 29, 2013 from http:// jobsearch.about.com/od/jobsearchglossary/g/unstructuredinterview.htm.

Doyle, A. (2013b). *Interview questions to ask an employer.* Retrieved December 29, 2014 from http://jobsearch.about.com/od/interviewquestionsanswers/a/interviewquest2.htm.

Farr, M. (2008). *Next day job interview: Prepare tonight and get the job tomorrow.* Indianapolis, IN: JIST Publishing, Inc.

Gottsman, D. (2013). *Suiting up for success: Job interview attire for women (part I).* Retrieved December 29, 2013 from http://www.huffingtonpost.com/diane-gottsman/job-interview-dress-tips_b_3569050.html

Kursmark, L. M. (2011). *Best resumes for college students and new grads: Jump-start your career!* Second edition. Indianapolis, IN: JIST Publishing, Inc.

Simply Hired Blog.(2013). *5 tips for making the most of your Skype job interview.* Retrieved December 20, 2103 http://blog.simplyhired.com/2013/08/5-tips-for-making-the-most-of-your-skype-job-interview.html

USI Office of Career Services and Internships. (2013). *20 most frequently asked interview questions. Retrieved December 29, 2013, from http://www.usi.edu/careersv/resumeinterview.asp*

Whittaker, A. (2013). *13 tips for nailing a Skype interview.* Retrieved December 20, 2013 from http://www.usatoday.com/story/tech/personal/2013/08/01/13-tips-for-a-great-skype-interview/2608915/

SECTION IV

FROM COLLEGE GRADUATE TO CAREER

POTENTIAL FIELD EXPERIENCE OPPORTUNITIES IN SPORT AND PHYSICAL ACTIVITY

SCENARIO #1 – FIELD EXPERIENCE/OBSERVATION - SOPHOMORE

Mary

> Mary is a sophomore and currently enrolled in a sport and physical activity field experience course (20 hours - 1 credit hour). Mary has only worked odd jobs during the summer not related to sport and physical activity. Mary is not for sure about her career choice in sport business but she is excited about the field experience course which allows her to observe professionals in the field. Mary makes a decision to observe the employees at a local theme park and resort.

SCENARIO #2 – PRACTICUM – JUNIOR

Eddie

> Eddie is a junior enrolled in a practicum course (150 hours – 3 credit hours). Eddie is taking classes but must complete a practicum before his senior year. Eddie wants to make sure he chooses a practicum that helps build his resume in pursuing a career as a Sports Broadcaster.

SCENARIO #3 – INTERNSHIP – SENIOR

Heidi

Heidi is a senior enrolled in an internship (450 hours – 9 credit hours). Heidi is interested in working for a non-profit sport and physical activity facility. Heidi became interested in the YMCA after reading Christen Mitchell's and Boyd Williams' career highlight (end of chapter). Christen has not been in the field for very long but has been able to work herself into Assistant Director of Health/Wellness at the YMCA. Although Boyd has not been at the YMCA for very long he has a considerable amount of experience with non-profit organizations and is currently the Executive Director at the YMCA in St. Louis. After careful consideration, Heidi decides to pursue an internship as a Health and Wellness Intern Coordinator.

You identified a potential career, stayed focused on your four-year plan, and you are nearing the end of you degree program. You have one more task to complete – the field experience. You have already taken the necessary professional preparation steps to help you obtain a field experience but it is up to you to do it! Begin the process by following the step-by-step procedures and guidelines in securing a field experience.

Securing the Field Experience

A field experience can be one of the most rewarding, career-enhancing strategies as long as you have a well-planned search and selection process. The search and selection process begins by realizing how important it is to secure a field experience where you can gain firsthand knowledge of skills needed to obtain a position in sport and physical activity (Bethell& Morgan, 2011; Bower, 2013). You may also need guidance in selecting the right field experience to secure a site, but you must also learn to take ownership and responsibility for the search by completing the step-by-step procedures, guidelines, and exercises throughout this chapter.

Several researchers introduced steps to secure a field experience in sport and physical activity (Foster & Dollar, 2010). This chapter combines the efforts of those researchers and the author in identifying steps for selecting and securing a field experience, which are performed at different stages in the process. The author has extended the steps by providing questions to provoke your thoughts about the field experience site. The steps are summarized in Exhibit 9.1 and exercises are located throughout the chapter to keep you organized while making sure important information is not omitted to obtain a field experience.

Exhibit 9.1 Step-by-Step Procedures and Guidelines in Securing a Field Experience
Focus the Search
1. Find out about your university requirements
2. Create a list of objectives you would like to accomplish during the field experience
Search and Apply
3. Identify potential sites that could help in reaching those objectives
4. Apply for the position
Secure the Field Experience
5. Interview for field experiences at several sites
6. Select the site that best suits your personal objectives and send letter of intent

Focus the Search

The first step in securing a field experience is to focus on the search. You must be aware of university requirements and create a list of objectives.

Step 1 — Awareness of University Requirements

A successful field experience can get you one step closer to a career in sport and physical activity. However, to be successful you need to become familiar with the formal educational objectives. You must first consult with your Field Experience Coordinator. The Field Experience Coordinator may provide you with a handbook familiarizing you with university requirements, expectations, and resources (Foster & Dollar, 2010). To begin the process of obtaining additional information about the field experience, Heidi begins by following a few basic steps. First, Heidi wants to get in contact with the Field Experience Coordinator. To do so, Heidi contacts the Department Chair, searched through the university catalog, and/or department website. Once Heidi locates the name of the Field Experience Coordinator she is able set-up a meeting to discuss her field experience. Heidi used Exercise 9.1 to identify her Field Experience Coordinator and you can do the same.

Exercise 9.1 Identify Field Experience Coordinator

General Information

Name _____

Office Building/Number _____

Phone Number _____

Email Address _____

University Website (if applicable) _____

Appointment

Date _____

Time _____

Location _____

There are several academic exercises university departments may propose you submit when accepting a field experience. These exercises are designed to establish a link between classroom theory and professional practice. The academic requirements allows you to test your sport and physical activity skills, to provide the Field Experience Coordinator with your ability to apply classroom knowledge to practical situations, and to help the university maintain its academic mission (Duerden, 2009). For example, Heidi used Exhibit 9.2 to ask about requirements, expectations, and resources for her field experience. You can do the same when you meet with you Field Experience Coordinator.

Exhibit 9.2 University Requirements Expectations, and Resources

1. A specific Grade Point Average (GPA)

2. The completion of paperwork, such as an application and work agreement

3. CPR/First Aid training

4. Professional liability insurance

5. Appropriateness of the Field Experience site

6. Number of hours required for each field experience

7. Number and frequency of evaluations

8. Additional assignments and projects (marketing plan for campus recreation program or developing bulletin boards for a corporate fitness facility)

Complete Exercise 9.2 in finding additional information about your university field experience requirements, expectations, and resources.

Exercise 9.2 University Requirements, Expectations, and Resources

Course Name _____

Course Number _____

Pre-Requisites _____

Academic Credit Hours_____

Hours Needed to Complete Field Experience _____

_____

Paperwork to be Completed _____

Additional assignments and/or projects _____

_____

Step 2 - Create a List of Objectives

Palomares (Foster & Dollar, 2010) reported the absence of a clear objective or focus on what you want to accomplish often inhibits your ability to seek a field experience. For example, Mary is young in her academic major and begins her field experience search by establishing clear objectives. Mary answered the following six questions to develop her objectives for the field experience:

- **How would you describe your idea job?** Mary identified her ideal job working in youth sports for a recreation department, private club, public school, and/or community service organization.

- **What type of field experience would provide you with the necessary skills in order to obtain this type of position?** Mary identified a youth fitness and sport program at a public middle school as an opportunity to gain the necessary skills to obtain a career in youth sports.

- **What population would you like to work with?** Mary identified her population as youth.

- **What type of work environment do you prefer working in (indoors, outdoors, busy place, office)?** Mary prefers to work indoors and outdoors (depending on activity) but does not want to work in a office setting.

- **Can you afford an unpaid field experience?** Mary can afford an unpaid field experience which provides her with many opportunities.

- **Do you mind relocating for the field experience?** Mary does mind relocating because she only has to complete a 20 hour field experience.

Exhibit 9.3 provides a list of objectives Mary developed in deciding on an appropriate field experience.

Exhibit 9.3 List of Objectives – Mary – Field Experience – 20 hours
1. I want a youth sports job working for a recreation department, private club, public school, and/or community service organization.
2. I prefer working indoors/outdoors but do not want to work in an office.
3. I can afford an unpaid field experience.
4. I want to do my field experience with a local middle school.

Searching and Applying

The first two steps were established to make sure you do not waste valuable time pursuing a field experience. Now you need to become aware of potential field experiences that match with your objectives.

Mary, Eddie, and Heidi realized that becoming aware of potential field experiences can be a challenge without proper guidance. Thus, Mary, Eddie, and Heidi sought guidance about potential field experience opportunities from their Field Experience Coordinator (Bethell& Morgan, 2011). One goal of this guidance is to view the field experience site as physically and psychologically safe and secure (Schoepfer & Dodds, 2010). By no means can the field experience coordinator force you to accept a specific placement (Schoepfer & Dodds, 2010), however the coordinator can ensure the field experience has substance, presents all aspects of working within an organization or industry, and is appropriate from a curricular standpoint (Schoepfer & Dodds, 2010). Your coordinator may also evaluate the attributes of the agencies supervisor since he or she is the most significant person in making a decision whether you have a meaningful work experience. For example, your coordinator may be able to determine whether the supervisor is able to communicate, well-qualified, and respected (Foster & Dollar, 2010). Exhibit 9.4 provides a list of ways you can find potential field experience sites.

Complete Exercise 9.3 to develop your own objective in finding a field experience.

Exhibit 9.4 Awareness of Potential Field Experience Sites

1. The universities career center
2. The sport and physical activity department website
3. Field Experience bulletin boards
4. Websites specific to sport and physical activity
5. Other websites not specific to sport and physical activity
6. Directories and professional materials
7. Other ways to discover field experiences (volunteering, job shadowing, graduates or peers, alumni)

Exercise 9.3 Six Questions for Creating a List of Objectives

1. Describe your ideal job following graduation? _____
   _____

2. What type of field experience would provide you with the necessary skills in order to obtain this type of position? _____
   _____

3. What type of population would you like to work with? _____
   _____

4. What type of work environment do you prefer working in? (indoors, outdoors, busy place, office)? _____
   _____

5. Can you afford an unpaid field experience? _____
   _____

6. Do you mind relocating for the field experience? _____
   _____

Take the items from the six questions above in listing objectives in discovering an ideal field experience.

1. _____

2. _____

3. _____

4. _____

5. _____

6. _____

The University Career Center. Many companies use university career centers to fill their field experiences and entry-level positions. The career center has valuable resources and information. Exhibit 9.5 provides examples of career services resources. You may come in contact with career services in person or by going to your university website and clicking on the appropriate link.

Exhibit 9.5 Career Services Resources
1. Information on Upcoming Job Fairs
2. Information on Potential Field Experience Opportunities
3. Information on Job Postings (part-time and full-time)
4. Hot Links to Jobs
5. Recruiting Events such as Career and Job Fairs
6. Job Search Books
7. Subscriptions to Job Information
8. Directories of Job Information
9. Graduate School Information
10. Employer Information
11. Computer Resources
12. Career Testing
13. Career Seminars
14. Mock Interviewing/Interview Coaching
15. On-Campus Interviewing
16. Resume and Cover Letter Writing

Academic Department Websites. Academic department websites usually provide information on field experience opportunities. The website may have a list of potential field experiences with descriptions and the application procedures. The department may also have a listserv that informs you about new field experiences as they become available. This list serve keeps you up-to-date on any sport and physical activity field experiences available.

Websites Specific to Sport and Physical Activity. There are numerous websites to help you find a field experience. Some sites provide you with the opportunity to be placed on the organizations listserv, thus keeping you up-to-date on sport and physical activity field experience opportunities. Exhibit 9.6 provides a listing of the sport and physical activity organization and website.

Exhibit 9.6 Field Experience Websites in Sport and Physical Activity

1.	www.sportscareer.com	29.	www.sportslink.org
2.	www.teamworkonline.com	30.	www.gymjob.org
3.	www.sportswebcom	31.	www.exercisejobs.com
4.	www.sportsmanagement club.com	32.	www.ymca.net
5.	www.sportsbusinessdaily.com	33.	www.aerobics.com
6.	www.pbeo.com	34.	www.nsca-lift.org
7.	www.onlinesports.com	35.	www.nifs.org
8.	www.nassm.com	36.	www.hfit.com/careers/
9.	www.sportsemploymentnews.com		field experiences.cfm
10.	www.bluefishjobs.com	37.	www.acsm.medcareer
11.	www.ncaa.org	38.	www.hpcareer.net
12.	www.jobsinsports.com	39.	www.sportsmana
13.	www.canadiansport.com/jobs		www.gementworldwide.com
14.	www.iaam.org	40.	www.sportsjobsusa.com
15.	www.workinsports.com	41.	www.workinsports.com
16.	www.athleticlink.com	42.	www.indeed.com
17.	www.sportsfitnessnetwork.com	43.	www.smarter.com
18.	www.coolworks.com	44.	www.careers.aahperd.org
19.	www.sportsfitnessnetwork.com		**Specific to Women**
20.	www.cooperinst.org	1.	www.athleticlink.com
22.	www.leisurejobs.us	2.	www.womensportsjobs.com
23.	www.wellnessconnection.com	3.	www.nacwaa.org
24.	www.exercisecareers.com	4.	www.womensportsfoundation.org
25.	www.healthandwellnessjobs.com	5.	www.womensportswire.com
26.	www.phfr.com	6.	www.womenSportsJobs.com
27.	www.exercisejobs.com	7.	www.womensportsservices
28.	www.athletictrainer.com	8.	www.wiscnetwork.com
		9	www.wiscfoundation.org
		10.	www.womenssportslink.com
		11.	www.wnba.com

Other Websites not Specific to Sport and Physical Activity. There are several non sport and physical activity websites that may help you to find an appropriate field experience. Exhibit 9.7 provides a listing of other websites that may provide additional field experience opportunities.

Exhibit 9.7 Other Field Experience Websites
1. www.internsearch.com
2. www.MonsterTRAK.com
3. www.careerbuilder.com
4. www.monster.com
5. www.experience.com
6. www.careerplanning.about.com
7. www.bls.gov/oco
8. www.myspace.com

Directories, ListServes, and Professional Material. Exhibit 9.8 provides a listing of directories, listserves, and professional material providing a list of available field experiences in sport and physical activity.

Exhibit 9.8 Directories, Listserves, and Professional Material
1. American Alliance for Health, Physical Education, Recreation, and Dance (AAHPERD)
2. Fitness Connection
3. Fitness Management
4. Executive Job Opportunity List
5. Field experience Contact Directory
6. NCAA News
7. North American Society for Sport Management (NASSM) Listserv
8. Personal Fitness Trainer
9. Sport Business Journal
10. Sport Marketing Directory
11. Women in NASSM (WIN)

Other Ways to Discover Field experiences. There are other ways you may find out about potential field experiences. You may volunteer or shadow a professional. Job shadowing was an ideal for Mary because she was completing a 20 hour field experience and shadowed a professional in the field. Mary began her search by asking her professor to help her find a volunteer site to complete her 20 hour field experience. Once Mary decided on an appropriate field experience she set-up an appointment to work alongside a professional. Mary followed the professional for a day and learned what may be expected of her if she chose this career.

Campus-sponsored job fairs can be a productive way of finding a field experience (Foster & Dollar, 2010). These job fairs are usually sponsored by the career center on campus, a sport and physical activity department, or a community organization. Heidi and Eddie decided to explore the university job fair. Heidi and Eddie decided upon a university job fair because it was held on campus, lines were shorter than with a community job fair, and they were familiar with the site and felt comfortable. Heidi and Eddie were also able to visit with recent graduates, peers, and alumni at many of the booths and ask questions specific to the field experience site. Heidi and Eddie found the university fair was a good way to market themselves to perspective employers. Complete Exercise 9.4 to discover potential field experience opportunities.

Exercise 9.4 Potential Field experience Opportunities

1. Go to your Career Center and ask about services that will help you identify potential field experience sites _____

   _____

2. Go to the academic department website and identify field experience sites

   _____

   _____

3. List two field experience opportunities from four websites specific to your career in sport and physical activity _____

   _____

4. List two field experience opportunities from two websites not specific to sport and physical activity _____

   _____

5. List two field experience opportunities from two directories, listserves, or professional material specific to sport and physical activity _____

   _____

6. Choose two other ways you are going to obtain information on potential field experiences _____

   _____

Step 4 - Applying for Positions

Once Heidi and Eddie collected enough information about the agencies, matched their objectives to the field experience, and identified potential sites it was time for the application process. Each organization has its own application procedure in applying for a field experience. The cover letter and resume is the most common application process utilized by employers. For example, Heidi's initial contact was to email a copy of her cover letter (Chapter 4) and resume (Chapter 3) to the employer. Some employers prefer mail, but if given the choice it is more efficient and effective to use email. Next, Heidi was called by the employer to set-up a phone interview (Chapter 8) because she was one of the top candidates for the position. Heidi's phone interview was so impressive the employer invited her for an onsite interview.

Since you may not have the opportunity to be a finalist for all field experiences it is important you have many opportunities to interview by sending cover letters and resumes to multiple potential employers. If you do not hear from the employer within a week, make a follow-up phone call. The objective in obtaining a field experience is to "seal-the-deal" during your onsite interview.

Securing the Field experience

There are three steps in securing the field experience: (a) to interview at various sites, (b) to select a site, and (c) to sign a work agreement.

Step 5 — Interview at Various Sites

Once Heidi had an onsite interview scheduled she referred back to Chapter 8. She participated in mock interviews and focused on various aspects of the interview process. Since Heidi interviewed for more than one position she had many opportunities to select a site and therefore continued to the next step.

Step 6 —Select the Site

Heidi decided to revisit all the sites before making a decision. Heidi also requested the organization to supply her with the names and emails of previous interns so she could speak to them about their experiences at the site. It was important for Heidi to review all of the sites that contacted her and showed an interest. She had to think about all of the information collected and the conversations made with the employers. Heidi finally made a decision by asking herself a series of questions. The example below provides answers to one potential site (YMCA) she was highly considering:

- **Does the YMCA meet the needs of my objectives?** Heidi wants to eventually work for a non-profit health and fitness facility. The YMCA was a great field experience opportunity for her to complete.

- Will you have multiple exposures to different segments of the facility programming (read the field experience description, ask the supervisor, or research the organization website)? Heidi has a variety of experiences at the YMCA working with the youth and adult fitness center, wellness programming, group exercise, the pool, and facility management.

- Does the YMCA provide financial benefits during the field experience? Heidi discovers the field experience does not have financial benefits but feels like this is her best opportunity.

- Does the YMCA have a history of hiring interns part-time or full-time after completion of the experience? Heidi was excited to hear there were job opportunities following the field experience. Although the position may not be local she was willing to relocate.

- Will you be actively involved in the programming offered at the YMCA? Heidi would be in charge of the Fit for Kids programming.

- Will the field experience at the YMCA help to extend my existing skills? Heidi needed additional experience with wellness programming and realized this would be an opportunity to expand on those skills

- Will you accept the YMCA field experience? Heidi decided to accept the position at the YMCA and turn down the other offers.

If you have more than one site to choose from then it may be beneficial for you to complete Exercise 9.5.

Exercise 9.5 Questions to Ask when Selecting an Field experience

1. Does the site meet the needs of my objectives?

   Site 1 _____

   Site 2 _____

2. Will I have multiple exposures to different segments of the facility programming (read the field experience description, ask the supervisor, or research the organization website)?

   Site 1 _____

   Site 2 _____

3. Does the field experience site have any financial benefits?

   Site 1 _____

   Site 2 _____

4. Does the facility have a history of hiring interns part-time or full-time after graduation?

   Site 1 _____

   Site 2 _____

5. Will you be actively involved in the management of the activity?

    Site 1 _____

    Site 2 _____

6. Will the field experience help you to develop and extend your existing skill set?

    Site 1 _____

    Site 2 _____

7. What kind of supervision and feedback will be available?

    Site 1 _____

    Site 2 _____

8. Identify the final field experience selection

    _____

After Heidi made her final decision she notified all employers. Heidi decided to call all of her employers, although she did have a well-written letter indicating her intent to accept or withdraw from consideration. Exhibit 9.9 provides a sample of Heidi's withdraw from consideration to one of her potential sites. Heidi chooses to send this message to the other sites via email.

Exhibit 9.9 Withdraw from Consideration

November 22, 2014

John Simmons

The Fitness Zone
Director of Health and Wellness
1324 Main Street
Boulder, CO 34567

Dear Mr. Simmons:

I wanted to thank you for the offer to complete my field experience Fitness Zone. I do not believe the field experience at Fitness Zone meets the needs of my goals and objectives. Therefore, I am withdrawing my name for consideration. Thank you again for the opportunity.

Sincerely,

Heidi Gail

Heidi Gail

Step 7 - Sign the Field Experience Work Agreement

The final step for Heidi was to have all parties, including representative of the university, the academic program and the sponsoring organization to sign an appropriate field experience agreement. Heidi's field experience work agreement was two pages and consisted of demographic information about herself and the field experience site, learning objectives, job responsibilities, supervision description, details about the evaluation process, and acknowledgment you are seeking credit (Foster & Dollar, 2010; Schoepfer & Dodds, 2010). Heidi had to sign the document and get signatures from her Field Experience Coordinator, and the site supervisor.

Summary

The field experience is an essential link between classroom knowledge and the "real world." There are many benefits of the field experience the agencies, and the university.

A well-planned field experience search and selection process illustrates you are taking responsibility in defining direction for your future career. It is now up to you to take full advantage of what the field experience has to offer.

Frequently Asked Questions

How do you know what is the best way to find an field experience?

The first step is to get in contact with your Field Experience Coordinator and allow him or her to point you in the right direction.

Do you really need to contact an organization if you do not accept the field experience?

You should never burn bridges. By contacting the organization you are building a network which can be extremely important if you need assistance in the future. You are also showing that you are professional and warrant consideration for future positions.

Is it better to contact the employer via phone, email or mail when withdrawing or declining an field experience offer?

A phone call would be the best method, however sending a withdraw or decline letter via email provides the employer with ample time to extend another offer.

Student Learning Activities

Complete the field experience exploration exercises throughout this chapter.

Form small groups and solicit each other's input regarding potential field experience sites.

➢ Potential Field Experience Opportunities Checklist
❑ Find out about your university requirements
❑ Create a list of objectives you would like to accomplish during the field experience
❑ Identify potential sites that could help in reaching your goals
❑ Apply for the field experience
❑ Prepare for the interview (s)
❑ Select an field experience site
❑ Sign an field experience work agreement
❑ Begin your field experience

CAREER HIGHLIGHT – ASSISTANT HEALTH & WELLNESS DIRECTOR (YMCA)

Christen Mitchell

Assistant Health & Wellness Director

Lowell & Helen Dunigan Family YMCA of

Southwestern Indiana

Evansville, IN

Education And Certifications

B.S. General Physical Education from University of Southern Indiana, Evansville, IN

CPR/First Aid, AED/Oxygen, Child Abuse Prevention, YMCA Cycling Instructor, YMCA Group Exercise Instructor, YMCA Personal Trainer, SilverSneakers MSROM & SilverSneakers II Cardio Circuit Instructor, YMCA Healthy Lifestyle Principles, YMCA Circuit Training

Years In Position

5 year

Previous Positions

Wellness staff positions at various facilities

Current Job Responsibilities And Hours

Supervisor responsibilities, recruits, trains, and develops part-time wellness staff, conduct performance appraisals, reward and discipline wellness staff, monitors and updates all required staff certifications, address complaints and resolves problems, conduct regular staff meetings for wellness and personal trainers, promote and incorporate YMCA mission and core values (respect, responsibility, honesty, caring, faith), participate in community health fairs, program statistics, monitor field experience program, assist in branch fundraising and special events, assume Health & Wellness Director responsibilities in her absence, scheduling of wellness staff and personal trainers, performs duties of fitness instructors, wellness staff and personal trainers as required by absence of staff, monitor daily operations, safety standards and policies. Typically works 30-35 hours a week.

Greatest Challenges

Finding enough time during the day to get the "paperwork" done and also interact with the members and provide great member service. Working for the YMCA you realize that the members truly are your number one priority. We strive to provide the best member service by enhancing their spirit, mind and body.

Career Advice

A great starting point would be to work as a staff person and do what you may eventually be asking them to do as an administrator. It is definitely beneficial to see exactly how it is on the wellness floor by working on the floor. As administrators we tend to be in and out and miss out on what is happening in our area. It is also a great way to earn the respect from your employees if they know that you have done what you are asking of them. Personally, I lead by example and would not ask my staff to do anything that I would not do myself. I feel like this has been very beneficial for my career. I would also suggest that you get as many certifications that you can and attend as many seminars or fitness events that you can as well. The more knowledge you have, the better the supervisor you can be.

CAREER HIGHLIGHT – EXECUTIVE DIRECTOR (YMCA)

Boyd A. Williams

Executive Director

Edward Jones Family YMCA

A Branch of the YMCA of Greater St. Louis, MO

Education And Certifications

BS in Physical Education with emphasis in Sport Management

Many within YMCA certification process: Trainer, Fiscal Management and Budgeting, Certified YMCA Senior Director

Years In Position

6 ½ years

Previous Positions

CEO of the Stevens Point Area YMCA, Stevens Point, WI

Associate Executive Director, Milwaukee, WI

Youth and Family Director, Neenah, WI

Current Job Responsibilities And Hours

Branch Operations, Fiscal Management and Budgeting, Board Development, Financial Development, Staff Supervision and Development, Membership Development - Typically works 50-60 hours per week in season.

Greatest Challenges

Maintaining a competitive, winning advantage over variables within the marketplace including like providers, economic factors, local business trends, employee training and maintaining high level of expectation for members and participants. Working in a not-for-profit, human service institution, and the ability to secure dollars in fundraising efforts has become increasingly difficult due to the number of organizations competing for the same dollars.

Career Advice

Number one, find a field you have a passion for. Determine what the motivating factors are that drives your interest in the field and determine if your interest is a sustainable, long-term interest. In my work with the YMCA, I have a passion for helping people and knowing the work the YMCA is doing in local communities has value and can help to make our communities a better place to work and live.

I recommend gathering as much information from the organization as one can to include volunteering, whether through an field experience or through the organization directly. One must determine if the field or interest matches their personal beliefs and values. All successful professionals I have met, in the YMCA or in other related areas have one characteristic in common, passion.

References

Bower, G. G. (2013) Utilizing Kolb's Experiential Learning Theory to implement a golf scramble. *International Journal of Sport Management*, Recreation, and Tourism, 12, (1), 29-56.

Bethell, S. & Morgan, K. (2011). Problem-based and experiential learning: Engaging students in an undergraduate physical education Theory. *Journal of Hospitality, Leisure, Sport, &Tourism Education*, 10(1), 128-134.

Duerden, M. D. (2010). Theory and practice of experiential education.*Journal of Leisure Research*, 42(4), 653-655.

Foster, S. B., & Dollar, J. E. (2010). *Experiential learning in sport management: Internships and beyond*. Morgantown: WV: Fitness Information Technology.

Schoepfer, K. L., & Dodds, M. (2010). Internships in sport management curriculum: Should legal implications of experiential learning result in the elimination of the sport management internship. *Marquette Sports Law Review*, 21(1), 182-201.

10

FINDING AND ACCEPTING FULL-TIME EMPLOYMENT IN SPORT AND PHYSICAL ACTIVITY

SCENARIO #1 – COMPLETED INTERNSHIP

Rachel

Rachel completed her internship, and she is ready to begin applying for full-time employment. Throughout her four years in college she made a considerable amount of professional development progress. She developed and focused on her four-year career plan in pursuing a career in sport and physical activity. Each field experience provided her with experience and a list of professionals for her network. Rachel needs to begin a new chapter of her life in seeking full-time employment. Rachel discovers that finding a job is competitive, but is confident in her abilities she could offer to a campus recreation facility. She developed one relationship through her internship with Indiana University Division of Campus Recreational Sports. She was supervised under the direction of Joanne Orrange (career highlight end of the chapter). Joanne Orrange was the Assistant Director of Special Events within IU Division of Campus Recreational Sports. Joanne provided her with a list of job opportunities to pursue. Rachel prepares herself by refocusing her sites on finding a job not a field experience.

You have completed your field experience and now you are ready to find a full-time job. How do you begin? Where do you look? Both of these questions are valid and each individual approaches the job search in a unique way. You do not need to begin from scratch because you have learned valuable ways to find employment. This chapter combines all of the exercises from this book and refocuses them in finding a full-time job. Rachel completed the step-by-step procedures and guidelines in finding and accepting a job. Begin with Exhibit 10.1 in taking one final look at what you need to do in order to obtain the job of your dreams.

Exhibit 10.1 Step-by-Step Procedures and Guidelines in Finding and Accepting a Job

1. Research job openings

2. Update professional development material

3. Apply for positions

4. Prepare for the interview

5. Evaluating a job offer

   a. culture

   b. location

   c. job responsibilities

   d. salary

   e. benefits

   f. professional development opportunities

   g. advancement opportunities

7. Accept or reject a job offer

8. On the job

   a. professionalism

   b. be a role model

   c. dedication and hard work

   d. respect for others

   e. accountability

   f. adhere to ethical standards

   g. stay up-to-date on new research findings

Step 1 – Research Job Openings

Once you have determined your career objective it is time to begin researching job openings. As mentioned in Chapter 9, there are many resources that assisted in finding a field experience. Take those same resources to find a job. Rachel chose to research her job openings by referring to her network and professional websites. Rachel sought guidance from her Internship Supervisor – Joanne Orrange. Joanne was able to refer her to two positions of interest. The first position was with Indiana University Southeast and the second position was with Kentucky Wesleyan. Rachel also sought guidance from www.nassm.org because of its reputation of being the premier internet portal for finding internships in sport and physical activity. Rachel listed all of her potential job openings by including the following information:

- Name of resource

- Name of organization or company

- Position

- Contact information

- Application protocol

Exhibit 10.2 provides a sample of how Rachel researched her job opening by using her network. Rachel used the same format as she researched job openings through the NASSM website.

Exhibit 10.2 Research Job Openings

1. **List resource** Joanne Orrange, Assistant Director Indiana University Recreational Sports_____

   Name of organization/company Indiana University Southeast Campus RecreationDepartment_____

   Position Special Events Coordinator for Campus Recreation _____

   _____

   Contact information Gail Kemp, Director of Campus Recreation at Indiana University Southeast _____

   Application protocol Resume and three references postmarked by October 2014

Complete Exercise 10.1 to research potential job openings.

Exercise 10.1 Potential Job Openings

1. List resource _____

    Name of organization/company _____

    Position _____

    Contact information _____

    Application protocol _____

2. List resource _____

    Name of organization/company _____

    Position _____

    Contact information _____

    Application protocol _____

3. List resource _____

    Name of organization/company _____

    Position _____

    Contact information _____

    Application protocol _____

4. List resource _____

    Name of organization/company _____

    Position _____

    Contact information _____

    Application protocol _____

Step 3 — Update Professional Development Material

Your professional development material needs to be updated before you can apply for a job. The professional development material that you want to focus on includes the following:

- Resume
- Cover letter
- Showcase portfolio

Resume

Chapters 1 and 3 discussed the absence of clear objective inhibiting your ability to seek a field experience that may lead to a career. You need to review the objective you listed on your resume in Chapter 3 (Exercise 3.2) specific to the field experience. This objective was good for the field experience but needs to be updated according to the job you are seeking. For example, Exhibit 10.3 shows Rachel's field experience career objective.

Exhibit 10.3 Resume Objective for Field Experience

Self-motivated college student with a strong work ethic evident through perseverance to finish projects and accomplish objectives. Seeking an internship with a recreational sports facility where I can utilize my knowledge of coordinating special events.

Rachel updated the objective to focus on the Special Events Coordinator within Indiana Southeast Campus Recreation Department (Exhibit 10.1). Notice in Exhibit 10.4 how Rachel is specific with the position she is applying for and the experience she gained by completing an internship with Indiana University.

Exhibit 10.4 Updated Resume Objective

Self-motivated graduate with a strong work ethic evident through perseverance to finish projects and accomplish objectives. Seeking the **Special Events Coordinator** position with Indiana University Southeast's Campus Recreation Department. Completed an internship with Indiana University Division of Campus Recreational Sports where I developed skills coordinating events such as the annual alumni golf outing, glow bowling, and NCAA basketball student tournament.

Cover Letter

The cover letter is also important to update before sending to an employer. The introductory material is a matter of including the appropriate date and the name and address of the employer where you are applying for the position. You also want to make updates to the first three paragraphs. For example, Exhibit 9.5 provides a sample of Rachel's first paragraph for the internship position she applied for at Indiana University.

Complete Exercise 10.2 to update your objective for the job you are seeking. Refer to your original objective and then focus on the research conducted to find your desired position.

Exercise 10.2 Career Objective

Original objective _____

_____

_____

_____

Desired job

List resource _____

Name of organization/company _____

_____

Position _____

Contact information _____

Application protocol _____

Updated objective _____

_____

_____

_____

_____

Exhibit 10.5 Original Cover Letter – First Paragraph

Please consider my application for the internship position at Indiana University that was advertised on the NASSM website. I am currently a student in the Sports Administration Program at the University of Kansas-Lawrence. My coursework provides me with a complete preparation for a variety of management positions in the sports industry within campus recreation.

Exhibit 10.6 provides an updated version of Rachel's cover letter in applying for the Special Events Coordinator at Indiana University Southeast. Notice how Rachel makes minor changes including where she found out about the position and the valuable experience she gained in completing an internship focused on special events.

Exhibit 10.6 Updated Cover Letter – First Paragraph

Please consider my application for the Special Events Coordinator at Indiana University Southeast. I recently graduated with a Sports Administration Bachelor of Science degree from the University of Kansas-Lawrence. I found out about the position from my former Internship Coordinator, Joanne Orrange. I recently completed my internship at Indiana University within the Recreational Sports Division. My focus during this internship was in special events. My knowledge and skills along with my degree in Sport Administration makes me an excellent candidate for the Special Events Coordinator at Indiana University Southeast.

Complete Exercise 10.3 to update the first paragraph of your cover letter specific to the job you are seeking. Refer to your original first paragraph of your cover letter and then focus on the job description to update the letter.

Exercise 10.3 Updated Cover Letter – First Paragraph

Original first paragraph_____

_____

_____

_____

Desired job List resource_____

Name of organization/compan _____

Position _____

Contact information _____

Application protocol _____

Updated first paragraph_____

_____

_____

_____

_____

Exhibit 10.7 provides a sample of Rachel's second paragraph.

Exhibit 10.7 Original Cover Letter – Second Paragraph

My work history includes the last two years as a Special Events Volunteer for the Parks and Recreation Department of Hendersonville, KY. I worked closely with Barb Huntington, Director of Athletics, and Joe Vincent, Director of Parks and Recreation Operations. During this time, I assisted with all of the major organizing and planning of sports leagues and events while also conducting both junior and adult sports clinics.

Exhibit 10.8 provides an updated version of Rachel's cover letter in applying for the Special Events Coordinator at Indiana University Southeast. Notice how Rachel incorporates her previous experience with her internship to make a clear connection that she has the background for the Special Events Coordinator at Indiana University Southeast.

Exhibit 10.8 Updated Cover Letter – Second Paragraph

In addition to my internship with the Indiana University Recreational Sports Department, I also worked two years as a Special Events Volunteer for the Parks and Recreation Department of Hendersonville, KY. I worked closely with Barb Huntington, Director of Athletics, and Joe Vincent, Director of Parks and Recreation Operations. I assisted with all of the major organizing and planning of sports leagues and events while also conducting both junior and adult sports clinics. Both of these experiences, along with my academic accomplishments, provide me with a strong background and knowledge that I believe is needed to become the Special Events Coordinator at Indiana University Southeast.

Complete Exercise 10.4 to update the second paragraph of you cover letter for the job you are seeking. Refer to your original second paragraph of your cover letter and then focus on the job description to update the letter.

Exercise 10.4 Updated Cover Letter – Second Paragraph

Original second paragraph _____

_____

_____

_____

_____

Desired job _____

List resource Name of organization/company _____

Position _____

Contact information _____

Application protocol _____

Updated second paragraph_____

_____

_____

_____

_____

Exhibit 10.9 provides a sample of Rachel's third paragraph.

Exhibit 10.9 Original Cover Letter – Third Paragraph

Please consider myself as a possible candidate for this internship. I am available for contact by telephone, 435-235-6859, or via e-mail, rthomas@kl.edu. Thank you and I look forward to hearing from you soon.

Exhibit 10.10 provides an updated version of Rachel's cover letter in applying for the Special Events Coordinator at Indiana University Southeast. Rachel simply changes the word "internship" to the specific job she is applying for.

Exhibit 10.10 Original Cover Letter – Third Paragraph

Please consider myself as a possible candidate for the Special Events Coordinator at Indiana University Southeast. I am available for contact by telephone, 435-235-6859, or via e-mail, rthomas@kl.edu. Thank you and I look forward to hearing from you soon.

Complete Exercise 10.5 to update the third paragraph of you cover letter for the job you are seeking. Refer to your original third paragraph of your cover letter and then focus on the job description to update the letter.

Exercise 10.5 Updated Cover Letter – Third Paragraph

Original third paragraph _____

_____

_____

_____

Desired job _____

List resource _____

Name of organization/company_____

Position _____

Contact information _____

Application protocol _____

Updated third paragraph_____

_____

_____

_____

Showcase Portfolio

There are several areas of the showcase portfolio that you want to update including those listed in Exhibit 10.11.

Exhibit 10.11 Showcase Portfolio
I.   Cover letter and resume
II. Self-Statement, Career Plan, and Academic Plan
III. Sample of Work Related and/or Service Materials
■ Academic
■ Employment
■ Volunteer
■ Field experience
IV. Professional Development Materials
■ Memberships to university and professional clubs and/or organizations

- ■ Certifications (i.e., first aid, CPR, personal training)
- ■ Continuing Education
- ■ Scholarship
- ■ Awards
- ■ Research Presentations
- ■ Research Publications

V. Support Materials - Letters of Recommendation (at least 3)

- ■ Professor
- ■ Advisor
- ■ Professional or employer in the field
- ■ Include faculty/employer biography for each letter of recommendation

Complete Exercise 10.6 to update all areas of your showcase portfolio.

➤ Exercise 10.6 Showcase Portfolio Checklist

❑ Cover Letter and Resume

❑ Self-Statement, Career Plan, and Academic Plan

❑ Sample of Work Related and/or Service Materials

- ■ Academic
- ■ Employment
- ■ Volunteer
- ■ Field experience

❑ Professional Development Materials

- ■ Memberships to university and professional clubs and/or organizations
- ■ Certifications (i.e., first aid, CPR, personal training)
- ■ Continuing Education
- ■ Scholarship
- ■ Awards
- ■ Research Presentations
- ■ Research Publications

Support Materials - Letters of Recommendation (at least 3)

- Professor
- Advisor
- Professional or employer in the field
- Include faculty/employer biography for each letter of recommendation

Exercise 10.7 Job Database

1. Name of organization _____

    Position _____

    Contact information _____

    Date applied _____

    Verification of receiving application information _____

    Follow-up phone call on the status of the position _____

2. Name of organization _____

    Position _____

    Contact information _____

    Date applied _____

    Verification of receiving application information _____

    Follow-up phone call on the status of the position _____

3. Name of organization _____

    Position _____

    Contact information _____

    Date applied _____

    Verification of receiving application information _____

    Follow-up phone call on the status of the position _____

4. Name of organization _____

    Position _____

    Contact information _____

    Date applied _____

    Verification of receiving application information _____

    Follow-up phone call on the status of the position _____

Step 3 — Apply for Positions

Now that you have researched specific job openings and updated your material it is time to apply for the positions. You want to prepare in the event someone contacts you about a job. You may choose to include your cellular phone number on the resume so the employer can get in contact with you at various times of the day. If you decide not to include your cellular phone then make sure you have an answering machine available for your home phone. The message should be appropriate and professional. You should also set-up a database of the jobs you applied for and those that have contacted you. This list of names can also be used to contact those employers you have not heard from. A handheld organizer can be used to set-up your interviews. Complete Exercise 10.7 to develop your job database.

Step 4 — Prepare for the Interview

You have been contacted by the employer about interviewing for a job. You referred to Chapter 6 and Exhibit 10.12 to prepare for the interview.

Exhibit 10.12 Step-by-Step Procedures and Guidelines to Interviewing
Step 1 - Preparation – Before the Interview
1. Knowing what you can do
2. Research perspective employer
3. Practice answering and asking questions
4. Appearance
Step 2 - Day of the Interview - Meeting the employer
5. Arrive early
6. Check appearance
7. Give a firm handshake and maintain good eye contact
8. Act interested
9. Avoid annoying behavior (tapping hand on desk, frequent "ummm," etc)
10. Use the employers formal name
11. Answering questions
12. Ask questions
Step 3 - The Follow-Up
13. Thank you letter
14. JIST Card

Step 5 — Evaluate Job Offer

How do you know this is the job to accept if offered the position? You can never be too sure, but taking your time and considering important job factors could make a difference in your decision to accept a position. For example, Rachel was offered the Special Events Coordinator position at Indiana University Southeast. Before Rachel accepted the position she made her decision by evaluating several factors related to the job offer including:

- Culture

- Location

- Job responsibilities

- Salary

- Benefits

- Professional development and advancement opportunities

Culture

The culture "includes a company's values, practices, and goals and the way it goes about achieving them" (Prete, 2011). The culture needs to be considered when evaluating a job because you want to make sure the values of the company or organization are in line with those you choose. Rachel discovered this information by researching Indiana University Southeast's website for their vision and/or mission statement, goals, and diversity information. Complete Exercise 9.8 to determine the values of the company or organization.

Exercise 10.8 Values of the Company

1. Name of organization _____

   Vision Statement _____

   _____

   Mission Statement _____

   _____

   Goals _____

   _____

   Diversity Information _____

   _____

2. Name of organization _____

   Vision Statement _____

   _____

Mission Statement _____

_____

Goals _____

_____

Diversity Information _____

_____

3.   Name of organization _____
     Vision Statement _____

_____

Mission Statement _____

_____

Goals _____

_____

Diversity Information _____

_____

Location

Although you may not have many options for your first job offer, location may
still play a factor into the acceptance or rejection of a job. Ask yourself a series
of questions before applying for a position that you would never accept due
to location. Are you willing to relocate? Is the job located where you want to
live? Is the job near shopping and restaurants? How long is your commute
to work? What mode of transportation is available? What is the cost of the
commute? Complete Exercise 10.9 to determine how much location is a factor
in accepting a position.

Exercise 10.9 Location Questions

1.   Are you willing to relocate? _____

2.   Is the job located where you want to live? _____

3.   Is the job near shopping and restaurants? _____

4.   How long is your commute to work? _____

5.   What mode of transportation is available? _____

6.   What is the cost of commuting? _____

Job Responsibilities

It is important to consider job responsibilities. What will your role be within the company? Is this role something you could play on a daily basis? Is the work challenging enough? Does the position match-up with my career goals? Will you have to travel and is this something you want to do? Complete Exercise 10.10 in finding your additional information on job responsibilities for the position.

Exercise 9.10 Job Responsibilities

1. What will your role be within the company? _____

2. Is this role something I could play on a daily basis? _____

3. Is the work challenging enough? _____

4. Does the position match-up with my career goals? _____

5. Will I travel and is this something that I want to do? _____

Salary

You do not want to accept the position on salary alone but it is an important aspect of the job offer. People working for salary alone tend to become unhappy once the newness of the position wears off (Collins, 2010). Will you be making enough money to cover cost of living? How often is your pay reviewed? How is your pay reviewed? Are there bonuses? Once you have found out specifics about salary then you need to make a realistic budget before making any decisions. Complete Exercise 10.11 to determine if the salary is something that you could live with if you accepted the position?

Benefits

You want to look at the benefits in terms of medical coverage, life insurance, holidays, sick leave, vacation, retirement plans, flex time, dental plans, and tuition reimbursement. The big question is what the employer is going to contribute to these plans? Not every company has these benefits and you need to decide what is best for your future. Complete Exercise 10.12 to answer your questions about benefits.

Exercise 10.11 Salary Expectations

1. Will you be making enough money to cover the cost of living? _____

2. How often is your pay reviewed? _____

3. How often is your pay reviewed? _____

4. Are there bonuses? _____

5. Develop a realistic budget:

Income

   Salary _____

   Other Income _____

Expenditures

   Rent or mortgage payment _____

   Electric _____

   Water _____

   Cable _____

   Phone _____

   Gas _____

   Garbage pick-up _____

   School loan _____

   Car _____

   Other debt _____

   Other debt _____

   Other debt _____

   Income – Expenditures = _____

Exercise 10.12 Benefits

What coverage is the employer going to contribute to these plans?

Medical coverage _____

Life insurance _____

Holidays _____

Sick leave _____

Vacation _____

Retirement plan _____

Flex time _____

Dental plan _____

Tuition reimbursement _____

Professional Development and Advancement Opportunities

It is very important that you continue to grow as a professional in your field. One area often overlooked when accepting a job is the professional development and advancement opportunities offered. Regardless if you see yourself in a management position you want to develop as a professional and funds needed to be available in order to do this. What opportunities are available for career growth? What specific programs are developed to prepare you for advancement? Is there a fund for professional development and if so what is the limit per employee? Complete Exercise 10.13 to determine the professional development and advancement opportunities of the job you are being offered.

Exercise 10.13 Professional Development and Advancement Opportunities

What opportunities are available for career growth? _____

_____

What specific programs are developed to prepare you for advancement? _____

_____

Is there a fund for professional development and if so what is the limit per employee? _____

_____

Step 7 – Accept or Reject the Job Offer

Although there is not a right or wrong way to determine whether to accept or reject a job offer the decision should reflect the factors discussed in the previous section. These factors are a reflection of your priorities and need to be considered before accepting or rejecting a job offer. You do not want to delay the acceptance of a job offer once you have established the job is right for you. The quickest way to accept the job offer is to call the employer (Collins, 2010). When calling the employer you need to make sure to follow these guidelines:

- Accept terms of employer's offer
- Reiterate terms of employment agreement
- Give specific starting date
- Express the willingness to complete training before the starting date
- Indicate confidence in doing the work set-forth
- Thank those involved in the hiring process
- Express excitement for the job

Complete Exercise 10.14 to prepare a script of what you may say to an employer when accepting a job. Have the script available when you call the employer.

Exercise 10.14 Accepting the Job Offer

Accept the terms of employment _____

Reiterate terms of employment agreement _____

Express the willingness to complete training before the starting date _____

_____

Indicate confidence in doing the work set-forth _____

_____

Thank those involved in the hiring process _____

_____

Express excitement for the job _____

_____

Take all of the sentences above and complete your script for the acceptance phone call _____

_____

_____

If you decide this job is not what you want then it is important to keep a good relationship with this employer. In other words you do not want to "burn bridges" because you never know what a good relationship with this employer could mean for your future. You want to make sure to follow these guidelines when calling an employer to reject a job:

- Express reason for rejecting job offer

- Thank those involved in the hiring process

- Be brief and to the point

- Thank the company or organization for consideration

- Close on a positive note

Complete Exercise 10.15 to prepare a script of what you may say to an employer when rejecting a job. Have the script available when you call the employer.

Exercise 10.15 Rejecting the Job Offer

Express reasons for rejecting the job offer_____

_____

Thank those involved in the hiring process _____

_____

Be brief and to the point _____

_____

Thank the company or organization for consideration _____

_____

Close on a positive note _____

Take all of the sentences above and complete your script for the rejection

phone call _____

_____

_____

_____

On the Job

You did it! You accepted your first job. You are now ready to venture into marketing yourself effectively to the employer in a professional manner. Professionalism means "exhibiting high levels of professional competence and conduct, possessing required credentials, presenting accurate and truthful information about the programs and services provided, and exemplifying a commitment to a healthy, active lifestyle" (Wuest, 2011, p. 396). To effectively market yourself and make a good first impression you must begin to understand the qualities of professionalism (Wuest, 2011) including:

- To be a Role Model

- Dedication and hard work

- Respect for others

- Accountability

- Adhere to ethical standards

- Stay up-to-date on new research findings

To be a Role Model

Being a good role model is "practice what you preach." First impressions do make a difference. You want to make sure you are dressing in the appropriate manner, are well-groomed, and take good care of yourself. For example, Rachel wants to make sure to take good care of herself because she is in a physically active profession. In taking good care of herself it is important she attempts to follow the professional model of an active lifestyle set forth through the National Association for Sport and Physical Education (NASPE) of 30 minutes a day of moderate physical activities on most days of the week and vigorous aerobic activities 3 to 6 times a week (NASPE, 2014). She also wants to participate in an activity strength training routine where she lifts 2 to 3 times a week and flexibility exercises 3 to 7 times a week (NASPE, 2014). Rachel believes this active lifestyle is important for all sport and physical activity professionals who want to model appropriate behavior while being committed to what they preach.

Dedication and Hard Work

As a working professional you need to dedicate yourself to the profession. This means setting goals to what you want to accomplish in this work setting. For example, Rachel set goals of showing up for work on time, staying late if the job warrants it, and being committed to Indiana University Southeast's mission statement.

Respect for Others

You must respect others at your workplace. You may not always agree with decisions but respecting others is important. In addition you must be aware sport and physical activity fields are becoming more diverse. You must understand the diverse needs of others so you become a professional that can effectively provide services in multicultural environments.

Accountability

Accountability is having the credentials you say you have when accepting a position. Accountability is a professional obligation that makes you an honest and trustworthy person. For example, Rachel indicated she had two years of experience working as a volunteer for Henderson Parks and Recreation Department. The Henderson parks and Recreation Supervisor may complete a reference check to confirm her information.

Adhere to Ethical Standards

Ethical standards are set to "serve as guidelines for actions and aid in decision making" (Wuest, 2011, p. 397). For example, Rachel discovered that Indiana University Southeast set an ethical standard where serious relationships may not exist between employees. Rachel must consider this ethical standard before making a decision to ask a fellow employee out on a date.

Stay Up-to-Date on New Research Findings

Just because you have a position does not mean it is time to relax and forget about what is happening in the field. You can stay up-to-date on the newest research findings by taking advantage of continuing education courses, workshops, conferences, and reading professional journals. You can also play an active role in advancing the field by sharing new research. As seen through the qualities of professionalism, there are many different meanings but overall we can agree professionalism reflects a commitment to the field, a respect for others and those in the field.

Summary

Congratulations! Your work has paid off. The professional development exercises you completed in this book has been the best investment you have ever completed in preparing yourself for a position in sport and physical activity. The dividends received from completing these exercises are worth the time and energy for you as a future professional. Although you may have your sights set on a particular job you need to remember that "every journey begins with a single step and with each new step, the objectives comes into clearer view and as always give back to those who are less fortunate than you. No matter how hard you have worked to get where you are now, there is always someone who has not had the same opportunities that you had in life. Do you best to give something back" (Krueger, 2003, pg 326). Best of luck with your journey after college!

Frequently Asked Questions

What if you cannot find a suitable job?

You need not be discourages. You may need more experience and should consider going back to school or accepting an additional internship. Maybe you need to expand your network or polish your resume to represent yourself better. Remember, the time you put into your job search is time well spent if you keep focused on goals. Continue searching and eventually you will find the job you were looking for.

Should you negotiate salary if you offered a position?

You need to learn about salaries for positions you are seeking. It is hard to negotiate salary when you are beginning your career. If you decide to negotiate salary be aware that you could possibly create tension between yourself and your future boss.

When offered a job is it okay to ask for a few days to think about it?

An employer is not going to be surprised if you take a few days to think about the position. However, you do want to stay away from saying phrases such as "I need time to think because I am waiting hear from another company," or "I need to check with my friends to see what they think." Consider saying, "This is a big decision so I need additional time," or "I would like some additional time to think this through."

Student Learning Activities

Complete the exercises throughout the chapter to find and accept a job.

Get into small groups and solicit each other's input regarding the potential jobs.

Practice your follow-up conversation with a fellow-student.

Accepting a Job Checklist

- ❑ **Research job openings**
- ❑ **Update professional development material**
- ❑ **Apply for positions**
- ❑ **Prepare for the interview**
- ❑ **Evaluate the job offer**
  - ❑ Culture
  - ❑ Location
  - ❑ Job responsibilities
  - ❑ Salary
  - ❑ Professional development opportunities
  - ❑ Advancement opportunities
- ❑ **Accept or reject the job offer**
- ❑ **On the job**
  - ❑ Professionalism
  - ❑ Be a role model
  - ❑ Dedication and hard work
  - ❑ Respect for others
  - ❑ Accountability
  - ❑ Adhere to ethical standards
  - ❑ Stay up-to-date on new research findings

CAREER HIGHLIGHT – ASSISTANT DIRECTOR RECREATIONAL SPORTS

Joanne Orrange

Assistant Director for Special Events

IU Division of Campus Recreational Sports

Bloomington, IN

Education and Certifications

-B.S.Recreation and Leisure Studies from State University of New York (SUNY) College at Brockport (1996); M.S. Recreational Sports Administration from Indiana University (1999)

-Certified Recreational Sports Specialist; CPR/First Aid Instructor Certified

Years in Position

9 years

Previous Positions

Assistant Director of Intramurals - Cornell University - 3 years

Graduate Assistant of Intramurals - Indiana University - 2 years

Current Job Responsibilities and Hours

Program Division Wide Special events such as: Summer Orientation, Welcome Week (RecFest), Semester Kick-Off, monthly Family Night, Jill Behrman Run for the End Zone 5K run/walk; Facility Use Counseling; Risk Management – oversee SET Instructors and assist with other aspects of the Division's Risk Management plan; Division wide special projects – coordinate and lead work groups in projects such as: Interior signage, furniture, recognition; Participants feedback system; Wellness Initiative Projects; Serve on Division and Campus Wide committees such as Outreach, CARE Committee, Disability Roundtable, etc.

The typical hours varies depend on what events are coming up. I definitely don't work a typical 9am-5pm day. I would have to say that I average about 40-50 hours a week. Some weeks are slower than others where I may work 20 or 30 and still be able to get done what needs to. Then there are other weeks where I am working 50-

60 hours to get everything done. It all evens out in the end and I enjoy the variety of this type of schedule. It never gets dull or boring! J

Greatest Challenges

Since I have been here for a little while now I am always trying to challenge myself to keep things new and fresh and not get complacent with the events that I program. I don't want things to become boring but always looking for ways to improve or try new ideas.

Motivation can be a challenge because I find that many of my events I need to motivate our entire staff to get on board during times of the year when everyone is stretched really thin. I also need to motivate a number of student volunteers who help with these events. So motivation is something that I continue to work with.

Career Advice

Get involved!! There are so many different areas within Recreation and the only way you will know which one will best suit you is to get out and experience as much as you can. Internships and summer jobs are a great way to have these experiences. I know that I learned so much from all the different experiences I had the opportunity to take advantage of. The other piece of advice is to never stop learning…..there is so much we can do to continue to improve the recreational experience that we cannot become complacent in what we do as professionals. We need to be open to learn from our participants, colleagues, and other professionals!

CAREER HIGHLIGHT – CONCESSIONS MANAGEMENT

Craig Spillman

Concessions Manager

VenuWorks of Evansville (Management Company of the Ford Center and Victory Theatre)

Education and Certifications

Indiana University

Bachelor of Science in Kinesiology, Sports Marketing and Management major, Business minor

Years in Position

Been working my current position since August 2011

Previous Position:

Director of Concessions – Grand Slam Catering/Birmingham Barons; Hoover, AL (September 2010-August 2011)

Promoted from Catering Intern (Summer 2007) and Concessions Intern (May 2010 - August 2010)

Compliance Intern – Indiana University Athletic Department; Bloomington, IN (May 2009 – April 2010)

Student Supervisor – RPS Dining Services; Bloomington, IN (August 2006 – May 2010)

Current Job Responsibilities and Hours:

I am in charge of staffing a variety of the Food and Beverage positions within the facilities, including Supervisors, Cash Room, Warehouse, Laundry, Concessions, Wait Staff, and Bartenders. I have a staff of roughly 125 employees. I do all of the hiring, firing, and payroll approval of those employees. I purchase/order the majority of the product/inventory we sell and have on hand. I handle our register system design and maintenance, along with product pricing. Hours variety tremendously based on the time of year/events in the building. On average, I probably work 30 hours/week in the summer months and probably 75 hours in the fall/winter months.

Greatest Challenge:

Staffing. When you have such a large part-time staff that is making min wage or just above it and the work is somewhat seasonal it is very hard to maintain a good staff. For busy events, we often have x-number of positions we need to fill and then we will have multiple employees call off work, so we will have to be to adjust on the fly. Each employee and personality is different and you have to know how to try and get the best out of each and every one of them.

Career Advice:

Sounds simple, but find something that you are passionate about and work hard to reach your goals.

References

American College of Sports Medicine. (2013). *ACSM's guidelines for exercise testing and prescription, 9ᵗʰ edition*. Baltimore, Maryland: Lippincott Williams &Wilkens.

Bethell, S. & Morgan, K. (2011). Problem-based and experiential learning: Engaging students in an undergraduate physical education Theory. *Journal of Hospitality, Leisure, Sport, & Tourism Education, 10(1)*, 128-134.

Collins, M. (2010).*Reasons why you should never choose a career based on salary potential alone*. Retrieved December 29, 2013 fromhttp://www.careerpath360.com/index.php/reasons-why-you-should-never-choose-a-career-based-on-salary-potential-alone-2-9080/

NASPE. (2014). *National Association for Sport and Physical Education*. Retrieved from http://www.aahperd.org/naspe/

Prete, J. (2011). *Will your next job be a good fit? Consider the company's culture*. Retrieved December 29, 2013, from http://www.recruitingblogs.com/profiles/blogs/will-your-next-job-be-a-good.

Schoepfer, K. L., & Dodds, M. (2010). Internships in sport management curriculum: Should legal implications of experiential learning result in the elimination of the sport management internship. *Marquette Sports Law Review, 21*(1), 182-201.

Wuest, D. (2011). *Foundations of physical education, exercise science, and sport: 17th edition*. Columbus, OH: McGraw-Hill

APPENDIX A

RESUME TEMPLATES

Name
Address
Cell phone
Email Address

POSITION DESIRED

SKILLS AND ABILITIES

Skill/Ability Supporting Evidence

Skill/Ability Supporting Evidence

Skill/Ability Supporting Evidence

Skill/Ability Supporting Evidence

Skill/Ability Supporting Evidence

EDUCATION/MILITARY EXPERIENCE

(paragraph format)

Degree, Name of School

Anticipated graduation Date

GPA or academic honors

EXTRACURRICULAR ACTIVITIES

Sports

Clubs

Sample 1 –Basic Skills Resume Template

Name

Address
Phone   **Email Address**

Profile   ■   Highlight qualifications

Specific Job
Skills   ■   Highlight skills

Education   ■   Degree, Name of School
                       ■   Anticipated graduation Date
                       ■   GPA or academic honors

                       ■   Thesis or research project

Relevant Coursework

■   **Course**   ■   **Course**■   **Course**
■   **Course**   ■   **Course**■   **Course**
■   **Course**   ■   **Course**■   **Course**

Professional
Memberships   ■   List Organization
                  ■   List Organization

Sample 2 – Basic Skills Resume Template

Name

Phone ■ Address ■ Email Address

Objective

Skills and Career Achievements

Skills   Paragraph of skills

Skills   Paragraph of skills

Skills   Paragraph of skills

Skills   Paragraph of skills

Education
Degree, Name of School

Anticipated graduation Date

GPA or academic honors

Thesis or research project

Professional Memberships
List organization

Extracurricular Activities
Name of activity, date

Name of activity, date

Sample 3 – Basic Skills Resume Template

NAME

Address

OBJECTIVE:

HIGHLIGHTS OF QUALIFICATIONS

- Qualifications
- Qualifications
- Qualifications

SKILLS

List by name (specific to field)

List by name (Specific to field)

List by name (Specific to field)

List by name (Specific to field)

EDUCATION ACTIVTIES

EXTRACURICULAR

Degree, Name of School
    Anticipated graduation Date

- Activity

GPA or academic honors

- Activity

Thesis or research project

- Activity

PROFESSIONAL MEMBERSHIPS PERSONAL ACHIEVEMENTS

- Organization
- Organization

- Personal achievement
- Personal achievement

Sample 4 – Basic Skills Resume Template

Name

Home Number
Address
Phone and Email Address

Objective
    Paragraph

Skills
- ■
- ■

Education

University with City, State
Degree and projected graduation month and year
GPA

Honors
Dean's Honor List and number of times
Academic scholarship (s)

Related Experience

Employer with City, State
Position Title   **Dates of Employment**
- ■ Position responsibilities
- ■ Position responsibilities
- ■ Position responsibilities

Employer with City, State
Position Title   **Dates of Employment**

- ■ Position responsibilities
- ■ Position responsibilities
- ■ Position responsibilities

Employer with City, State
Position Title   **Dates of Employment**

- ■ Position responsibilities
- ■ Position responsibilities
- ■ Position responsibilities

Sample 5 – Reverse - Chronological Resume Template

Name

Address ■ Phone ■ Email Address

OBJECTIVE: Write objective here

EDUCATION

Degree – Expected Graduation
Name of school – city, state
GPA or Academic honors/awards (if applicable)
-     Thesis or special projects (if applicable)
-     Scholarship/fellowship (if applicable)

RELEVANT EXPERIENCE (most recent first)

Employers name, Employers city, state, zip   Employment Dates
Position title

-     Duties and accomplishments
-     Duties and accomplishments
-     Duties and accomplishments
-     Duties and accomplishments

Employers name, Employers city, state, zip   Employment Dates
Position title

-     Duties and accomplishments
-     Duties and accomplishments
-     Duties and accomplishments
-     Duties and accomplishments

Employers name, Employers city, state, zip   Employment Dates
Position title

-     Duties and accomplishments
-     Duties and accomplishments
-     Duties and accomplishments
-     Duties and accomplishments

PROFESSIONAL MEMBERSHIPS AND/OR CERTIFICATIONS

-     List organization – list certification if applicable

EXTRACURRICULAR ACTIVTIES/LEADERSHIP ACTIVITIES

-     List extracurricular activities/leadership activities

Sample 6 – Reverse - Chronological Resume Template

Name
Address
Phone
Email Address

Related Activities

Education

Degree, Name of School
Anticipated graduation
Date GPA or academic honors

Thesis or research project

Relevant Experience

**Position Title, Employers Information
Dates**

- Duties and accomplishments
- Duties and accomplishments
- Duties and accomplishments
- Duties and accomplishments

**Position Title, Employers Information
Dates**

- Duties and accomplishments
- Duties and accomplishments
- Duties and accomplishments
- Duties and accomplishments

**Position Title, Employers Information
Dates**

- Duties and accomplishments
- Duties and accomplishments
- Duties and accomplishments
- Duties and accomplishments

Computer Skills

Paragraph of computer skills

Sample 7 – Reverse - Chronological Resume Template

NAME
Address
Phone
Email

Objective: Paragraph Style

Education: <u>University</u>, *City, State*

Expected Graduation Date

Work Experience: <u>Employer</u>, *City, State*

Position Title
Dates of Employment

❖   Responsibility
❖   Responsibility

<u>Employer</u>, *City, State*
Position Title
Dates of Employment

❖   Responsibility
❖   Responsibility

<u>Employer</u>, *City, State*
Position Title
Dates of Employment

❖   Responsibility
❖   Responsibility

<u>Employer</u>, *City, State*
Position Title
Dates of Employment

❖   Responsibility
❖   Responsibility

Computer Skills: Paragraph Style

Sample 8 – Reverse - Chronological Resume Template

Name
Address

OBJECTIVE

HIGHLIGHTS OF QUALIFICATIONS

- Qualification Highlight
- Qualification Highlight
- Qualification Highlight
- Qualification Highlight

EDUCATION

Degree, Name of School

Anticipated graduation Date

GPA or academic honors

SCHOLARLY WORK

Oral or poster presentation

Paper

PROFESSIONAL CERTIFICATIONS

Personal Training Group Exercise

EMPLOYMENT HISTORY

Employers Name, Employers city, state, zip   Employment Dates

Position title

   Paragraph Style

Employers Name, Employers city, state, zip   Employment Dates

Position title

   Paragraph Style

Sample 9 – Combination Resume Template

NAME
Address
Phone ■ Email Address

Objective
   Paragraph

Education
   Degree, Name of School
   Anticipated graduation Date
   GPA or academic honors

   Research Project – oral or poster
   presentations and/or papers

Related Experience
   Employers name, Employers city, state, zip   Employment dates
   Position title

   Duties and accomplishments (paragraph form)

   Employers name, Employers city, state, zip   Employment dates
   Position title

   Duties and accomplishments (paragraph form)

   Employers name, Employers city, state, zip   Employment dates
   Position title

   Duties and accomplishments (paragraph form)

Extracurricular Activities
   Name of activity, date
   Name of activity, date

Clubs and Organizations

   Name of Club or Organization, offices held, dates of membership
   Name of Club or Organization, offices held, dates of membership

Sample 10 – Combination Resume Template

NAME:

Address, Phone, Email

OBJECTIVE:

HIGHLIGHTS OF QUALIFICATIONS

- **Highlight Qualification**
- **Highlight Qualification**
- **Highlight Qualification**
- **Highlight Qualification**

EDUCATION	Employment History	
Degree and anticipated graduation University with City and State	Position Title Employer	Dates of Employment
Certification (s)	Position Title Employer	Dates of Employment
Honors	Position Title Employer	Dates of Employment

PERSONAL ATTRIBUTE	**PERSONAL ATTRIBUTE**
o Paragraph style – example reinforcing the personal attribute mentioned above o Paragraph style – example reinforcing the personal attribute mentioned above	o Paragraph style – example reinforcing the personal attribute mentioned above o Paragraph style – example reinforcing the personal attribute mentioned above
TRANSFERABLE SKILL	**TRANSFERABLE SKILL**
o Paragraph style – example reinforcing the transferable skill mentioned above o Paragraph style – example reinforcing the transferable skill mentioned above	o Paragraph style – example reinforcing the transferable skill mentioned above o Paragraph style – example reinforcing the transferable skill mentioned above
COMPUTER SKILLS	**CLUBS AND ORGANIZATIONS**
o List computer skill o List computer skill	o List club or organization o List club or organization

Sample 11 – Combination Resume Template

Name

Address
Phone
Email

PROFILE AND OBJECTIVE

Paragraph Style

SKILLS

- Skill
- Skill
- Skill
- Skill

EDUCATION

Degree and anticipated graduation
University with City and State

Certifications

Honors

EXPERIENCE

Position Title	Dates of Employment
Employer	City and State
Paragraph Style	

Position Title	Dates of Employment
Employer	City and State
Paragraph Style	

Position Title	Dates of Employment
Employer	City and State
Paragraph Style	

Sample 12 – Combination Resume Template

APPENDIX B

RESUMES

B

Resumes for Students in Sport and Physical Activity

Skills Resume Sample	Anticipated Degree	Position Segment
1	B.S. Recreation & Leisure Studies	Campus Recreation
2	B.S. Exercise Science with an emphasis in Cardiac Rehab	Cardiac Rehab
3	B.S. Sports Studies Minor Coaching	Intercollegiate athletic coaching
4	B.S. Recreation, Parks, and Tourism Concentration in Hospitality Management and Commercial Recreation	Parks and Recreation
5	B.S. Exercise Science Minor Biology	Physical Therapy
6	B.S. Sport Administration	Sport Event Management
7	B.S. Kinesiology Concentration in Personal Training and Group Exercise Instruction	Commercial fitness
8	B.S. Kinesiology Minor Athletic Training Specialization in Strength and Conditioning coach	Sport Specific Training
Reverse-Chronological Resume Sample	**Anticipated Degree**	**Position Segment**
9	B.S. Sport Management	Sports marketing and promotion
10	B.S. Sport Administration	Intercollegiate Athletic Administration
11	B.S. Exercise Science Specialization in Fitness Instructor and Nutrition	Community health
12	B.S. Exercise Science Concentration in Special Populations	Corporate fitness
13	B.S. Sport Administration	Sport Facility Management
14	B.S. Kinesiology Specialization in Sport Management	Interscholastic Athletic Administration
15	B.S. Sport Management	Sport Governing Body
16	B.S. Athletic Training Minor Psychology	Physical Therapy
Combination Resume Sample	**Anticipated Degree**	**Position Segment**
17	B.S. Exercise Science	Personal Trainer
18	B.S. Exercise Science Minor in Coaching and Nutrition	Sport Specific Training
19	B.S. Exercise Science Minor – Health Promotion	Health Promotion/Health Education
20	B.S. Sport Management Minor Broadcasting	Media/PR/Broadcasting
21	B.S. Exercise Science	Health Resort
22	B.S. Sport Management	Professional Sport
23	B.S. Kinesiology Minor Nutrition/Dietician	Private Fitness Club
24	B.S. Kinesiology Minor Sport Nutrition	Private Fitness Club

ANDREA MARTIN

1345 Clairview Drive * Ithaca, NY * 34567
Home: (432)567-8965
Cell Phone: (342)546-4356
E-mail: Amartin@netcom.net

POSITION DESIRED

Self-motivated college student with a strong work ethic evident through perseverance to finish projects and accomplish objectives. Seeks field experience with a **recreational sports** facility where I can utilize my knowledge of intramurals.

SKILLS AND ABILITIES

Hardworking/ Multitasker	I am able to proficiently juggle academics (16 credit hours), part-time employment (20 hours a week as a lifeguard), and volunteer activities (Race for the Cure), while consistently committing 100 percent to the task at hand.
Reliable	Excellent attendance record; I was an Amigo (freshmen orientation leader) who addressed incoming freshmen on academic requirements and college life. I assisted the freshmen in registering for class and never missed the 6 training sessions or 5 orientation sessions.
Punctual	I carried 16 hours and never missed opening the swimming pool as a lifeguard for the students and faculty of Ithaca University.
Leadership	I was a Summer Sports Camp Counselor for two basketball camps. I supervised 30-60 sports camp participants during the basketball camps. I oversaw dormitory stay and ensured timely arrival at camp and meals. I also developed relationships with coaches, staff and sport camp participants.
Communication	I have good written and verbal presentation skills. I use proper grammar and have a good speaking voice. I receive A's in all my English and Communication courses.
Attention to Detail	My work is orderly and attractive. I take pride in completing quality work.

EDUCATION/MILITARY EXPERIENCE

Pursuing a **Bachelor of Science in Recreation and Leisure Services** from Ithaca College in Ithaca, NY. My project graduation is May of 2014. I have completed introductory courses in Recreation, Parks, and Tourism. I maintain a GPA of 3.45/4.00.

Reserve Officers Training Corps (ROTC), 2004 to present
Instruction and training given both in the classroom and at Army installations range from strategic studies to tactical exercises – air-land battle doctrine, rappelling, and marksmanship.

EXTRACURRICULAR ACTIVITIES

Team captain of the bike club on campus. Enjoy participating in all intramural events held at our university, leading my basketball, softball, flag football, and soccer teams to two consecutive tournament wins.

Sample 1 – Basic Skills Resume

Kristy L. Price
3 Graham Street
Grove City, PA 16126
Home: 412.678.9875
Cell: 435.678.9086
Email: krislpri@ren.com

Objective

To obtain an internship at a Cardiac Rehab facility while completing my degree in Exercise Science with an emphasis in Cardiac Rehab.

Qualifications

- Good written, verbal, and interpersonal communications
- Ability to prioritize; complete multiple tasks under stressful situations
- Highly organized and dedicated, with a positive attitude
- Proficient in Microsoft Office 2013 (Word, PowerPoint, Excel), e-mail, SPSS, and Internet Resources.

Education

Bachelor of Science: Exercise Physiology   Expected Graduation May 2014
Emphasis: Cardiac Rehab
Gettysburg, College, Gettysburg, Pennsylvania
Certified American Red Cross CPR/AED/First Aid

Relevant Experience & Skills

Related Employment Experiences 2006-Present
- Assist with a physical activity program for the Belview Assist Living Community.
- Create and lead group exercise classes to meet the abilities of elderly residents at the Atria Community Home.
- Experience as a personal trainer at the Gettysburg University Fitness Center administering initial consultations (health history and goals), exercise testing (heart rate, blood pressure, height, weight, Bioelectrical Impedance, Submaximal testing, strength, and flexibility), and orientations of the equipment.

Research & Analysis
- Experience in collecting, analyzing, and interpreting data for a Gettysburg University wide Coronary Heart Disease Study. 2007-Present
- Demonstrated the ability to administer heart rate, blood pressure, body composition, blood glucose, and cholesterol screening at the Employee/Student Health Fair at Gettysburg College. Spring 2008

Sample 2 – Basic Skills Resume

Pam Anderson

176 Green Street, Corvallis, OR 05142
(803) 345-5678 Panderson@sigecom.net

Objective
- To obtain a position within intercollegiate athletics. Specific interest is in coaching women's basketball.

Profile
- Currently enrolled in Sport Management Courses
- Sport Management Club Member
- Member of NASSM and SRLA

Specific Job Skills
- Effective communication, listening and interpersonal skills
- Basketball tournament experience
- Highly proficient computer skills in Illustrator, Adobe Photoshop, Microsoft Word, and PowerPoint.

Education
- BS, Oregon State University
  Corvallis, Oregon (anticipated graduation May 2014)
- **Sports Studies with a Minor in Coaching**
- 3.7/4.0

Relevant Coursework
- Coaching Team Sports
- Sport Event Management
- Sport Publicity/Promotion
- Sport Marketing
- Sport and the Law
- History of Women in Sport

Relevant Experience
Oregon State University, Corvallis, Oregon Summer 2007
Basketball Camp Counselor
- Taught basketball skills to girls ages 6-18
- Responsible for camp participants staying overnight

Extracurricular Activities
- Member of the University of Oregon Women's Basketball team 2010-present
- Co-Captain for the Race for the Cure team (2009)
- High school varsity basketball and softball at Corvallis High School(2009)

Sample 3 — Basic Skills Resume

Jonathen Taylor

1546 Market Street
Miami, FL 33181
(987)567-4356 (Home)
(567)435-6589 (Cell)
jtaylor@trevort.edu

OBJECTIVE:
Undergraduate student seeking a position with the Vanderburgh Parks and Recreation Department.

COMPUTER SKILLS:
Proficient in Microsoft Windows, Microsoft Word, Microsoft PowerPoint, Microsoft Outlook

EDUCATION:
University of Florida, Gainesville, FL

Bachelor of Science degree - anticipated graduation in May 2015

Major: Recreation, Parks and Tourism

Concentration: Hospitality Management and Commercial Recreation

WORK EXPERIENCE:

United States Air Force
Personnel Specialist, Miami, FL (November 1997-July 2009)
- Organized, maintained and reviewed personnel records including pay documents.
- Entered and retrieved personnel information using an automated information system.
- Prepared organizational charts, wrote official correspondence and maintained reports.
- Provided current information about personnel programs and procedures to employees and administrators.

HONORS:
- Honor Graduate, United States Air Force Airman Leadership School (2003);
- Twice Awarded Air Force Commendation Medal (2002);
- Letter of Appreciation for Outstanding Performance during Combined Federal Campaign Fundraiser (2002);

ACTIVITIES:
- Volunteer worker for Miami Air Force Base Youth Basketball League (November 2007)
- Head Coach, AFROTC Detachment 330, University of Florida Intramural Basketball Team (January 2009)
- Organizer for Home of Future Stars Youth Football Camp (June 2009)

Sample 4 – Basic Skills Resume

Nathan Green
3176 Navy Road   Ph.(812)345-9087
Newburgh, IN 47630   NGreen24@hotmail.com

Objective:

Seeking a field experience offering me the opportunity to obtain hands-on experience using spinal specific and supportive progressive resistance exercises, soft tissue management, and specific stretching protocols tailored to each patient.

Skills:

Courteous, compassionate, detailed oriented and highly motivated

Education:

University of Southern Indiana, Evansville, IN
Bachelor of Science – **Exercise Science**
Specialization – **Biology**
Anticipated Graduation – December 2014
Dean's List 2008, 2009
Cumulative GPA – 3.5/4.0
Kinesiology Club

Military experience:

Indiana Army National Guard, Evansville, IN March 2003 – Present
As a cadre I am responsible for the development and sustainment of new enlistees prior to shipping to basic training:
- Physical fitness instruction
- Drill and ceremony
- Maintaining personnel file

Honors and activities:

Military

■ Primary Leadership Development course Honor Graduate

■ Basic non Commissioned Officers course Honor Graduate

■ Combative Instructor

■ Ranger Challenge Team Commander

Certification:
American Red Cross CPR/AED/First Aid, December 2011-present

Sample 5 – Basic Skills Resume

Tonya Kemp

405 Egley Rd
Hendersonville, KY

864-456-9876
TonyK@Ken.edu

OBJECTIVE

To obtain a Special Events Position within the United States Olympic Committee (USOC) where I can assist the marketing department with implementation and execution of game night planning and entertainment

PROFILE

Innovative, diligent, self-motivated individual seeking an exercise laboratory internship offering growth and advancement. Quick learner that is proficient and organized with attention to detail. Known as a leader and motivator with ardent ability to multi-task. Strong written and verbal skills.

ADDITIONAL SKILLS

Talent for building rapport and trust with clients
Values organization and time management for efficiency and professionalism
Open to new ideas, enjoys brainstorming Flexible and adaptable...assimilates quickly in transitions
Resourceful problem solver...analyzes problems then formulates solutions

EDUCATION

University of Kentucky, Lexington, KY
Major: **Sport Administration** (COSMA accredited)
Bachelor of Science degrees anticipated May 2014
Cum GPA 3.9/4.0
Proficient in Microsoft Office and Email

ACTIVITIES & AWARDS

University of Kentucky Board of Overseers Mentoring Program, 2012
Pi Beta Phi Thelma K. Long Award, 2012
Dean's Scholar, 2012
Academic Commonwealth Scholarship, 2011-2012
Pi Beta Phi Fraternity for Women, Member & Vice President of Communications, 2011 to Present
Dean's List, 2011,2012,2013
Member, Sports Officials of Deal, 2010-2011
Member, Resident Student Association & Vice President of United Tower, 2010-2011
Member, Golden Key International Honor Society 2010-2011
Member, National Society of Collegiate Scholars 2010-2011
Member, Phi Eta Sigma National Honor Society 2010-2011

WORK HISTORY

University of Kentucky Special Events Office, 2010 to Present

Student Assistant
Assist with special events such as the Midnight Madness, In-Season Festival, Fan Appreciation Day, and other football game day activities on an on-going basis.

Sample 6 – Basic Skills Resume

John Smith

34 Main Street * Norfolk, VA 23507
(804)555-9832 Home
(804)760-6875 Cell

jsmith@yahoo.com

OBJECTIVE:	Seeking an internship that requires personal training and group exercise instruction. Position should require the involvement of a variety of tasks, including sales, initial consultations, evaluations, exercise recommendations, orientations, and teaching of a variety of group exercise classes.
QUALIFICATIONS:	Highly organized and dedicated with a positive attitude. Resourceful with good written, verbal and interpersonal skills. Ability to prioritize and work under stressful situations. Experience in personal training settings where I utilized my skills of communicating during initial consultations, evaluations, and orientations. I am also a group exercise instructor teaching classes of muscular conditioning and cycling.
EDUCATION:	Bachelor of Science, Kinesiology **Concentration, Personal Training & Group Exercise Instructor** Anticipated Graduation May 2014 University of California, Irvine, CA Deans List 2012, 2013 GPA 3.6/4.0
VOLUNTEER EXPERIENCE:	Newport Beach Fitness Center December 2009 to Present **Personal Trainer – Newport Beach, CA** • Initial Consultations • Evaluations • Exercise Recommendations • Orientations **Group Exercise Instructor** • Teach Muscle Conditioning • Teach Cycling Classes
PROFESSIONAL CERTIFICATIONS:	American Red Cross CPR/AED/First Aid, August 2011-Present American Council on Exercise, Group Exercise, August 2011-Present National Strength & Conditioning Association, October 2012-Present

Sample 7 – Basic Skills Resume

Kevin Jones

1254 Pacific Shores Place
Malibu, CA 95678
Mobile (324)456-0987

Education:

Pepperdine University, Malibu, CA Expected   Graduation May 2015

Objective – To obtain a position where I can develop skills in order to train athletes. I would like to be involved in programs including speed, agility, quickness, strength, vertical jump, flexibility training, and overall anaerobic conditioning.

B.S. Kinesiology with a concentration in Strength and Conditioning Coach Minor in Athletic Training

Academic All-American 2013, 2014

Profile:

➢ Student athlete participating in football at Pepperdine University
➢ Knowledgeable about strength and conditioning training protocols
➢ Strong leadership skills (team captain)
➢ Energetic, motivated, and disciplined
➢ Effective communicator (quarterback)
➢ Mature and focused (dedicated to meeting or exceeding team goals and objectives)

Volunteer Experience:

➢ Summer football camp counselor for Pepperdine University
➢ Field experience within athletic training room at Pepperdine University
➢ Youth football Instructor

Selected Coursework:

➢ Strength and Conditioning I and II
➢ Methods of Personal Training
➢ Program Design for Athletes
➢ Exercise Physiology
➢ Exercise Testing and Prescription
➢ Weightlifting

Certification:

➢ American Red Cross CPR/AED/First Aid   2010 – present

Sample 8 – Skills Resume

Mark O'Reilly

15 North 1234 East
Salt Lake City, Utah
(988)434-5687 Morelly@aol.com

Objective: To obtain a Sport Advertising Internship for a minor league baseball team where I can have the opportunity to utilize my solid understanding of sport marketing and advertising strategies in providing public service announcements, press releases, flyers, banners, and obtaining local radio stations for advertising and entertainment.

Competencies: Advertising Communications * Press Releases * Electronic Media * Radio Media * Media Interviewing * Web page development and design * Proficient in computer skills of Adobe * Photoshop * PageMaker

EDUCATION
University of Wisconsin, Madison, WI 54308
B.S. Sport Management - projected completion May 2015

SCHOLARLY WORK
O'Reilly, M., & Thomas, B. (May, 2013). *Take me out to the ballgame: Satisfying the season ticket holder.* Presented at the North American Society for Sport Management, Clearwater, FL.

Thomas, B., Martin, S., & **O'Reilly, M**. (2012). Factors affecting baseball club season ticket holders' satisfaction. *Journal of Sport Management,* 24(5), 246-252.

Related Experience:
University of Wisconsin Sport Management Department, Madison, Wisconsin.

Marketing Liaison   **October. 2013-Present**

- Student liason for sport management annual golf tournament. Communicate and market the benefits of participating in the annual faculty golf tournament to faculty, students, and the community.
- Developed marketing strategies and communications to student body and University of Wisconsin constituents in promoting the event.
- Developed and maintained Web pages for the annual golf tournament University of Wisconsin Athletic Department, Madison, WI.

Student Worker in Marketing Department   **August 2004-Present**

- Work with Athletic Department in developing brochures for teams.
- Monitor media interviewing schedule with basketball personalities.
- Relay information from leader board to media continuously throughout basketball tournaments University of Utah Athletic Department, Salt Lake City, Utah.

Community Affairs Volunteer   **Summer 2012**

- Created fundraisers and events for the Utah Athletic Summer Camps.
- Coordinated Utah player appearances for each sport camp.

Sample 9–Reverse - Chronological Resume

Kevin Friedan (754)345-8756

4387 Auburn, AL 38647   kfriedan@daisy.edu

Professional Profile

Seeking an athletic administration position where I may continue with my experience in Education, Coaching, and Sport Leadership.

- Alabama High School Athletic Association Official
- National Archery Association Certified Teacher
- 2008-2009 Eastern University Campus Recreation Student Board Member· Alabama Recreation Association Member 2009 - present
- American Red Cross CPR & First Aid Certified 2007 - present
- Speak basic Spanish and French
- N.I.R.S.A. Official
- Trained in Microsoft Office & Dream Weaver computer software

Education

BA Sport Administration   University of Alabama   Anticipated Graduation
                                                                                   May 2013

Professional Accomplishments

University of Alabama Recreational Sports Department   2009 - Present

- Assist in all aspects of daily operations of campus intramural sports
- Train and supervise forty-seven students to be officials in various sports
- Set-up daily events, administer events, and break down events

Southern Alabama Youth Football League   Summer 2008

- Officiated youth football games
- Maintained game control from players to fans
- Made sure the playing field is safe and playable

Vanderburgh County High School   2007-2008

- Assistant coach varsity football
- In charge of special teams
- Maintained scouting reports
- Updated current stats to local media

Sample 10 – Reverse - Chronological Resume

Bethany Dubner

568 Circle Drive * Columbus, OH 43211 * Cell: (813)555-7658
Email: bethdunbner@hotmail.com

OBJECTIVE

To work with the general and special populations in a community wellness center where I can utilize my skills in fitness testing, exercise prescription, working with special populations, exercise instruction, and assistance with education/health promotion programs.

RELEVANT WORK EXPERIENCE

Hastings Lancaster Company, Evanston, IL

Group Exercise Instructor   October 2010-present
- Instructor for employees, employees' spouses, and retirees of the company - Kickboxing, Spinning, Abs Class, and Breakfast Club (Retiree Class)

The Fitness Gym, Evanston, IL
Group Exercise Instructor   September 2009-present
- Instructor of Kick-N-Cardio to the adult population (ages 18 and older)

Northwestern University, Evanston, IL

Manager of Recreation and Fitness Center   August 2009-present
- Supervising 25 student employees: Welcome Greeters and Fitness Consultants
- Monitoring the welcome desk, laundry room, group exercise room, basketball courts, locker rooms, track, exercise machines, and equipment check-out, then writing a daily report for the facility
- Performing fitness tests on Northwestern Kinesiology and Sport students
- Managing the cash register and daily purchases

Group Exercise Instructor   August 2005-present
- Instructor of Kickboxing, Spinning, Circuit Training, Body Sculpt, Six Pack, and Butts-N-Guts to Northwestern students and staff members (ages 18 and older)
- Helped organize the Spring 2011 group exercise schedule for the facility

Fitness Consultant   August 2008-August 2010
- Created individualized workouts for students and staff
- Motivated individuals through their workouts
- Cleaned and cared for the facility's exercise equipment
- Greeted the facility's guests at the front desk

EDUCATION

Northwestern University, Evanston, IL   August 2009-present
- Bachelor's Degree in **Exercise Science**, Minors in **Nutrition** and **Fitness Instructor** Anticipated graduation in December 2014 - Dean's List, 2011,2012,2013; Study Abroad (Australia, Spring 2006)

PROFESSIONAL CERTIFICATIONS

- AFAA Group Exercise Instructor Certification, January 2011 – present
- American Red Cross Adult, Infant and Child CPR Certification, January 2011 – present
- American Red Cross Standard First Aid Certification, January 2011 – present

Sample 11–Reverse - Chronological Resume

Hilary K. Adams
20 Kellog Drive
Quincy, IL 60601
HKadams@aol.com
(345)456-2345

OBJECTIVE:

To obtain an internship with the Kennedy Space Center (KSC) Health Education and Wellness Program (HEWP) where I can gain valuable experience in disseminating health information, health screening, cardiovascular disease reduction, women's health, worksite lectures, nutrition education, health fairs, and other developing programs.

Membership and Fitness Coordinator, Personal Trainer, Group Fitness Instructor

YMCA of Greater Illinois, Quincy, IL (November '09-present)
I assist in the development and management of member fitness programs. I implement fitness programs and coach members of all fitness levels. I also handle office administration and maintenance.

Step Aerobics Instructor

University of Illinois, Champaign, Illinois (August '09-present)
I teach Step Aerobic classes as part of the core courses required for all students.

Group Fitness Instructor, Personal Trainer

Sportfirst International, Champaign, Illinois (January '07-April '09)
I instructed members in step and Hi/Lo Aerobics, Cardio Kickboxing, Muscle Conditioning, and Yoga classes. I also accumulated 200 personal training hours on an annual basis.

VOLUNTEER INVOLVEMENT:

O YMCA Youth Baseball Coach at the Northeast Family YMCA in Wheaton, IL: August 2006-2010.

O YMCA Youth Soccer Coach at the Northeast Family YMCA in Wheaton, IL: August 2009.

O Girl on the Run Running Coach in Wheaton, IL: August 2005-2009.

O Team YMCA mini marathon and marathon training coach in Rochester, CO: January 2004 – 2008.

EDUCATION:
Quincy College,
Quincy, IL
B.S. Exercise Science
Specialization - Special Populations
Anticipated graduation in May 2014

HONORS:
GPA: 3.75/4.00; Dean's List spring 2012, 2013

CERTIFICATIONS:

ARC
First Aid/AED/CPR-June '11 - Present

AFAA
Group Exercise Instructor-January '10-present
Personal Training
Spinning - March '10 – present

YMCA Instructor
Personal Training - February '10-'11
Healthy Back - November '09 – '10

Sample 12–Reverse - Chronological Resume

John Sampson Smith
3450 Forklift Drive
Brentwood, NY 11435
(784) 435-5897
Jsampson@mall.net

Education: Bachelor's Degree in Sports Administration from the State University of New York at Old Westbury, Westbury, NY
Expected graduation May 2015

OBJECTIVE:

To obtain a sport facility management internship where I can learn more about personnel supervision, budget development and administration.

Experience:

Landscaping Plus, Brentwood, NY   August 2011 to Present

Gardner/Landscape Assistant - I worked directly with the owner on a 5-person team to maintain or improve landscapes for affluent client base.

Winter Parks Resort, Winter Park, CO   December 2009 to present

Life Operator - supervised ski-lift equipment, monitored equipment for mechanical problems, greeted guest, and provided information about facilities and services (including snow conditions, hours of operation, weather conditions, and trails).

Sample 13 – Reverse - Chronological Resume

Patrick W. Limbaugh

345 Crystal Street
Atlanta, GA 43590
(745)657-8965
E-mail: patwlim05@hotmail.com

Objective:	To supervise organized high school athletic program, and to become involved with the athletes, parents, as well as people in the community.
Education:	University of Georgia, *Atlanta, GA*
	B.S. Kinesiology with a Specialization in Sport Management Expected Graduation Date June 2015
Work Experience:	Georgia Parks, *Atlanta, GA*
	Operations Manager
	August 2010-Present

- ❖ Organize different recreational events
- ❖ Hire volunteers search for special sponsors for event.
- ❖ Organize and supervise concessions during special events

University College Tribune, *Atlanta, GA*
Contributing Writer, Desk Clerk
February 2007 – August 2009

- ❖ Reported on local sporting events
- ❖ Interviewed coaches, player, and fans
- ❖ Wrote exceptional stories edited stories, answered phones
- ❖ Collected game data and transferred it onto computer

University of Georgia Athletic Department, *Atlanta, GA*
Student Athletic Assistant
August 2004 – February 2007

- ❖ Helped with confirming scheduled events
- ❖ Took notes for the athletic director during meetings
- ❖ Called different schools to set-up dates for events
- ❖ Organized concessions during special events

Computer Skills:	Worked with Windows XP, Word, Access, Power Point, and Mac computers
Certification:	American Red Cross CPR/AED/First Aid, January 2011 – present

Sample 14 – Reverse - Chronological Resume

Mary Thompson

School Address
1356 Saddle wood Drive
Manhattan, KS 66502
(432) 768-9045 Cell

Permanent Address
44811 WCR 35
Pierce, CO 80650
(457)534-7689 (Fax)

mathompson@hotmail.com

OBJECTIVE:
To obtain a position with NCAA or other regulating agency where I can gain knowledge of the responsibilities in overseeing sport organizations.

EDUCATION:
Kansas State University, Manhattan, KS
B.S. Sport Management   **Anticipated Graduation May 2015**

Awards and Honors:
- University of Washington Athletic Directors Honor Roll (2012-2013)
- Academic Honor Roll (2012, 2013, 2014)
- Dean's List, three Semesters (2012, 2013, 2014)

EXPERIENCE:
- **Women's softball Association of America**
  Turf Management Intern   **Summer 2014**
  - Responsible for assisting the Director for Grounds relating to maintenance of facilities for major events including the Big 12 Softball Championship, the NCAA Women's College World Series, the ASA Junior Olympic Hall of Fame Tournaments, and other events as assigned.

- **Kansas State University, Manhattan, KS**
  Softball Camp Counselor Intern   **Summer 2013**
  - Responsible for teaching softball skills to girls ages 12-15.

- **Colorado High School, Pierce, CO**
  Softball Volunteer   **Summer 2012**
  - Promoted Youthhagen High School summer softball camps.
  - Served as coach to girl ages 7-8 teaching basic softball skills.

- **Summer Olympics, Athens, Greece**
  Softball Volunteer-Field Crew Assistant   **Summer 2011**
  - Served as field crew assistant maintaining a playing field and two practice fields.

ACTIVITIES AND COMMUNITY SERVICE:
- Scholarship Athlete- Kansas State University, softball team   **2012-present**
- Boys and Girls Club- Middletown Recreation Clinic   **Summer 2011**

Sample 15 – Reverse - Chronological Resume

NATALIE CLAYTON

4356 Whitesboro Way
Austin, TX 78750

Ph. 987-098-7654
nclayto@hotmail.com

Objective:

To obtain an internship where I can gain valuable experience and skills in Physical Therapy.

Work Experience:

Progressive Health of Texas: Austin, TX
June 2006-Present
Physical Medicine Technician

- Assist physical/occupation therapists
- Help patients ambulate
- File paperwork throughout hospital
- Transport/move patients
- Clean/sterilize equipment

Dick's Sporting Goods: Austin, TX
March 2005
Fitness Associate/Personal Trainer (IFPA)

- Loaded equipment into customer vehicles
- Demonstrate proper equipment use
- Stock/Organize merchandise
- Properly fitted customers for bicycles
- Provided customer assistance as needed

Gilles Cycling and Fitness: Austin, TX
Sales Associate March 2007 – February 2008

- Ordered all merchandise for running department
- Organized equipment
- Demonstrated proper use of equipment (treadmills, bikes)
- Fitted customers for bikes
- Assembled bikes

EDUCATION

Southwest Texas State
B.S. Athletic Training
Minor Psychology
Anticipated graduation May of 2015

HONORS

National Society of Collegiate Scholars

Dean's List
2012
2013
2014

ACTIVITIES & AWARDS

Member of SMART Youth Fitness and Nutrition DVD 2013

NCAA National Qualifier in Track and Field
2012-2013

Frances & Guy Cornell Memorial Scholarship,
2012-2013

Exercise Science Department Scholarship
2012-2013

Member of Southwest Texas Track and Field Team
2011-2012

CERTIFICATION

American Red Cross CPR/AED/First Aid
2011-present

Sample 16 – Reverse - Chronological Resume

Stephanie McCullough

2345 Deed Street, #15
Maiden, NC

864-456-9876
Jane.McC@wiscon.edu

Seeking a practicum where I can improve my personal training skills (sales, initial consultation, fitness assessment, program design, and orientation) and gain valuable business knowledge. I am qualified by a unique blend of personal training, sport and physical activity skills.

HIGHLIGHTS OF QUALIFICATIONS

- Recipient of "Outstanding Group Leader Award"
- Good communicator in group exercise classes and monthly nutrition seminars
- Completion of advanced personal training seminar
- Interact with clients and employees in a professional manner

EDUCATION

Majors: Exercise Science (NASSM/NASPE accredited)
Bachelor of Science degrees anticipated May 2015
Specialization in Sport Management
Cum GPA 3.9/4.0
University of Wisconsin, Madison, WI.

SCHOLARLY WORK

Binh, N. X., McCue, C., & O'Brien, K. (2008, April). *An integrated approach to training core stability.* Poster session presented at the American College of Sports Medicine Annual Conference, Indianapolis, Indiana.

PROFESSIONAL CERTIFICATION

American Council on Exercise, Group Exercise Instructor, 2010-present
National Strength & Conditioning Association Personal Trainer, November 2011-present
American Red Cross CPR/AED/First Aid, June 2010-present

EMPLOYMENT HISTORY

YMCA of Southwestern Wisconsin, Madison, WI   **August 2009 - Present**
Wellness and Fitness Instructor

I observe the fitness and wellness center. I help members with any problems, questions, spotting and program suggestions. I provide equipment orientations to members, clean all equipment, provide members with fresh towels, test, and record any problems with equipment.

Wisconsin Physical Activity Center, Madison, WI   **August 2007-August 2009**
Building Monitor

I set-up and teared down equipment for volleyball and basketball games. I provided athletes with clean uniforms, completed cleaning duties, made work schedules for the semester, completed time sheets, organized purchasing of equipment, and cleaned athletic lockers

Sample 17 – Combination resume

Brent Maxwell
543 Fourth Avenue
Duluth, Minnesota 55876
Email: Bmaxwell@minnestor.edu

PROFILE AND OBJECTIVE

I am an energetic, motivated, team player seeking an internship with a professional sports team where I can learn more about becoming strength and conditioning specialist.

EDUCATION

University of Minnesota, Duluth MN
Bachelor of Science Anticipated'14
Major: Exercise Science
Minor: Coaching and Nutrition

SKILLS

- Leadership abilities – Team captain - Led my soccer team to three NCAA Division I conference championships
- Team player – I support team unity
- Dependable and responsible – I have never missed a game or practice in the last three years as a player on the Men's Soccer team.
- Solid understanding of the game of soccer and specificity of training athletes

SCHOLARSHIPS/AWARDS

Aug '13 to present – Jan '12 to Present

- Men's Soccer Scholarship
- Academic All-American

EXPERIENCE

University of Minnesota Athletic Department
August 2010 to Present

During the summers I worked for the University of Minnesota Athletic Department where I was a student strength and conditioning coach and a sports camp counselor.

SERVICE

Sept '12 to present – May '13 present

- Susan B. Komen Team Volunteer
- Summer Youth Sports Camps – Soccer Coach

Student Youth Strength and Conditioning Coach, August 2010 to Present
I am integral part of the development and implementation of the strength and conditioning camps offered through the University of Minnesota Athletic Department. This program is offered to Youth ages 15-18 who participated in workouts specific to their sport.

ORGANIZATIONS

NSCA – Jan '11 to present
NSCA Member – Jan '13 to present

Youth Sports Camps Counselor, May 2010 to present
I am a counselor and coach for the Men's summer soccer camp where I guide youth boys ages 8-18 in improving their soccer skills.

Sample 18 – Reverse - Combination Resume

Nancy B. Casey

407 Walters Hall
Sarasota, FL 34236

Cell: 617-555-8856
E-mail: nancybcas@hotmail.com

OBJECTIVE: To gain experience in the health promotion/health education field.

**SKILLS
PROFILE:**   Leadership and organizational skills, excellent customer service, computer proficiency with Microsoft Word, Excel, and PowerPoint

EDUCATION: Arizona State University – West; Phoenix, AZ
Bachelor of Science in Exercise Science
Minor: Health Promotion
Anticipated graduation May 2014

Professional Honors & Activities: Exercise Science Club, Intramurals

**RELEVANT
COURSES:**

Principles/Application in Fitness Training	Exercise Physiology
Measurement and Evaluation in P.E.	Kinesiology
Biomechanics	Exercise Leadership

**RELEVANT
EXPERIENCE:**   **Arizona State University Fitness Center,**   **Phoenix, AZ**
Student Consultant
December 2012-Present
- Administer exercise tests
- Develop exercise recommendations
- Provide orientations of the facility

Chrysler Corporate Fitness Center,   **Auburn Hills, MI**
Intern
August 2012 – December 2013
- Administered health assessments
- Taught health education workshops
- Taught fitness classes

Sarasota County Government,   **Sarasota, FL**
Intern
Summer 2012
- Implemented various health and wellness promotion programs
- Developed employee games
- Marketed programs and special events

CERTIFICATIONS: ACE Personal Trainer, August 2012
ACE Group Exercise Instructor, March 2011
AFAA Group Exercise Instructor, February 2011
American Red Cross CPR/AED/First Aid, January 2011

Sample 19 – Reverse - Combination Resume

HOLLY O'REILLY

15 Island Road; Guilford, CT 06437
(988)434-5687 HSmith@aol.com

Objective

I am seeking an athlete assistant internship with ASA entertainment in their Competition and Demo Events Department.

Skills

Proficient with Microsoft Word and Excel - Familiar with Macs
Exceptional written and verbal communication skills
Creative writing experience
Possess the ability to take initiative, prioritize, and multi-task

Education

Boston University
B.S. Degree projected completion May 2013 in **Sport Management**
Minor: **Broadcasting**
3.56/4.0 GPA – Dean's Honor List (2011, 2012)

Related Experience

Boston University Athletic Department
Sports Information Assistant   **January 2012-Present**

- Maintain up-to-date stats for media under the direction of the SID.
- Assist in media coverage of the men's and women's basketball competitions.
- Assist with the development of featured stories and arranged interviews.
- Assist in produces media guides, promotional brochures, and event programs.

Boston University Athletic Department
Student PR Assistant   **December 2011-February 2013**

- Assisted in preparing media guides, arranging/conducting press briefings, coordinating press and conferences, sending news releases to media
- Maintained files and scrapbook

Boston University Athletic Department
Ticket Sales   **August 2011 –January 2013**

- Responsible for opening and closing ticket booths before and after Men's and Women's home basketball games.

Sample 20 – Reverse - Combination Resume

Nadine Jackson

4356 High Street, Ojai, CA 43506
(321)564-8967
njackson@ruler.com

Objective: To obtain a health and fitness position at a Health Resort.

Skills: Planned and organized health activities; managed health events; reputation for reliability; professionalism; planning; team player; and interpersonal skills

Related Activities

Education
B.S. **Exercise Science**, University of California, Oakland, CA
Anticipated Graduation Date December 2014
3.62/4.00 – Certified CPR/AED/First Aid, October 2013-present

Relevant Experience

The Oaks at Ojai   **Summer 2013**
Ojai, CA - Intern
  ♦ Assisted guests with stress reduction, fitness gain and weight loss, and provided education on the basics of healthy living.
  ♦ Worked with the management team, teaching fitness classes, front desk, reservations, in the kitchen and housekeeping departments.

The Sport and Health Company   **Summer 2012**
McLean, VA - Intern
  ♦ Provided fitness evaluations, exercise program design, promotional fitness programming, programs for special populations, and water fitness programs.

Sporting Goods Store   **Summer 2011**
Southwest, TX – Sports Apparel Consultant
  ♦ Provided personal insight and experiences to shift target market of mall.
  ♦ Consulted with owner on fashion purchasing and shopping experiences.

Fitness Related Activities

Susan B. Komen Race for the Cure	Spring 2012
University Health Fair worker	Fall 2011
YMCA volunteer	Summer 2011

Sample 21 – Reverse - Combination Resume

Jenna Patel
2456 156th street * Clemson, SC 98685 * jholloway@wash.edu

OBJECTIVE
To obtain a position where I can gain valuable experience in becoming a sport agent.

EDUCATION
Clemson University, Clemson, SC -**B.S. Sport Management – Anticipated May 15**

SKILLS SUMMARY
- Strong academic skills; hands-on experience planning; implementation of programs and projects for athletic events.
- Strong organizational skills; takes initiative; excellent customer service leadership qualities
- Computer competent; demonstrated ability using Microsoft Word, and Excel

WORK EXPERIENCE
University of Washington, Athletic Department, Seattle, WA
Internship (August 2012 – December 2013)
- Networked with Varsity Club to increase membership and helped improve on support of the athletic program
- Worked in the ticket office by selling and accepting tickets during the games.
- Worked the concession stand
- Prepared mailing lists for alumni, students, and varsity club members for the monthly newsletter and publications

Seattle Pacific University, Athletic Department, Seattle, WA
Sports Camp Counselor (May 2011 – July 2012)
- Coached 14-18 year old girls at a tournament sponsored by the University of Setho.
- Conducted practice sessions leading to skill development for the girls.
- Assisted in developing tournament brackets for a double-elimination tournament.
- Supervised 70-80 sport camps participants in the dormitories and during the camp.

University of Washington, Athletic Department, Seattle, WA
Student Manager Women's Basketball (August 2010 – May 2011)
- Assisted with the pre-season conditioning and regular season practice by timing the players, setting up equipment, running copies of the workout routine, and attended all practices and team meetings.
- Set-up film room for coaches following each game which consisted of making copies of stats for each coach and player. Gave campus tours for recruits during site visits

Sample 22 – Reverse - Combination Resume

Maria Smith
3245 Johnson Lane
Salt Lake City, UT 854690
845-890-7645
Msmith@gmail.com

OBJECTIVE

To obtain a comprehensive internship program that will prepare me for every aspect of the club industry.

EDUCATION

University of Utah, Salt Lake City, UT
B.S. Kinesiology
Minor in Nutrition/Dietitian
American Red Cross CPR/AED/First Aid, June 2012-present
Anticipated Graduation May 2014

WORK EXPERIENCE

Tri-State Athletic Club, Salt Lake City, UT   **January 2012 - Present**
Fitness Instructor
  ➢ Conduct exercise testing and prescription for client ages 19-45.
  ➢ Assist in the maintenance of outdoor recreational pool, indoor lap pool, indoor track, state of the art free weight and cardiovascular facilities.
  ➢ Aerobic class instruction (spinning, cardio kickboxing).
  ➢ Indoor basketball program development for youth ages 11-14.

The Athletic Club Boca Raton, Boca Raton, FL   **Summer 2012**
Intern
  ➢ Maintained indoor basketball, racquetball, squash & tennis courts.
  ➢ Aerobic class instructor in kickboxing and spinning.
  ➢ Exposed to strategies in membership retention, marketing, and business management.

The University Club, Houston, Salt Lake City, UT   **Summer 2011**
Group Exercise Instructor
  ➢ Taught aerobic classes of step and muscular conditioning.
  ➢ Developed an incentive program to encourage members to join classes.

EXTRACURRICULAR ACTIVITIES

I enjoy running, biking, swimming, and rock climbing. I am an energetic, proactive health and fitness professional.

Sample 23 – Reverse - Combination Resume

OBJECTIVE

To obtain a position that allows me to learn skills needed to manage and work in a private club industry with special focus on creating personalized service in an athletic setting.

EDWARD CRAGER
234 CANDLEWOOD COURT
MANHATTAN, KANSAS 66508
856-908-6734
ECRAGER@TROY.EDU

EDUCATION

Kansas State University, Manhattan, KS   **Anticipated Graduation May 2015**
B.S. Kinesiology
Minor: Sports Nutrition

WORK EXPERIENCE

Kansas Health and Fitness Facility, Kansas City, Kansas   **August 2012-present**
Fitness Specialist
* ❖ Provide exercise tests and prescriptions to youth and adults.
* ❖ Develop and implement incentive programs.
* ❖ Participate in the mobile health unit providing blood pressures and heart rates.

Manhattan Private Club, Kansas City, Kansas   **December 2011-present**
Front Desk Clerk
* ❖ Graduate of star service program.
* ❖ Client and customer interaction.
* ❖ Provide personalized service to all members who came in contact with me.

Kansas State University Recreation Center, Kansas City, Kansas   **December 2011-present**
Welcome Greeter
* ❖ Student, faculty and employee check-in
* ❖ Check-out locks, radios, towels and incentive awards.

PROFESSIONAL ACTIVITIES

* ❖ Student member of the Washington American Association for Health, Physical Education, Recreation and Dance (WAAPERD)   **December 2012 to Present**
* ❖ Organized WAPERD State Conference social   **January 2011 to Present**
* ❖ Student member of the American Association for Health, Physical Education, Recreation, and Dance (AAHPERD)   **December 2010 to Present**

CERTIFICATION

* ❖ American Red Cross CPR/AED/First Aid   **December 2012 to present**

Sample 24 – Reverse - Combination Resume

APPENDIX C

COVER LETTER TEMPLATES

Your Name

| Address | email address | Cell Phone |

Date

Name of Company
Address

Dear Mr. or Ms. Last name:

Opening paragraph — focus on thanking the individual for the interview

Middle paragraph — skills and experience relevant to the needs of the employer

Closing paragraph — assertive not aggressive

Sincerely,

Your Name

enclosure: resume

Font Notes: Text Font – Times New Roman, 12 pt.
              Name – Arial Rounded MT, 18 pt.

Sample 1 – Paragraph Style Cover Letter Template

YOUR NAME   Cellular Phone

Email address   **Address**

Date

Name of Company
Address

Dear Mr. or Ms. Last name:

Opening paragraph — focus on thanking the individual for the interview

Middle paragraph —bullet points of relevant skills and experience focused on the needs of the employer

- Bullet Point 1
- Bullet Point 2
- Bullet Point 3

Closing paragraph — assertive not aggressive

Sincerely,

Your Name

enclosure: resume

Font Notes: Text Font – Arial Black, 11 pt
               Name – Copperplate Gothic, 18 pt

Sample 2 – Bullet Style Cover Letter Template

Your Name
Address
Phone
Email Address

Date

Name of Company
Address

Dear Mr. or Ms. Last name:

Opening paragraph — focus on thanking the individual for the interview

Middle paragraph — skills and experience relevant to the needs of the employer

Closing paragraph — assertive not aggressive

Sincerely,

Your Name

enclosure: resume

Font Notes: Text Font – Times New Roman, 12 pt
              Name – Verdana, 18 pt

Sample 3 – Paragraph Style Cover Letter Template

YOUR NAME

Home Number and Address ◇ Cellular ◇ Email

Date

Name of Company
Address

Dear Mr. or Ms. Last name:

Opening paragraph — focus on thanking the individual for the interview

Middle paragraph — bullet points of relevant skills and experience focused on the needs of the employer

- Bullet Point 1
- Bullet Point 2
- Bullet Point 3

Closing paragraph — assertive not aggressive

Sincerely,

Your Name

enclosure: resume

Font Notes: Text Font—Bodoni MT, 11 pt
              Name—Castellar, 18 pt

Your Name
Address

Sample 4 – Bullet Style Cover Letter Template

NAME   HOME NUMBER AND ADDRESS   PHONE   EMAIL

Date

Name of Company
Address

Dear Mr. or Ms. Last name:

Opening paragraph- Thank you for taking the time to meet with me

Middle paragraph – reinforce your skills and experience that you can bring to the company

Closing paragraph – assertive not aggressive

Sincerely,

Your Name

enclosure: resume

Font Notes: Text Font—Times New Roman, 12pt;
                 Name—Copper Plate Gothic

Sample 5 – Indented Paragraph Style Cover Letter Template

YOUR NAME

Date

Name of Company
Address

Dear Mr. or Ms. Last name:

Opening paragraph — focus on thanking the individual for the interview

Middle paragraph — bullet points of relevant skills and experience focused on the needs of the employer

- Bullet Point 1

- Bullet Point 2

- Bullet Point 3

Closing paragraph — assertive not aggressive

Sincerely,

Your Name

enclosure: resume

Your Name
Address
Phone
Email Address

Font Notes: Text Font—Bodoni MT, 11 pt
Name—Perpetuna Tilting MT, 26 pt

Sample 6 – Bullet Style Cover Letter Template

Address
Phone

NAME

Date

Name of Company
Address

Dear Mr. or Ms. Last name:

Opening paragraph- Thank you for taking the time to meet with me

Middle paragraph – reinforce your skills and experience that you can bring to the company

Closing paragraph – assertive not aggressive

Sincerely,

Your Name

enclosure: resume

Font Notes: Text Font- Times New Roman, 12pt;
             Name- Cloudy Stout, 18pt

Sample 7 – Indented Style Paragraph Cover Letter Template

YOUR NAME
Address
Phone, Email

Date

Name of Company
Address

Dear Mr. or Ms. Last name:

Opening paragraph — my resume outlines or I am enclosing my resume for your review or I saw your advertisement

Middle paragraph — bullet points of relevant skills and experience focused on the needs of the employer

- Bullet Point 1

- Bullet Point 2

- Bullet Point 3

Closing paragraph — assertive not aggressive

Sincerely,

Your Name

enclosure: resume

Font Notes: Text Font—Arial, 11 pt

Name—Engraver MT, 18 pt

Sample 8 – Bullet Style Paragraph Cover Letter Template

APPENDIX D

COVER LETTERS

Paragraph Style Cover Letter	Anticipated Degree	Position Segment
1	B.S. Kinseiology Specialization - Coaching	Interscholastic Athletics
2	B.S. Sport Administration	Professional Sport
3	B.S. Sport Administration	Parks & Recreation
4	B.S. Sport Administration	Sport Marketing
5	B.S. Exercise Physiology	Cardiac Rehab
6	B.S. Kinesiology	Public Safety
7	B. S. Exercise Physiology	Sports Specific Training
8	B. S. Exercise Science Minor - Strength Training	Sports Specific Training
Indented Paragraph Style Cover Letter	**Anticipated Degree**	**Position Segment**
9	B.S. Sport Management Emphasis - Marketing	Sport Retail
10	B.S. Sport Administration	Professional Sport
11	B.S. Sport Administration	Professional Sport
12	B.S. Kinesiology	Fitness
13	B. S. Sport Administration Minor - Marketing	Professional Sport
14	B. S. Sport Administration Minor - Marketing	Professional Sport
15	B. S. Sport Administration	Professional Sport
16	B.S. Exercise Science/Sport Medicine	Athletic Trainer
Bullet Style Cover Letter	**Anticipated Degree**	**Position Segment**
17	B.S. Exercise Science	Physical Therapy
18	B.S. Sport Administration	Interscholastic Athletics
19	B.S. Exercise Science	Commercial Fitness
20	B.S. Exercise Science Minor Nutrition	Corporate Fitness
21	B.S. Exercise Science Minor Health Promotion	Corporate Fitness
22	B.S. Sport Administration	Sport Event Management
23	B.S. Exercise Science	Private Fitness Club
24	B.S. Sport Administration	Intercollegiate Athletics

PATTY THOMAS

3245 Dover Parkway
Bloomington, IN 32456   pattyhom@earthink.net   Mobile 543-908-9543

November 3, 2014

Ms. Cathy Martin
Head Basketball Coach
Lincoln High School
1324 Dame Kate
Bloomington,IN 32456

Re: Field Experience

Dear Ms. Martin:

I am interested in applying for a field experience coaching position at Lincoln High School during the Fall of 2014. I am a student-athlete (women's basketball) at Indiana University Purdue University at Indianapolis (IUPUI) pursuing a Bachelor of Science Degree in Kinesiology with a specialization in coaching. My coach speaks highly of you and your team.

While I have not had much experience in the area of coaching, I feel as though my experience as a student-athlete coupled with my educational background and my desire to learn and grow makes me an asset to your coaching staff and team.

I would like to learn more about the current field experience position. I am confident my skills enables me to make an immediate contribution to your organization. I can be reached at (812)564-8790 after 5 pm or pthomas@iupui.edu
Thank you for your time and I look forward to hearing from you soon.

Sincerely,

Patty Thomas

Patty Thomas

enclosure: resume

Sample 1 – Paragraph Style Cover Letter

LANCE H. McKINNEY Jr.

4369 Jackson Lane, Tampa, FL 43567
lhmkinney@insightbb.com
M (324)657-9874

January 23, 2014

Mr. Don Franklin
Personnel Director
Boston Mariners
345 West Main Street
Suite 325
Boston, NC 34528

Dear Mr. Franklin:

I am applying for the position of public relations intern in response to your ad on the National Basketball Association website. I was particularly attracted to the position because of my interest in community relations, NBA team management, and the opportunity to apply the skills I am learning as a student in the Sport Administration Program at Southwest Florida College.

I have extensive experience and skills that are relevant to this position. My particular field of expertise is in public and community relations management. This seems like a perfect opportunity to combine my 11-year military experience in the public relations field with the possibility of an exciting future working in the sports industry.

I will make an excellent candidate for the public relations intern position and, look forward to hearing from you. I can be reached at (453) 678-5489 or via e-mail at lhmkinney@insightbb.com. Thank you for you consideration.

Sincerely,

Lance H. McKinney Jr.

Lance H. McKinney Jr.

enclosure: resume

Sample 2 – Paragraph Style Cover Letter

Bill Foster

3456 Carmel Drive, Box 122
Kansas City, MO 32456
bfoster@kl.edu
Mobile 213-876-5987

February 23, 2014

Jackson Smith
Tennis Associates of Kentucky
456 Lawson View, Suite 112
Hendersonville, KY 45367

Dear Ms. Smith:

Please consider my application for the internship that was advertised at the 2013 Fifth Third Tennis Classic in Hendersonville, KY. I am currently a student in the Sports Administration Program at the University of Kansas-Lawrence. My academic coursework provides me with complete preparation for a variety of management positions in the sports industry including professional and intercollegiate sports.

My work history includes the last two years as an intern and tennis instructor for the Parks and Recreation Department of Hendersonville, KY. I worked closely with Barb Huntington, Director of Athletics, and Joe Vincent, Director of Tennis Operations. I assisted with all of the major organizing and planning of sports leagues and events while conducting both junior and adult tennis clinics.

Please consider me as a possible candidate for this internship. I am available for contact by telephone, 435-235-6859, or via e-mail, bfoster@kl.edu. Thank you and I look forward to hearing from you.

Sincerely,

Bill Foster

Bill Foster

enclosure: resume

Sample 3 – Paragraph Style Cover Letter

Joshua Kubeck

745 Commission Drive
Indianapolis, IN 23458

321-546-9087

joshk@aol.com

March 14, 2014

Justin Peters
Head of Human Relations
Silver Marketing
145 South Reminton Road
Tampa, FL 32987

Dear Mr. Peters:

I am writing to be considered for the internship position available in your sports marketing division. I learned about the position via the website Monster.com, on August 14, 2014. This position sparked a particular interest because of an unquenchable desire to become a leader and trend setter in the sports marketing industry.

I financed my education by working as a coach, at the Metro Sports Center in Indianapolis, IN for five years and more recently at the Fitness and Sport Arena in Tampa, FL. Staying immersed in sports has allowed me to keep up with trends and patterns of our modern sports industry.

I want to couple the experience of working with your company with the my academic preparation. I am graduating with a degree in advertising and I am currently working on my second degree in sports administration, scheduled for completion December of 2015. I would love the opportunity to sit and talk with you in more detail as to how I can become an asset to Silver Marketing. Feel free to contact me for an interview time at (321)546-9087, or by correspondence at the address listed. Thank you for your time and effort.

Sincerely,

Joshua Kubeck

Joshua Kubeck

enclosure: resume

Sample 4 – Paragraph Style Cover Letter

CAROL JONES

1234 Country Club Blvd.
Kent, OH 34256
(453)890-7658

April 23, 2014

Mr. James Hobesound
The Institute for Wellness and Sports Medicine
Testing Coordinator
210 West Hospital Drive
Hattiesburg,MS 39404

Dear Mr. Hobesound:

Mr. John Hamilton suggested I contact you in regards to an internship position within your Wellness Center. I am currently a student at Kent State University in Kent, OH, and I am anxious to begin my career in Cardiac Rehab. I heard about your 42,000 square foot facility which houses Phase II and III Cardio/Pulmonary Rehabilitation programs, and I thought this would be an excellent place to complete my internship.

My strength is being able to work with people in the community. I have volunteered for several health fairs and completed a field experience at St. Mary's Cardiac Rehab facility in Kent, OH. I have also been working with Dr. Hamilton on a senior fitness program at Kent, OH. This program develops patient health education programs for those individuals in Cardiac Rehabilitation facilities. In addition to the program I have also had academic experience in Advanced Cardiac Rehab, Exercise Testing and Prescription, and Program Design for Healthy and Special Populations.

I am excited about the opportunity to work with professional staff members in helping to further my career in cardiac rehab. I have enclosed my resume to provide additional information on my strengths and career achievements. I am also prepared to show a preliminary portfolio of my work. I can be reached M-F after 3 pm. Thank you for your consideration.

Sincerely,

Carol Jones

Carol Jones

Enclosure: Resume

Sample 5 – Paragraph Style Cover Letter

Danielle Long

922 Lakeview Lane	832-980-7654
Macon, GA 31206	Dlong@mac.edu

October 3, 2014

Ms. Marybeth Price
Public Safety Medical Services (PSMS)
Lewisville, Texas 75467

Dear Ms. Price:

I am interested in being considered for the internship position at Public Safety Medical Services. I am currently a student working towards a Bachelor of Science Degree in Kinesiology with a minor in nutrition from Macon University in Macon, GA. My father is a fireman and that is what has sparked an interest in this career path.

During my last four years at Macon University I had the opportunity to work in adult fitness programs at the university and within the community. I have volunteer experience for the university health fairs, family day and after school programs. My coursework has prepared me for an internship such as the one you are offering. I have taken courses in Exercise Testing and Prescription, Exercise Physiology, Program Design for Healthy and Special Populations and Health Promotions.

If you want a dynamic, goal-oriented individual with a strong background to succeed and lead others to success, look no further. I am a driven and focused individual who knows how to set goals and work to achieve them. I would appreciate the opportunity to interview for the internship. I can be reached at 832-980-7654

Sincerely,

Danielle Long

Danielle Long

Enclosure: Resume

Sample 6 – Paragraph Style Cover Letter

NATALIE GREEN

4356 Student Drive
Pittsburgh, PA 15261
843-867-9087
ngreen@pitts.edu

September 07, 2013

Mr. James Eggimann
Manager
4356 Sports Lane
Indianapolis, IN 43567

Dear Mr. James Eggimann:

I am currently a senior pursuing a Bachelor of Science degree in Exercise Physiology from the University of Pittsburgh, and I anticipate graduating in May of 2015. I would like to be a track and field coach in the near future and I believe interning for the Indianapolis Invaders would help me gain experience working with athletes.

I have had a passion for track and field ever since I started running competitively in seventh grade. I was an NCAA national qualifier my sophomore and junior years at the University of Pittsburg and was awarded fifth place at the national level in the distance medley relay. I am fascinated with the USA Track and Field National team. I have worked for the past three summers at Sports Acceleration Center as a strength consultant. I believe a combination of my experience and enthusiasm in sports allows me to make a positive contribution to your organization.

After reviewing my resume and application, I believe you will find that I am a well-qualified candidate for the internship with the Indianapolis Invaders. I look forward to discussing the internship with you in more detail in the near future. You may reach me by telephone 843-867-9087 or email at ngreen@pitts.edu. Thank you for your time and consideration.

Yours Truly,

Natalie Green

Natalie Green

Enclosure: Resume

Sample 7 – Paragraph Style Cover Letter

Brett Gilman

1234 University Drive
Rochester, MI

867-890-6789
bgillman@aol.com

January 21, 2014

Mr. Steven Bonner
Manager
Carmichael Training Systems
110-B South Sierra Madre Street
Colorado Springs, CO 80903

Mr. Bonner:

I am interested in an internship with the Carmichael Training Center in Colorado Springs, CO. I am currently a student pursuing a Bachelor of Science Degree in Exercise Science with a specialization in Strength Training. For the past five years I have been a consultant and trainer for individual athletes and teams at Rochester High School in Michigan. During those experiences I have learned many different styles and techniques to help athletes attain their peak physical performance.

I wish to continue my experience in sports training with new conditions and settings. I heard about your Hybrid style of weightlifting, and I am interested in learning more about the protocol through a hands-on internship experience. I believe in a well-rounded education and experience, and I know an internship with the Carmichael Training Facility would help further my career in sports training.

I respectfully ask that you consider my request for an internship. I would like to set a time to meet you and discuss the different ways I can be a benefit to your program. I am available by phone at 867-890-6789 or via email pthomas@iupui.edu.

Truly,

Brett Gilman

Brett Gilman

Enclosure: Resume

Sample 8 – Paragraph Style Cover Letter

Jane G . Dove
2345 Mile Lane Rd, Tampa, FL 43567 * 743-908-7546 * jdove@verizon.net

June 29, 2014

Mr. Timothy English
Executive Director, Dicks Sporting Goods
4356 Fourth Street
Atlanta,GA 43547

Dear Mr. English:

I am an energetic, motivated, assertive individual pursuing a Bachelor of Science degree in Sport Management with an emphasis in Marketing from University of Florida. I anticipate graduating in May of 2014. My career goal is to become a manufacture representative selling products to sport teams and sporting good stores. I definitely want to be a part of this booming business, and therefore I am extremely interested in the position you advertised in sport retailing through the University of Florida Career Services Center.

The majority of my previous work experience has been with local department stores. Although these positions have been outside the sport industry they have provided valuable interpersonal skills and the ability to identify individual needs. Both of these attributes are beneficial for this position. Recently, I accepted a position with Dick's Sporting Goods. I am responsible for selling exercise equipment. This position is a good match because of my knowledge in knowing the brands and specifications for the equipment. In addition to my work experience I have also taken courses in sport financing and sport business which are important to the position.

I would like to meet with you at your convenience to discuss the position in further detail. You can reach me at my home telephone number in the morning and evening at (743)908-7456 or through my email jdove@verizon.net. Thank you for your consideration. I look forward to hearing from you.

Sincerely,

Jane G. Dover

Jane G. Dove

Enclosure: Resume

Sample 9 – Indented Style Cover Letter

Tommy Harford

1234 Goundview Dr, Ames, IA 32456
thartford@gmail.com, 654-987-0943

May 16, 2014

Braddock Tempers
Director of Group Sales
Montgomery Wildcats
302 West State Street
Lake Mary, FL 32564

Dear Mr. Tempers:

Please consider my resume for the Montgomery Wildcats internship that I inquired about in an email on May 1, 2014. I am currently a student enrolled in the Sports Administration program at Iowa State University. I plan to graduate in December of 2014.

I have completed courses that taught me about current trends, sports marketing, and sports information. My work history includes working for Iowa State University Athletic Department. I helped with game day operations and promotions to bring fans to soccer, volleyball and field hockey events. I helped create ideas for halftime shows that involved fans, helped with promotional giveaways and helped put together game programs. I would be extremely interested in this internship and the chance to work with the Montgomery Wildcats baseball team.

Please consider an interview to further discuss my qualifications and this internship opportunity. I may be contacted by phone at 654-987-0943 or via email thartford@gmail.com. Thank you for you consideration.

Sincerely,

Jason Burns

Jason Burns

Enclosure: Resume

Sample 10 – Indented Paragraph Style Cover Letter

Kris Brussel

5423Parkway Drive
Carbondale, IL 62901
854-890-7654
kbrussel@hotmail.com

October 7, 2014

Christian Carlson
General Manager
South Bend Silver Hawks
P.O. Box 4218
South Bend, IN 46634

Dear Mr. Carlson:

 Please consider application for an internship in ticket sales, concessions, marketing and promotions, and stadium operations that was posted on www. sportmanagementclub.com. I am currently a sophomore at the University Southern Illinois, Carbondale and I plan to major in Sport Administration in May 2014. My courses will include Sport Management, Sport Governance, Sport Marketing, and Financial Principles in Sport.

 For the past two years I have been serving in the United States Army Reserves. Some qualities the Army has helped instill in me consist of discipline, moral values, integrity, leadership, and confidence. Through my experiences in the Army and other jobs, I have learned that taking initiative is a key to success. I trust that I possess the willingness to learn and do well in this internship.

 Please consider an interview with me in the future to discuss my opportunities with the South Bend Silver Hawks. The best way to contact me is via email at the following address: kbrussel@hotmail.com. Thank you for taking the time to consider me for this internship and I look forward to hearing from you.

Sincerely,

Kris Brussel

Kris Brussel

Enclosure: Resume

Sample 11 – Indented Style Paragraph Cover Letter

Samantha Becker

117 Greenbriar Way * Tucson, AZ 85721
312-989-8765 * sbecker@arizona.edu

January 3, 2014

John Bryant
Metro Sports Center
2345 Metro Lane
Tucson, AZ 85720

Dear Mr. Bryant:

I am interested in the internship position offered next spring at the Metro Sports Center. I am a senior at the University of Arizona completing a Bachelor of Science Degree in Kinesiology with a specialization in Sport Management. My academic preparation in conjunction with a wide variety of previous experience makes me an ideal candidate for the internship at Metro Sports Center.

My experience in leadership, after school sports programs, sports clubs, athletics and community involvement, combined with my academic courses, has provided me with the background necessary for this position. Metro Sports Center has an excellent reputation for providing the community with organized athletic leagues and tournaments.

I welcome the opportunity to explore my potential contributions to your program. I will contact you within a week to arrange a meeting. Should you have any questions before that time, you may reach me via phone 312-989-8765 or via email at sbecker@arizona.edu.

Sincerely,

Samantha Becker

Samantha Becker

Enclosure: Resume

Sample 12 – Indented Style Paragraph Cover Letter

Heather Sparks

1038 Independence Rd.
Carrollton, GA 30118
432-879-0987
hsparks@geo.edu

January 15, 2014

John Adams
Internship/Employment Coordinator
Chicago Bulls
1901 West Madison Street
Chicago, IL 60612-2459

Dear Mr. Adams:

I am interested in speaking with you about a marketing internship with the Chicago Bulls that was advertised in the *Chicago-Tribune* on January 10, 2014. As an avid follower of the business and marketing side of the sports industry, who is currently pursuing a bachelor degree in Sport Administration with a minor in marketing at State University of West Georgia, I am excited about the possibilities of working for the Chicago Bulls.

I have gained valuable experience marketing "The Yellow Pants" at the State University of West Georgia. The "Yellow Pants" is a pep rally program to begin the athletic season at State University of West Georgia. I was responsible for advertising of this yearly event. I have also completed courses in sport marketing, sport finance, sport facility management and sport event management. I also belong to the sport administration club at State University West Georgia.

Please consider my request for this internship because I believe I have the work ethics and competitive drive that would show great benefits for the organization's marketing team. I may be contacted at 432-879-0987 or via e-mail at hsparks@geo.edu. Thank you for your time and consideration. I will be in touch and hope to hear from you soon.

Sincerely,

Heather Sparks

Heather Sparks

Enclosure: Resume

Sample 13 – Indented Paragraph Style Cover Letter

Bryce Williams

456 Creek Lane
New Orleans, LA 70118
756-987-0987
bwilliams@yahoo.com

August 24, 2014

Mr. Michael Payton
Senior V.P. and Chief Creative Officer
OTT Communications
PO Box 99529
Louisville, KY 40269-0529

Dear Mr. Payton:

As a current student at Tulane University studying Sports Administration with a Marketing minor, I was very interested to see your company has just started a new professional sports marketing firm here in New Orleans. I seek to learn all the facets of the marketing world and gain the experience to make a difference within a professional sports setting.

I have been working in restaurants for two years now, and have gained important people skills. I can multi-task and have the ability to do so on the move and in stressful situations. Knowing that this business is very competitive I would attack it in the same way I attacked being a Division-I football player at the Tulane University. Knowing, not just hearing, and seeing how hard it is to be an athlete gives me a respect and appreciation that will aid me immensely in this business. I know I am qualified to handle any job you have to offer me.

I am very excited about the opportunity to work with your sports marketing firm and welcome the chance to talk to you about any open position. You can contact me at any time on my cell phone 756-987-0987 or by e-mail at bwilliams@yahoo.com. Thank you for your consideration.

Yours Sincerely,

Bryce Williams

Bryce Williams

Enclosure: Resume

Sample 14 – Indented Style Cover Letter

Brandon Lennon

1111 University Drive
Wayne, NE 68787
432-987-6543
Blennon@wayne.edu

August 28, 2013

Mr. Robert Thomas
Personnel Director
Charlotte Bobcats
129 West Trade Street
Suite 700
Charlotte, NC 28202

Dear Mr.Thomas:

      I would like to express my interest in the National Basketball Association and the available public relations intern position on your agency's website. I am studying Sport Administration at the University of Nebraska with an emphasis in community relations. I expect to graduate in May of 2014. I am particularly attracted to the position because of the opportunity to expand my knowledge of NBA team management.

      My particular field of interest is in public and community relations management. I have experience and skills that are relevant to this position including public and community relations as a student worker within the University of Nebraska Extended Services Division. This seems like a perfect opportunity to combine experience with an exciting future working in public relations.

      I am eager to speak to you about the internship possibilities. I can be reached at 432-987-6543.

Sincerely,

Brandon Lennon

Brandon Lennon

Enclosure: Resume

Sample 15 – Indented Style Cover Letter

Mary Short

132 Sparks Drive
Springfield,MA 01109
765-980-7654
mshort@springfield.edu

August 30. 2014

Ms. Georgia Parks
Kentucky Orthopedic Rehab Team
601 S. Floyd Street, Suite 220
Louisville, KY 40202

Dear Ms.Parks:

I am extremely interested in obtaining an internship with the Kentucky Orthopedic Rehab Team. I am currently a senior at Springfield College and was given your name by my Exercise Science Internship Coordinator. I am currently in the Exercise Science and Sports Medicine Program at Springfield College, and I am graduating in May 2014. The majority of course work I have completed has involved athletic rehabilitation, anatomy, and physiology. I also have completed extensive course work in biology and chemistry. Through my previous employment I have had contacts with the public and work well with people in many different situations.

While I have not had much experience in the field of physical therapy, I feel as though I can be an effective member of your team. I am still searching for what specific career I desire, but I know I would like to do something in the field of physical therapy. This opportunity will allow me to become familiar with the field and make contacts that could contribute to my future endeavors.

Please consider my desire to be a part of your team. I am requesting an interview to further discuss your expectations for internships and how I can contribute to your team. You can contact me at 502-460-0518 or via e-mail at wsbent01@louisville.edu. Thank you for your time and consideration and I hope to meet and talk with you soon.

Sincerely,

Mary Short

Mary Short

Enclosure: Resume

Sample 16 – Indented Paragraph Style

Jim Royce

School Address
762 University Blvd
Evansville, IN 47712
(812)435-6789

Permanent Address
1513 Lakes Trail
Indianapolis, IN 46234

Jroyce@att.net

June 25, 2014

Mr. Frank Weatherwood
Rehabilitation Institute of Michigan
262 Mack Avenue
Detroit, MI 48202

Dear Mr. Weatherwood:

I am extremely interested in an internship with the Rehabilitation Institute in Michigan. I am currently pursuing a Bachelor of Science degree in Exercise Science at the University of California at Berkeley. I anticipate graduating in May of 2015. My field experience, practicum, and volunteer work with the University of California at Berkeley and local high schools have provided me experience in physical therapy. My academic experience coupled with my work experience makes me a viable candidate for your organization.

My education, experience, and extracurricular activities are all indicators of a successful career as a physical therapist. I have been working within the University of California at Berkeley Athletic Training Department as a volunteer for the past three years. This experience has allowed me to gain valuable skills that complement athletic training/physical therapy:

- Prevention of athletic injuries
- Recognition and evaluation of athletic injuries
- Rehabilitation of athletic injuries
- Educational counseling of student athletes

In summary, I hope my past coursework and additional skills described in my resume, illustrated I can make a direct contribution to the Rehabilitation Institute of Michigan. I would like to further discuss my qualifications in relation to this internship opportunity. You may reach me at (324-897-9086) from 2:15 p.m. until 4:00 p.m. any day of the week or via email at Jroyce@att.net. I look forward to speaking with you soon. Thank you for your time and consideration.

Sincerely,

Jim Royce

Jim Royce

enclosure: resume

Sample 17 – Bullet Style Cover Letter

Warren Stuart

3425 Courtview Drive, Mooney, WA 90001
436-897-9086 * wstuart@yahoo.com

September 5, 2014

Russell Smith
Athletic Director
New Castle High School
324 Technology Parkway
Mooney, WA 90001

Dear Mr. Smith:

Please consider me for the Student Assistant intern to the Athletic Director at New Castle High School advertised in the Evening News Sports section on September 3, 2014. Currently, I am studying sport administration at Washington University.

For a little over two years I have worked as a student assistant within the Mooney Washington University Athletic Department. As a student assistant I have learned many responsibilities of an athletic director including:

- ✓ Scheduling, handling compliance issues
- ✓ Event preparation
- ✓ Organization of staff

I believe this experience is invaluable and can be an asset to the Student Assistant Internship opening at New Castle High School. I look forward to being in contact with you and hope you will consider my request for an interview to discuss more about the job opportunity as well as my qualifications. I can be contacted at 436-897-9086 or by e-mail at wstuart@yahoo.com. Thank you for your consideration and I look forward to meeting you soon.

Sincerely,

Warren Stuart

Warren Stuart

enclosure: resume

Sample 18 – Bullet Style Cover Letter

Audra Pessington
RR3 Box 345
Melbourne, FL 32919
apessington@aol.com

November 20, 2014

John R. Martin
Lifetime Fitness
345 Chestnut Street
Omaha, NE 32457

Dear Mr.Martin:

Recently, I discovered that Lifetime Fitness posted an intern position on the University of South Florida Career Services and Placement job postings. I am highly interested in gaining valuable work experience at your facility, and I would like to be considered for an internship position. I am anticipating graduating from the University of South Florida with a Bachelor of Science in Exercise Science in May of 2015.

Through my experiences, I have demonstrated the ability to adapt quickly to a variety of situations, and I feel that my professional and analytical qualities will allow me to make a positive contribution to your facility:

> Worked part-time as a welcome greeter, fitness consultant, and fitness instructor for the University of South Florida Recreation Center.
> Worked part-time for the South Florida Health and Fitness Center as an sport specific trainer.
> Experiences at South Florida Gym as a desk worker.

I would appreciate the chance to meet with you to discuss the position further. If you have any additional questions and would like to speak with me personally, please contact me by telephone at (456) 347-0987 or by email at apessington@aol.com. Again, thank you for your time and consideration.

Sincerely,

Audra Pessington

Audra Pessington

Enclosure: Resume

Sample 19 – Bullet Style Cover Letter

Anna P. Night

435 View Crest Drive, New Brunswick, New Jersey * 432-908-7645 * an@hotmail.com

September 6, 2014

Ms. Evelyn Lawrence
Health Fitness Corporation
3500 American Blvd.
Minneapolis, MN 55432

Dear Ms. Lawrence:

I am currently a senior at Rutgers University pursuing a Bachelor of Science Degree in Exercise Science with a minor in Nutrition and Fitness Instruction. I heard several positive comments about the community of Minneapolis and Health Fitness Corporation. Please consider this letter and resume as an indication of my strong interest in completing my internship at your facility.

I have several experiences that I may offer to Health Fitness Corporation. These experiences in the fitness field have helped me develop an excellent work ethic and strong leadership skills.

- ❖ Group exercise instructor experience teaching kickboxing, Pilates, and Yoga at a community and a university campus recreation facility
- ❖ Fitness consultant experience where I conducted initial consultations, exercise testing and prescription, and orientations at a university campus recreation facility
- ❖ Student manager experience where I worked alongside the Assistant Director of the facility in learning leadership skills.

Furthermore, my love for fitness adds to my caring personality and great organizational skills that will be a positive asset to any organization.

After reviewing my resume and qualifications, I believe you will find that I would be an excellent student to have as an intern at Health Fitness Corporation. I look forward to meeting you and learning more about the facility in a personal interview. You may reach me by telephone at 432-908-7645 or email at an@hotmail.com.

Sincerely,

Anna P. Night

Anna P. Night

enclosure: resume

Sample 20 – Bullet Style Cover Letter

Heather Alberts
18 Porter Avenue
Shreveport, LA 71115
*(812)243-4567

December 23, 2014

Daniel Thomas
WELLSTAR Health Place/Mobile Health Services
320 Kennestone Hospital Blvd
Marietta, GA 30060

Dear Mr.Thomas:

I am interested in the internship at WELLSTAR Health System. The enclosed resume is in accordance with the instructions stated on the www.internshipsearch.com website. I would like to be considered for the position because I am interested in adult fitness and health promotion. I am currently pursuing a Bachelor of Science degree in Exercise Science and a minor in Health Promotion from Louisiana State University. I anticipate graduating in May of 2014.

Highlights of my college career include the following:

> ➤ Team captain for the Louisiana State University women's softball team; led my team to three consecutive conference championships.
> ➤ Excellent academic record; Since entering Louisiana State University, I have consistently maintained a 4.00/4.00 GPA while competing in athletics
> ➤ Communications and Public Relations Skills – In my athletic role I was the spokesperson for the team.
> ➤ American Red Cross CPR/AED/First Aid Certifications

I am anxious to launch my career, and I believe the WELLSTAR Health System would be a wonderful beginning. I look forward to hearing more about the internship. Should any questions arise regarding the information on my resume, please do not hesitate to contact me at (812)243-4567. I look forward to hearing from you in the near future.

Sincerely,

Heather Alberts

Heather Alberts

Enclosure: Resume

Sample 21 – Bullet Style Cover Letter

Elizabeth Minter

1245 Washington Ave * Chestertown,
MD 21620 * (502) 419-7301 * eminter@yahoo.com

September 28, 2014

Colette Patel
Event Coordinator
9200 World Cup Way, Suite 202
Frisco, TX 75034

Dear Ms. Patel:

I am responding to your advertisement on the TeamWork Online website regarding the Event Operations Internship. Please find enclosed my resume showing my education, experience, and background. I am currently a student in the Sport Administration program at the Washington & Lee University. I anticipate completion of degree in May of 2015.

My recent and upcoming job experiences include working with a variety of organizations such as:

❖ AAA-Baseball (Washington Raiders) and Arena Football 2 (Evansville ACES) teams as well as event operations with the Tour de Washington and ESPN. With the Raiders and the ACES, I helped compile information from the fans attending the event. The information included but was not limited to what could possibly be done to make the 'fan experience' better at the games.

❖ The Tour de Washington is a city-wide charity bike-race in Washington, I am volunteering my time for this wonderful event on October 1st, 2009.

❖ My main purpose with ESPN was helping in event operations for a nationally televised college football game. I helped set-up cameras and ran connections through the stadium to make sure everything was hooked up properly. I also was a camera operator for this ESPN nationally televised collegiate football game.

Please consider my request for an interview to further discuss my qualifications and this job opportunity. I may be contacted at (502) 419-7301 or via e-mail at Eminters@ washington.edu. Thank you for your consideration.

Sincerely,

Elizabeth Minter
Elizabeth Minter
Enclosure: Resume

Sample 22 – Bullet Style Cover Letter

Lesley Harris

432 Howard Drvie • Austin, Texas 78465• (845)324-9085 • lharris@hotmail.com

January 25, 2014

Mr. Andrew Johnson, Lake Shore Athletic Club
c/o Lakeshore Athletic Club
4536 West Shell Court
Chicago, IL 60602

Dear Ms. Johnson:

Currently, I am a senior Exercise Science major at Southwest Texas State University. As part of my graduation requirements I must complete an internship. My professors have always spoken highly of the Lake Shore Athletic Club. While reviewing the Lake Shore Athletic Club's internship program online, I quickly realized that its focus on management services for corporate wellness would be a great match with my career goals.

My first-hand experience in the fitness industry combined with my educational background in Exercise Science provide me with necessary skills applicable to this internship. I have completed the majority of the course work required for my major while maintaining a 3.7/4.0 GPA. Through my course work I have learned valuable skills such as:

- Taking skinfold measurements and cardiorespiratory fitness testing;
- Measuring blood pressure, height, weight and flexibility;
- Conducting fitness assessments and health screenings

My two years of experience at Bally Fitness and my two-and-a-half years of experience as a group fitness instructor at a variety of facilities has helped me to gain a better understanding of the day-to-day operations of a fitness center.

After reviewing my resume and application, I believe you will find that I am a well qualified candidate for the internship at Lake Shore Athletic Club. I look forward to discussing the internship with you in more detail and will call you next week to confirm your receipt of my application materials. You may reach me by telephone at 845-324-9085 or email lharris@ hotmail.com. Thank you for your consideration.

Sincerely,

Lesley Harris

Lesley Harris

enclosure: resume

Sample 23 – Bullet Style Cover Letter

Bobby Mancino

1324 York Drive, Idaho Falls, Idaho 432567
432-905-9874 * bmanchino@home.net

January 15, 2014

Mr. Ray E. Tucker
Athletic Director
Office of the President
3245 Alumni Hall, Suite 456
Harrisburg, PA 34549-8976

Dear Mr. Tucker:

I am applying for an internship position with York College (York, PA). I was informed about this open position through the National Association of Collegiate Directors of Athletics website, posted on Jan. 10, 2013.

I am currently a student at Idaho State University in the Sports Administration Program. I am completing my course studies to graduate in May of 2015. My studies have included courses in:

- ✓ Sport Communications
- ✓ Sport Management
- ✓ Sport Marketing
- ✓ Legal Aspects of Sport

I understand this position requires administrative experience in intercollegiate athletics, excellent communication and presentation skills. The coursework and my recent internship with Idaho State University have prepared me for the skills asked of me for this Job.

My training in this field seems to match all of your requirements for this job. I am very confident that I will be an excellent intern for York College. I have been around winning programs all of my life and I am sure this will be no different. Please consider my request for an interview to discuss my interest in this position. I may be contacted at 432-905-9874 or via email at bmanchino@home.net. I will be available at your convenience. Thank you for your consideration.

Sincerely,

Bobby Mancino

Bobby Mancino

enclosure: resume   Sample 24 – Bullet Style Cover Letter